## SCIENCE FICTION WRITING SERIES

# *World-Building*

Science Fiction | EDITED BY Ben Bova | Writing Series

# World-Building

## Stephen L. Gillett

**WRITER'S DIGEST BOOKS**
Cincinnati, Ohio

This hardcover edition of *World-Building* features a "self-jacket" that eliminates the need for a separate dust jacket. It provides sturdy protection for your book while it saves paper, trees and energy.

Other fine Writer's Digest Books are available from your local bookstore or direct from the publisher.

00   99   98   97   96      5   4   3   2   1

**Library of Congress Cataloging-in-Publication Data**

Gillett, Stephen Lee.
   World-Building / Stephen L. Gillett.
      p.      cm.—(Science fiction writing series)
   Includes bibliographical references and index.
   ISBN 0-89879-707-1
   1. Science fiction—Authorship. 2. Astronomy—Authorship. I. Title. II. Series.
PN3377.5.S3G55   1995
808.3'8762—dc20                                                                    95-25826
                                                                                          CIP

Edited by Ben Bova
Designed by Angela Lennert Wilcox
Cover illustration by Bob Eggleton

# ACKNOWLEDGMENTS

An author can't write a book without a lot of help over the years from many people, and I would like to thank them here. I'd first like to thank Stanley Schmidt, editor of *Analog*, and Kim Mohan, editor of *Amazing*; much of the material herein previously appeared in articles in their magazines. Stan gave me my first outlet for popular writing and encouraged my attempts, and Kim gave me the opportunity to do a science column. Of course, I'd also like to thank Ben Bova, the editor of this series, for the opportunity to put together this book, and for his encouragement.

I'd like to thank Rob Quigley, chairman of the Department of Physics and Astronomy at Western Washington University, Bellingham, Washington, specifically for current information on bolometric magnitudes, and also for all the discussions over the years. Thanks also to Poul Anderson, for the opportunity to conduct the "world-building" sessions at "Contact: Cultures of the Imagination" every spring and for the inspiration through the years from his fiction. Martyn Fogg also made useful suggestions on an early draft.

I also thank Jerry Oltion, for his thorough critiques of the original articles before they were submitted to the gaze of the outside world, for permission to quote from some of his collaborative works— and for his friendship since our somewhat bizarre introduction to organized science-fiction fandom at Norwescon '83!

And finally, to my family: Joyce my wife, and Travis, my son, for their forbearance.

Last, a few stylistic notes: Technical terminology, like everything else, is always in flux, and where choices exist I've tried to opt for the more straightforward versions.

So, first, I've used regular plurals for such technical but thoroughly naturalized words as "nebula," "aurora," "supernova" and so on. Although this is in defiance of most of the astronomical literature, the Latinate plurals ("nebulae," etc.) are beginning to seem affected, and in any case are distracting. Anyway, if *Scientific American* can decide that the plural of "millenium" is "milleniums," I'm in good company!

Second, I capitalize "Earth," "Moon" and "Sun" when they refer specifically to the astronomical bodies—as is becoming standard in the technical literature, and as only makes sense. This usage also makes possible two useful distinctions: The words "sun" and "moon," lowercased, refers generically to any star or any planetary satellite. (I have *not* gone so far, however, as to make "earth" a generic word for an Earthlike planet!)

Third, I've used the generic terms "pericentron" and "apocentron" for the closest and farthest points, respectively, on an orbit. The traditional literature contains a plethora of alternative forms ("perigee"/"apogee," "periastron"/"apastron," "perihelion"/"aphelion," etc.) that merely depend on the nature of the primary body. Such archaic distinctions only add intellectual clutter without enhancing understanding.

Stephen L. Gillett

Carson City, Nevada

June 1995

# ABOUT THE AUTHOR

Steve Gillett got his undergraduate degree in geology at Caltech in 1975. After a brief period with the U.S. Geological Survey, he received his Ph.D., also in geology, from SUNY Stony Brook in 1981. In the early and mid-1980s, Gillett worked as a consulting geologist in the Pacific Northwest. There he was involved in introducing advanced technology to the oil business.

While in the Northwest, Gillett also taught astronomy at a community college, and he's since returned to academia full-time. He's currently a research associate at the Mackay School of Mines, University of Nevada, Reno, where among other things he works on Paleozoic paleomagnetism, and on seismic risk at Yucca Mountain, Nevada, the proposed high-level nuclear waste repository, as well as teaching undergraduate geology. He's published technical papers on such diverse topics as the statistics of directions and possible lunar resources. Recently he's become interested in the implications of nanotechnologies for the geological sciences, in particular for the resource business.

Gillett has also written many popular science articles. He's a frequent contributor of speculative science articles to *Analog*, and was the science columnist at *Amazing Science Fiction* from January 1991 until that magazine ceased publication in early 1995.

He has also written science fiction under a pseudonym, often in collaboration with Jerry Oltion, and has conducted the world-building seminar at "Contact: Cultures of the Imagination," hosted by Cabrillo College of Santa Cruz every year in the Bay Area.

Gillett was born in El Paso, Texas, but grew up in Las Vegas, Nevada, after his family moved there in the mid-1950s. His father worked for one of the prime contractors at the Nevada Test Site, the U.S. nuclear-weapons testing facility, and he vaguely remembers seeing some of the aboveground tests from a mountainside about fifty miles away—back around 1960, when they were considered just nifty fireworks!

He now lives in Carson City, Nevada, with his wife Joyce (a veterinarian), their son Travis, a cat and an Australian Shepherd. His hobbies include outdoor activities such as camping and hiking, model rocketry (with Travis!) and ragtime piano.

# TABLE OF CONTENTS

**CHAPTER 1**

*Why World-Build?*.................................................................1

The necessity of using real science to create a sense of wonder in your SF, and how this book will help you to achieve this.

**CHAPTER 2**

*The Astronomical Setting*................................................6

Some important differences between planets and stars; understanding and calculating astronomical scales, gravity, horizon distance and orbits; variables that affect planets, such as year length, change of seasons and tidal action.
• Gravity • Orbits • 'Tis the Season . . . • Dances With Gravity

**CHAPTER 3**

*Making a Planet*................................................................37

How the details of a planetary system reflect vagaries in its formation, and how this element of historic contingency provides lots of storytelling options.
• Elementary Considerations • The Collapse of a GMC (Giant Molecular Cloud) • For Healthy Growing Planets . . .
• Stirring the Ingredients • Some Elementary Variations

**CHAPTER 4**

*The Earth*...........................................................................54

Lots of things make an Earth, and they're all interconnected. A look at some of the Earth's aspects and some possible variations that may lead to interesting worlds.
• Powering a Planet • Plate Tectonics • Water and Air: The Volatiles • The Atmosphere • The Ocean • The Magnetic Field and Magnetosphere • The Colors of a Planet • Day and Night
• A Thought Experiment: The Ice World

**CHAPTER 5**

*The Ancient Earth*...........................................................94

Avoiding the "Cenozoic Earth Syndrome" by understanding the ancient Earth and using it for inspiration.
• The Planets Earth • Deep Time • The Ancient Atmosphere
• The Archean Earth • The Dance of the Continents
• Ice Ages • Life!

**CHAPTER 6**

*The Other Planets* ............................................................109

> With the wealth of data from space probes, the other planets
> aren't just lights in the sky anymore. Instead, they and their
> planets are a "reality check" and a source of inspiration for
> what can happen in the real Universe.
> • The Planets in the Sky • The Other Rocky Planets: Aborted
> Earths • The Gas Giants (and Their Companions)

**CHAPTER 7**

*Stars and Suns* ..............................................................127

> The parent star warms the planet, drives the weather, and
> provides the ultimate energy source for life. Only stars like our
> own Sun can support interesting planets!
> • Color and Spectrum • Magnitudes • Beyond the Main
> Sequence • Under Twin Suns • Galaxies

**CHAPTER 8**

*Not as We Know It* ........................................................154

> Differences in volatile content provide major scope for
> variation in a world. A review of some possibilities.
> • Volatile Mixtures • Wetworlds • Nitroworlds
> • Brimstone Worlds • Exotica

# CHAPTER 1

# Why "World-Build"?

*The bloody light of Reddawn spilled across the morning landscape. Lurid shadows, black against red, stretched away from gaunt trees limned against the sky, and icicles flamed crimson as they caught the dim light. Overhead, aurorae pulsated, dim with the coming dawn but still visible.*

from "Contact," by Jerry Oltion and Lee Goodloe

*Red or white, the planet below was the most beautiful thing she'd seen in months. Sheets of fluffy clouds Coriolis-spun into storm whorls, with dark ocean below occasionally reflecting sunlight. Nothing but ocean below, by the look of it, though. . . .*

from "Waterworld," by Lee Goodloe and Jerry Oltion

*The surface was so alien . . . Masha shuddered. Like a simulation where the parameters are wrong: turquoise-green sky, pale greenish sun, fuzzy blackish plain running off into greenish haze, white trees with tiny black leaves that sparkled when they caught the sun, glinting like frosty snow on a bright day. . . . You wanted to reach over and tweak the knobs till the colors were right. Mars or the Moon looked positively homelike by comparison.*

A sense of wonder. How many times have we heard that advanced as the reason for science fiction? For most SF readers, that's what drew them to the genre in the first place. And yet how many stories and books wring out that "gosh, wow" reaction?

One reason, no doubt, is the lack of a sense of immersion in the story. If the story doesn't take itself seriously, why should the reader? The sense of wonder critically requires the reader's believing that this could *really be*. And *that's* probably the main reason to use real science in a story. Skillfully done—as background, not lecture—it imbues a sense of reality that can carry your reader along, that can elicit the willing suspension of disbelief almost unconsciously.

You sometimes hear authors sniff that using a scientific background "stifles creativity." But that's nonsense. For one thing, the real world is far more varied than authors' imaginations. Human minds have enough trouble keeping track of the complexities of the real universe, let alone devising a new one ex nihilo! True, using real science imposes a framework; but claiming *that* inhibits creativity is like claiming that using a language, rather than arbitrary combinations of letters, stifles creativity. Aazr bk eorf xcx? Sure, lots of letter combinations are prohibited by the rules of English—but no one seriously considers that a drain on creativity. Are sonnets less an art form because their rules are restrictive?

Craftsmanship is another reason. Most readers (even those pooh-poohing the use of real science in science fiction) expect a lot of research to lie behind a historical novel. Nearly everyone would be put off by a story in which, say, the characters tripped over beer cans in Victorian England, or in which the author was under the impression that Julius Caesar and Attila the Hun were contemporaries. People *expect* research in a historical novel, and properly so.

Of course, there are levels. A novel set in medieval Europe that might entertain—and impress—me might thoroughly exasperate a medieval scholar, who could pick out all the flaws and anachronisms I'd miss. Similarly, I routinely find serious flaws in worlds designed by the hardest of hard SF writers; but then, I do planets for a living!

Still, if the effort is there, it lends a coherence and substance to a story that can never hurt. Although it can't make a bad story good, it can make good stories out of fair ones, and even great stories out of good ones.

And this isn't to say you can't finagle, too. Just as a historical novelist will fit unhistorical characters and incidents into a generally true-to-life background, so the SF writer might fit, say, faster-than-light (FTL) travel into an otherwise hard SF novel, despite the fact that FTL is utterly forbidden by physics as currently understood. So hard an SF writer as Poul Anderson finagled the physics of special relativity in his quintessential hard SF novel *Tau Zero*. After all, you've got a story to tell! But if you need to bend the rules a bit, you need to do it in a manner that doesn't jar your readers. If they drop out of the story with a bump, because they crash into a scientific howler, it's *your* problem. At all costs, you don't want to break the spell. And lots of SF readers are sophisticated, too. You need to be at least as sophisticated.

Of course, this doesn't mean you have to bore your reader with big expository lumps, either. In my younger years, I never found that the readability of Thomas B. Costain or Samuel Shellabarger suffered from the background they had to work into their historical novels. Similarly, part of the SF writer's job is to introduce the background without disrupting the narrative flow; indeed, by enhancing it if possible.

Moreover, researching a scientific background is not such a chore as is made out. It gives the sense of the breadth of a world—interesting planets will be as multifarious and varied as is the Earth—and fills in background for you almost automatically. And that very framework imposes a sense of verisimilitude that's particularly valuable in long fiction. It keeps you consistent. It's also a source of details. Anyone who writes fiction knows the value of the advice to use a few vivid details in descriptions, rather than a catalog of generalities. A well-thought-out world generates such details automatically.

In this book, although I'll talk about planets in general, I'll focus on Earthlike planets in particular. A great deal of SF is set in "exotic Earth" settings for all sorts of perfectly valid narrative reasons: An interesting shirtsleeve environment is available, interaction with the planet and its life forms furnish numerous possibilities for conflict, and so on. And your reader can bring to the story a vast background of experience; after all, we *live* on a planet! It's also hardly a new observation that an environment affects its inhabitants profoundly, and that goes especially for an alien world. Working out how their planet will affect its inhabitants (and any visitors) is a fruitful source of the conflicts and details that animate a story.

I'll also look far more at the "edge of the envelope" than would, say, a textbook. Lots of the fun SF settings lie in the special cases, unusual circumstances, and speculations that, although not known to be forbidden by current knowledge, lie beyond current information. Pulling such material out of standard references can be a challenge, especially if you want to get on with telling the story! I've also gathered an extensive reference list together at the end of the book, along with suggestions for research help.

Some simple "cookbook" calculations for such things as a planet's surface gravity, how far it needs to be from its sun to receive a certain amount of sunlight, and how long its year is in such an orbit are similarly included. Personal computers have now made multiple calculations nearly painless, even for those who view the prospect of mathematics with about the same enthusiasm they'd view a root canal. I find spreadsheet programs such as Lotus 1-2-3, QuattroPro, or Excel particularly useful. They make the calculations easy: once you've typed in the values you don't need to start all over again if you make a mistake; just retype the incorrect value, and watch all the calculations correct themselves automatically. With a calculator you have to reenter all the numbers even if just one is wrong.

A spreadsheet also makes it easy to try out lots of different scenarios. See how the year and illumination change as you type in different values for the distance. Watch how surface gravity changes as a planet's radius and density change. Playing with the numbers will give you a far better feel for your planet and its environment than any number of equations. (They're a lot more fun than taxes, too!)

I've also isolated most of the calculations in sidebars, so that you can read through without distraction, and only turn to the actual formulas when you have something to calculate. Other sidebars contain supplementary or background information with which you may already be familiar, so it can be skipped over easily.

---

## A NOTE ON UNITS

Some measurements will be given in "absolute" units: meters, miles, pounds, kilograms and so on. Most of these will be in metric units, simply because they're vastly more convenient for calculation, as you'll find when you go to calculate! Of course, some measurements will also be given in U.S. conventional units, to give their flavor in everyday terms. Some astronomical measurements are given in special but traditional units (e.g., light years), simply because the distances they measure are much too big for everyday measures to be convenient. Temperatures much different from everyday values are usually given in kelvins (formerly called "degrees Kelvin"), which is simply the Celsius ("centigrade") scale in which the zero point is absolute zero. $0 \, K = -273.15°C =$ absolute zero. Room temperature is ~300 kelvins (27°C). (The symbol "~" means "about" or "approximately.")

Most measurements, however, will be presented in *relative* units; that is, where the value of some parameter for a familiar object (generally the Sun or Earth) is set equal to one. This gives a better sense of scale; it's often much more illuminating to say your planet's surface gravity is, say, 1.2 times Earth's, rather than 12 meters/sec². Such units also often make calculations more straightforward.

For big numbers, *scientific notation* is handy. This simply consists of expressing the number as a factor times ten raised to some power. It's more readable, for example, to say there are $~6 \times 10^{12}$ miles in a light year than ~6,000,000,000,000 miles. For one thing, it's easier to keep track of the zeros!

Finally, granted that using real science is important, at least in anything that professes to be hard science fiction, why should we even care about planets? Lots of hard SF is set off planets, and there's even a school of thought that says planets are obsolete. Our descendants (so they say) will colonize space in the future (if they even bother; maybe they'll just send intelligent robots instead).

But we're storytellers, not foretellers. Planets automatically provide varied and diverse story settings, and easily provide that all-important sense of wonder. And another point: planets are *spacious*, as a character once commented in Arthur C. Clarke's *Imperial Earth*. Even the largest space colony will not give the sense of wide-open spaces you get on a planet.

# CHAPTER 2

# The Astronomical Setting

To begin with, Earth, of course, is a *planet:* a big ball of rock and (in the center) metal. Planets are worlds. They're not self-luminous, which means they're cool bodies, at least on the outside. They shine instead by reflected sunlight. Depending on the angle from which they're illuminated, they can show "phases" such as crescent, half, full, and so forth (page 110).

Earth also spins around an *axis*: an "imaginary" (that is, dynamically defined) line. This *rotation* has major effects. It causes sunrise and sunset. It spreads the Sun's heating around more or less evenly, like a roast rotating on a spit. It distorts the circulation of air and ocean currents, which has an absolutely profound effect on weather systems. And it slightly deforms the planet itself. All these effects will be discussed in more detail later.

Earth is *orbiting* (moving in a closed path around) a *star*, the Sun, under the influence of gravity (pages 11-12). It's one of several planets making up the *Solar System*. Although the only planets we can observe directly are around our own Sun, current thinking is that planetary formation is common around stars. By the early twenty-first century space-based telescopes may be able to see planets around nearer stars (a detail for your story).

So, stars are suns. They shine by their own light with energy from nuclear reactions in their center, where intense pressures and temperatures force nuclear fusion. They come in different kinds, depending largely on two things. First is *mass*, the amount of matter in them. This determines the intensity of stars' nuclear reactions. The larger they are, the hotter they burn. Thus massive stars are bright and short-lived, and not good places for Earthlike planets. Second is *age*. Old stars are running out of fuel and have very different structures, as different nuclear reactions now dominate in them. They're also typically bright but geologically short-lived. They're also not good places for an Earthlike planet, but may provide some unusual settings.

The most important difference between stars and planets is simply *mass*. Stars are much more massive. A planet is too small to "turn on the nuclear fires" at its center. Even gas giant planets, which are rich in hydrogen, the nuclear fuel of ordinary stars, can't do so. Planets also differ among themselves in composition. Small rocky planets like the Earth are very different from a large ball of gas like Jupiter (page 109).

## ASTRONOMICAL SCALES

Special units prove to be convenient in dealing with astronomical distances, because the distances are *much* greater than everyday. In the Solar System, the average distance from Earth to Sun is a convenient measure. It's the astronomical unit (AU), and is ~93,000,000 miles or ~150,000,000 kilometers (Table 1). This is very large by everyday standards. It would take ~177 years to travel one AU at 60 miles per hour. Pluto averages ~40 AU from the Sun; comets lie hundreds to several thousand AU away.

The distances between planets are far greater than their sizes. The diameter of Earth is 12,756 km (~7970 miles), or less than one-millionth its distance to the Sun. Even the diameter of the Sun (1,390,000 km) is less than $\frac{1}{10,000}$ the distance. Thus the planets are vastly smaller than the distances separating them, and "dust in a void" is the correct image.

The Solar System is dominated by the Sun. Its mass $(1.991 \times 10^{30}$ kg) is some 330,000 times Earth's, and even Jupiter, with a mass 318 times Earth's, is still a thousand times smaller.

Even so, nearby stars lie so *much* farther away that the vast and empty Solar System looks very cozy indeed. Even the AU becomes cumbersome, so we use a couple of new units. One is the *light year*, which is simply the distance light travels in a year. So it measures distance, not time! One light year is $9.46 \times 10^{12}$ km, or ~6,000,000,000,000 (6 trillion) miles, or 63,200 AU. The nearest star, Proxima in the Alpha Centauri system, is about 4.2 light years away; or almost 1600 times the distance to Pluto.

The other unit is the *parsec*, which is based on measuring distances by *parallax*. Parallax is the amount an object seems to shift against the background when viewed from different positions. By measuring this shift, and knowing the distance between the viewing positions, you can calculate the distance to the object. For measuring star distances astronomers use either side of the Earth's orbit, vantage points 186,000,000 miles apart. Even so, the distances to the nearest stars are still barely measurable. Something that lies at a distance of one parsec has a *par*allax of one *sec*ond of arc. As there are 3600 seconds of arc in a degree (and 360 degrees in a circle), this is obviously a small angle indeed! It's the width of a quarter from three miles away. And yet no star is even as close as one parsec (a parsec works out to be 3.26 light-years).

Finally, *galaxies* are vast systems containing billions to hundreds of billions of stars. They're thousands of times larger than the distances between neighboring stars, and so are measured in *kilo* (thousand) parsecs (kpc). The scale of the Universe itself is conveniently reckoned in *mega* (million) parsecs (Mpc).

## GRAVITY

Gravity is the force that holds the Universe together. It holds together planets and stars, and holds things down on their surfaces; it chains planets and satellites in their orbits; it holds the very galaxies together. So, gravity is fundamental when considering the setting in which planets and stars are found. In this section I'll include a general description of how gravity works, with some "cookbook" formulas for useful calculations, and then discuss some of the complications that arise in complicated, real-world systems—complications that let you set up exotic and little-used planetary settings.

Gravitational force follows an inverse-square law: two bodies attract each other with a force proportional to their masses, and inversely proportional to the square of the distance between them. Or in mathematics,

$$F = GMm/r^2$$

where $F$ is the force exerted, $M$ and $m$ are the masses of the bodies, $r$ is the distance between their centers of mass, and

$$G = 6.667 \times 10^{-8} \text{ dyne cm}^2/\text{g}^2 = 6.667 \times 10 \times^{-11} \text{ newton m}^2/\text{kg}^2$$

is a universal constant. As we'll see, this equation is exactly true *only* for point or spherical masses, and that fact has some useful implications for world-building. (A *dyne*, or gram centimeter/sec$^2$, is the unit of force in the centimeter-gram-second (cgs) version of the metric system. A *newton* (kilogram meter/sec$^2$), is the unit of force in the meter-kilogram-second (MKS) system. Use the value of $G$ depending on whether the masses and distances are expressed in grams and centimeters, or kilograms and meters. The force $F$ will then be correctly expressed in dynes or newtons, respectively.)

Gravity also forces planets (and stars) into spheres. Any planet-sized blob of matter will flow like water. So don't write about non-spherical planets, unless the non-sphericity is maintained *dynamically*, that is by ongoing forces, as with the equatorial bulge from the planet's rotation (page 88). Larry Niven's elongate planet Jinx, for example, with its ends sticking out of the atmosphere, is impossible; you might as well try building a house out of tapioca. James Blish's *Earthman Come Home* has a similar flaw: The crust of the planet He was supposed to be stabilized by a giant iron latticework bled off the planet's core. Cooked spaghetti would work as well as iron.

Galileo explained this weakness of matter in bulk: Strength goes up as the *square*, but mass as the *cube*. If you double the size of a column, for example, it becomes 4 ($2 \times 2$) times as strong, but 8 ($2 \times 2 \times 2$) times as massive. The legs of a human-sized ant would collapse. The giants of myth would need skeletons of much stronger material than bone if they had human proportions. An iron beam as long as a planet couldn't support its own weight, much less a planet's. And a planet . . . well, a planet collapses in on itself as much as it can, to form a sphere.

## MATTERS OF GRAVITY

### Surface Gravity

The gravitational acceleration ("pull") felt by something at the surface of a spherical body, such as a planet, is given by

$$g = GM/r^2$$

where $g$ is the acceleration, $G$ is the universal gravitational constant, $M$ is the mass of the planet, and $r$ is its radius. Note that $g$ does not depend on the mass of the body at the surface. As Galileo pointed out, heavy objects fall at the same rate as light ones, in the absence of air resistance.

On the average, $g = 9.8$ m/sec$^2$ on Earth, or 32 feet/sec/sec. For planet-designing, it's often more useful to express the above equation in terms of Earth values:

$$g_p = M_p/r_p^2 = r_p(\rho_p/\rho_e),$$

where $g_p$, $M_p$, $r_p$ are the values for the other planet if Earth = 1 (e.g., $M_p = 1.2$ would mean the planet has 1.2 times the mass of Earth), $\rho_p$ (Greek letter rho) is the mean density of the planet, and $\rho_e$ is the mean density of Earth (5.5 g/cm$^3$ = 5500 kg/m$^3$).

Note that $g$ depends on both the density and the radius of the planet. For the same surface gravity, a low-density planet is larger. For example, on solving the above equation for $r_p$, a planet with a density of 4.0 but Earth-normal gravity must have a radius of 1.38 Earth's. Conversely, even a small planet can have high surface gravity if it has high density. For example, the Earth's iron core (page 50) has a density of about 10 and a radius of 0.55, so the gravity at the top of the core is about 0.99, or almost the same as at the surface! (Calculating surface gravity as a function of density and radius is an excellent example of where a spreadsheet program is very useful. It becomes very easy to try different combinations to tailor your planet the way you want.) Finally, note that the *mean* density of the entire planet is all that matters. Earth would have far less surface gravity if it didn't have that high-density core. Typical surface rocks have densities of about 2.6 g/cm³, less than half the mean density of the Earth.

The surface gravity is a good source of story detail, as well. For example, because things fall faster on high-gravity worlds, people on such a planet are likely to be more injury-prone. Not only will things hit harder, but their reflexes, tuned to a more leisurely pace, will be too slow. They also are likely to suffer from heart problems; Larry Niven makes a point of this about the high-gravity world Jinx. Other things being equal, mountains are likelier to be lower and weathering more effective: raindrops hit harder and landslides are more frequent.

Finally, surface gravity varies slightly from place to place, because no planet is a perfect sphere. First, there's the rotational flattening from the planet's spin (page 88). Due to this alone, Earth's sea-level value varies from ~9.83 m/sec² at the poles to 9.78 at the equator. (If you need an exact formula, see a standard geophysics text such as Stacey in the References.) The gravity variation has two causes: the different distances from the center of the Earth (the poles are closer than the equator), and the fact that the centrifugal force offsets gravity slightly, with the maximum at the equator. For slowly rotating planets like Earth this variation is negligible for practical purposes, but it would become important on a rapidly spinning world. Hal Clement used this to good effect with the giant world Mesklin in his classic novel *Mission of Gravity*. In addition, tidal distortion (page 23) causes minor variation, and finally there are *very* slight (and local) variations due to the differences in the density of subsurface rocks.

## ORBITS

An orbit is the path of one body around another under the influence of gravity; or more properly, the path of the bodies *around each other.* The Universe consists of bodies orbiting each other in a set of hierarchies: satellites around planets, planets around stars, stars around stars, stars and star systems around the center of a galaxy. They orbit their common center of mass (CM), the point around which mass vs. distance is evenly distributed. The balance point of a teeter-totter is an example.

The fundamental orbit type is the two-body problem, which was solved by Isaac Newton. It treats two bodies orbiting each other (see page 13). To start with, you can nearly always ignore other bodies, because they're far enough away not to have much effect.

---

## ESCAPE VELOCITY

"Escape velocity" is how fast something must be going to escape the gravity of another body completely. Something thrown directly away from a body at escape velocity would never fall back. This value is important for more than just space travel! It's also one of the parameters that determines whether a planet can keep an atmosphere (page 63).

It's given by:

$$v_{esc} = \sqrt{(2GM/r)} = kr\sqrt{\rho}$$

where $r$ is the radius of the planet, $M$ its mass, $\rho$ (Greek letter rho) its mean density, and $G$ the gravitational constant. Thus $k = \sqrt{(8\pi G/3)} = 2.36 \times 10^{-5}$ (metric units) is also a constant. For Earth $v_{esc} \sim 12$ km/sec or 7 mi/sec.

---

## Calculating an Orbit

Here are some "cookbook" formulas for the two-body problem. They can be derived from Newton's Laws of Motion and the Law of Gravitation, but we won't do that here! The derivation is given in any standard reference on celestial mechanics, such as Danby (see the References). The formulas are useful for basic, simple calculations for finding orbital periods, given the masses of the bodies. A planet around a star, a satellite around a planet, two stars around each other in a binary star system: They're all the same. In general, we speak of "primary" and "secondary" masses for the larger and smaller bodies.

The two-body problem is summarized in Kepler's laws (as amended):

1. an orbit is an *ellipse* with the *center of mass* at one *focus* (figure 1, next page). Here $F_1$, $F_2$ are the two foci, $a$ is the semimajor axis, and $b$ the semiminor axis. The mean distance between the masses is also $a$. By definition, the sum of the distances from the two foci to any point on the ellipse is constant. It's equal to $2a$. Equivalently, the equation of the ellipse is:

$$x^2/a^2 + y^2/b^2 = 1.$$

   The *eccentricity* of an ellipse measures its deviation from a circle:

$$e = \sqrt{(a^2 - b^2)} \, / \, a.$$

   The farthest point from the focus (apocentron) is $a(1+e)$, whereas the nearest point (pericentron) is $a(1-e)$. The eccentricity of a circle is zero: both foci coincide at the center, and both semimajor and semiminor axes are equal, and equal to the radius.

2. The *radius vector* sweeps out equal areas in equal times; the "law of areas." The radius vector is the line connecting the occupied focus of the ellipse with the object in its orbit. Thus the areas in the diagram (figure 2, page 15) are equal. This in turn means that bodies move faster near pericentron, slower near apocentron, and the difference gets greater the more elliptical the orbit. This law follows directly from the conservation of angular momentum (page 43).

3. The *square* of the period is proportional to the *cube* of the semimajor axis.

$$a^3/p^2 = G(M + m)/4\,\pi^2$$

   where $P$ is the orbital period, $a$ is the semimajor axis, $M$ is the mass of the primary, $m$ the mass of the secondary, $G$ the gravitational constant, and $\pi = 3.14159\ldots$ This relation simply means that the farther apart the bodies, the longer the orbital period.

   If $m$ is much smaller than $M$, as with a planet and its star, then $M+m$ is almost the same as $M$, and we can use the

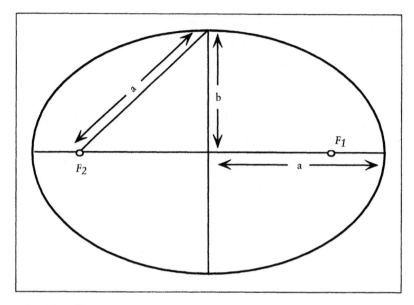

**FIG. 1** An Ellipse.

The positions of the foci $F_1$ and $F_2$ are shown, as are the lengths of the semimajor axis $a$ and semiminor axis $b$.

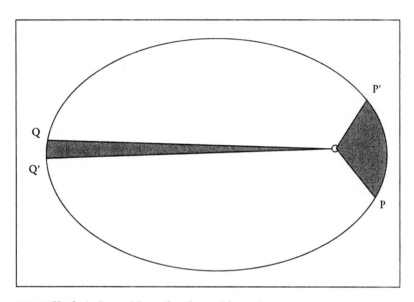

**FIG. 2** Kepler's Second Law, the "Law of Areas."
The areas of the two shaded segments are equal, so the planet (or satellite, or binary star) takes the same amount of time in going from P to P' as it does in going from Q to Q'.

approximate form:

$$a^3/p^2 = GM/4\ \pi^2.$$

For a small planet of any star:

$$P = \sqrt{(\ a^3/M\ )}$$

where $P$ is the revolution period (in years), $a$ is the mean distance (AU), and $M$ the star's mass relative to the Sun. Finally, if $e$ is small, the orbit is nearly a circle, the radius $R$ of the circle is nearly the semimajor axis $a$, and so

$$P = \sqrt{(\ R^3/M\ )}.$$

However, you must use the exact equation if the masses of the bodies are comparable, as with a binary star.

Spreadsheet calculations are also very handy when calculating orbits. It's easy to try many different combinations of parameters to, say, see how a planet's year changes with the star mass, the distance, etc. They're a lot more fun than financial what-ifs, too!

Here's another useful relation. If $m$ orbits $M$ at a distance $R$ (between centers of mass), then the orbital velocity of $m$ is:

$$v_o = \sqrt{(GM/R)}.$$

For a (small) satellite orbiting Earth, this works out to ~8 km/sec (~5 mi/sec) at $R = r =$ radius of Earth (~6370 km).

Finally, note that gravity depends *only* on mass, not on the nature of that mass. Earth's orbit wouldn't change if, say, the Sun were replaced with a neutron star of the same mass. Of course, lots of other things would!

---

## HORIZON DISTANCE

How far is the horizon on a perfectly even surface, say a ship on a flat sea? That can be another vivid background detail; on a large diameter world, for example, it's farther to the horizon. This lends a sense of vastness that can make your characters feel overwhelmed. It was used by Jack Vance in *Big Planet* and Poul Anderson in *The Man Who Counts*. Conversely, on a small planet the horizon is close and the planet seems cut off, as in the photos on the Moon. Of course, the horizon distance may not be noticeable if it's misty or hazy.

For small heights $h$ above the ground, the distance to the horizon is approximately $\sqrt{(hR)}$ on a planet of radius R. For Earth at human eye level, this is ~5 km. An object of elevation $e$ can be seen at a distance ~ $\sqrt{(Re)}$.

## 'TIS THE SEASON . . .

A year is the time it takes for a planet to complete one orbit around its star: its *revolution period*. One obvious effect on a planet is seasons! They occur because a planet's axis is generally tilted with respect to the plane of its orbit; 23.5°, in the case of the Earth right now. This tilt, or *obliquity*, causes the seasons, because over the course of the year each hemisphere is tipped alternately toward and away from the Sun (figure 3, next page). During winter, when the Earth is tipped away, solar heating is less effective, both because the sunlight is impinging at a shallower angle, and because the days are shorter so the sun doesn't shine as long. Just the opposite happens during summer.

So, the intensity of the seasons obviously depend on the latitude. Conditions at the equator hardly change over the year, whereas the poles go from uninterrupted daylight to uninterrupted darkness! Even in temperate latitudes, though, the effects aren't small. At 40°N, for example, the latitude of San Francisco, Reno and Denver, the total heating on the summer solstice, the longest day of the year (June 21) is three to four times as much as on the winter solstice six months later.

The obliquity and the seasons are also intimately related to climatic zones. The Arctic (and Antarctic) circles, which define the "polar" regions, are 23.5° from the poles, a distance set by the 23.5° tilt of the Earth's axis. These circles are simply the outer limit at which the Sun doesn't rise (or set) on at least one day of the year (figure 3, next page). Similarly, the tropics of Cancer and Capricorn, which are 23.5° from the Equator, mark the latitudes farthest from the Equator at which the Sun will be directly overhead on at least one day out of the year (figure 3, next page). They define the tropics,

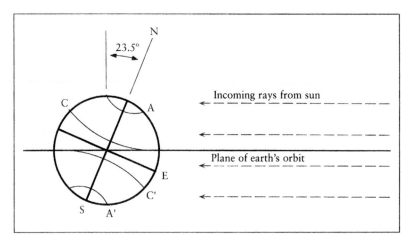

**FIG. 3** Seasons and Climatic Zones on the Earth.

The diagram shows the situation on June 21, the longest day in the northern hemisphere (and the traditional beginning of summer). Sunlight strikes the northern hemisphere, which is tipped toward the Sun, more directly and the days also last longer. Both these effects cause summer. Just the opposite obtains in the southern hemisphere, which is tipped away from the Sun and therefore entering winter. *N* and *S* are the north and south geographic poles (i.e., the ends of the spin axis), respectively; *E* is the Equator. *A* and *A*' are the Arctic and Antarctic Circles, respectively, each of which is 23.5° from the pole—the amount of Earth's axial tilt. They represent the limits at which the Sun does not rise (or set) for at least one day out of the year. *C* and *C*' are the tropics of Cancer and Capricorn, respectively, which lie 23.5° from the Equator. They reflect the farthest latitudes off the Equator at which the Sun is directly overhead on at least one day of the year, and are conventionally taken to delimit the tropics or "torrid zone." (Note that on June 21 the Sun is directly above the tropic of Cancer.)

or "torrid zone," the climatic belt in which the seasons are barely noticeable. The temperate zones lie between these extremes.

The intensity of the seasons is set by amount of axial tilt. Thus, seasons aren't inevitable. If the planet's axis were upright, they wouldn't occur, and the year would be noticeable only by the changing patterns of the constellations in the night sky. Perhaps those changes have arcane religious significance on such a world. Moreover, on such a planet the sun never rises high in polar latitudes. In Poul Anderson's "Queen of Air and Darkness," this added to the mysterious mood because the auroras (page 85) dominated illumination.

A small tilt also has some more subtle implications, though. For example, much of the water supply in temperate climes comes from snowmelt. If there's no winter, there will be no snow, and thus deserts are likely to be more widespread. Because the poles always receive little heating, climatic zones are also more extreme. *Some* tilt (like Earth's 23.5°) helps even out the heating over a planet. For comparison, the value of tilt that evens out the heating received by both poles and equator, over the course of a year, is ~54°.

So, too much tilt will also cause extreme seasons, and that will lead to extreme climate. For a planet with a tilt of 90°—that is, lying on its side—the Arctic and Antarctic circles coincide with the equator, and there are neither tropical nor temperate zones. Seasons are extreme indeed; over nearly half the planet the sun would never set during the summer, and never rise during the winter. Only during spring and fall, when it would shine from the side, would the sun rise and set as we're used to. A Solar System example is Uranus, which with an obliquity of 98° lies nearly on its side.

Poul Anderson's *The Man Who Counts* had a generally Earthlike planet with such a tilt. An intelligent species coped with the extremes by migrating from hemisphere to hemisphere over the course of the year—and that drove fundamental conflicts in the plot.

A oddball result, unused in SF so far as I know, is that for a planet with such an extreme axial tilt, the equatorial regions may be better places to grow glaciers than the poles. The poles have half-year winters, to be sure; but they're followed by half-year summers, and it's hard to preserve any snowfall. Glaciers result when snow is preserved from year to year, so that it can build up into ice (page 101). By contrast, the "tropics" are milder year-round, and some models suggest they could accumulate snow into glaciers.

We also can't speak of *the* tilt of a planet's axis; it will vary, perhaps substantially, over geologic time! The initial obliquities and rotation rates probably come from the vagaries of the last few gigantic impacts toward the end of planetary formation (page 47). Thus you can start out with any value that's convenient for your story. Some recent work also suggests that the obliquities of most planets undergo large changes over geologic time, however, because of perturbations by the other planets (page 22).

Year length is an obvious variable in designing a planet. It's not a completely free parameter, though, since a planet must be at a certain distance from its star to get the right amount of heating— and at that certain distance the year length is set by the star's mass, from Kepler's Third Law. For example, there must be unusual circumstances to have a long year, as it implies a very bright star. Thus the star is either a "highly evolved" one, such as a red giant (page 144), or else it's very massive (page 135). Neither is geologically long-lived. A more subtle consequence comes from remembering that much of the water supply in the temperate zones comes from the winter's snow. So, if the year's too long, all the snow melts before season's end and you have a *real* drought. An extra season comes between summer and fall: the "dry!" The glorious Summers on Ursula LeGuin's planet Werel (in *City of Illusions*), which had a year sixty-odd Earth years long, would get a mite thirsty.

A short year, on the other hand, implies the planet is very close to its star, and that implies a dim star. When the year becomes weeks or even days long, there's hardly room for a season as we're used to it! This is especially true since the day length in such a case is likely to be long, because of tidal braking (pages 20, 138).

As many authors have suggested, a notably elliptical orbit could probably provide seasons in lieu of (or in addition to) the axial tilt. For example, a planet whose orbit has an eccentricity of 0.25 (somewhat greater than Mercury) varies its distance by 50 percent from its sun. From page 13, if the mean distance ( = semimajor axis) is taken as one, then the pericentron distance (closest approach) is $1 - 0.25 = 0.75$, while the apocentron distance (farthest point) is $1 + 0.25 = 1.25$. Since the drop-off of sunlight follows an inverse-square law (page 131), this in turn means the planet experiences $1.25^2/0.75^2 = 2.78$ times as much heating at pericentron compared to apocentron. This is roughly the same difference as experienced by temperate latitudes from summer to winter on Earth.

Seasons caused by ellipticity will have one major difference from those caused by axial tilt, though: The whole planet will have the same season at the same time! That should have major implications for climate; even on Earth, the ice ages correlate most strongly with the slight variation in eccentricity (page 102). By contrast, seasons due to axial tilt don't change the *total* heating of the planet, because when it's winter in one hemisphere it's summer in the other.

An elliptical orbit can also stabilize the rotation of a very close-in planet by thwarting a 1:1 tidal lock (page 28). A signficantly elliptical orbit can also provide unusual local color. For one thing, the size of the sun in the sky will change perceptibly over the year, as the planet approaches and then retreats in its orbit. Even more bizarrely, *if* (and only if!) the planet's rotation period is a significant fraction of its year length, the very motion of its sun across its sky is uneven. On Mercury in our own Solar System, for example, the Sun can even back up briefly in the sky during the course of a day (pages 114-115). This comes about because the planet's speed in its orbit varies due to Kepler's Second Law.

## DANCES WITH GRAVITY

The solution of the two-body problem is exactly true *only* for point masses or spheres, because a perfect sphere acts as though all its mass is concentrated at the center. Now, it's true for all practical purposes for *any* masses as long as the distance between the masses is much greater than their sizes. If the distance is large enough, each looks like a point from the other. That's why the two-body solution works so well as a first cut. Nonetheless, (1) there are more than two bodies in the Universe; and (2) none of them are perfect spheres.

Both these differences become important over geologic time because they affect the long-term stability of planetary orbits. They also can change the axial tilts, with major effects on climate.

Such subtleties have been underutilized for world-building in SF. Most obviously, intricate systems can yield exotic story settings, and of course you can deepen the simple "gosh, wow" reaction by showing how such a setting will affect cultures, societies and religions. Ring systems, or co-orbiting planets, or the slow but chaotic tumbling of a world's spin axis are but a few of the "exotica" that could be used.

That slow but inexorable changes occur over geologic time in a real planetary system also mean that profound changes can happen long after planetary formation has settled down. Oscillations of climate obviously have implications for both life and culture. But even more catastrophic changes can occur: imagine a tidally decaying satellite finally coming within Roche's limit (page 29) and breaking up, or two satellites colliding because their orbits finally crossed. Such occurrences could provide unusual disaster settings indeed!

## Perturbations

Because the other gravitational tugs are typically modest, the changes are *perturbations*, in which the orbit parameters change very slowly. In *cyclic* perturbations, a value changes more or less systematically between limits, at least for very long periods of time. All real orbits undergo small cyclic perturbations. Earth's Milankovich variations (page 102), small changes in the Earth's orbit and obliquity, are good examples. Since the Milankovich variations seem to have driven the recent Ice Ages, this also shows that even very small orbital changes can have big climatic effects if conditions are right. (It seems Earth's climate right now is very finely balanced (page 102), so that small changes have disproportionate effects.)

A *secular* perturbation, on the other hand, is a consistent change in one direction. Thus they're fundamentally unstable and must be very slow to persist over geologic time. Commonly they're driven by the tidal losses described below. By the same token, they can make for spectacular changes! Consider the havoc in a satellite system, for example, if orbit paths begin to cross as a result of secular changes.

Worlds are not exactly spherical for a number of reasons. One is the equatorial bulge from the planet's rotation (page 88). An important effect of this is obliquity variations. Gravitational tugs from other bodies on the bulge change the obliquity over geologic time. Systematic variations in Mars's orbit and obliquity may have caused drastic changes in its climate, for example. Indeed, two recent studies indicate that the obliquity of the inner planets, other than Earth, changes chaotically over geologic time. Long-term Martian climate may be haphazard indeed!

Such drastic changes don't happen on Earth because the Moon

prevents them. In effect, another planet has to perturb the entire Earth-Moon system, which is much more difficult. The Moon all by itself causes most changes in Earth's obliquity, which are modest although a major component of the Milankovich variations. So the value of the Moon may lie in the obliquity stabilization, and thus climate stabilization, it provides.

Gravitational effects from the equatorial bulge also keep close satellites nearly in the plane of a planet's equator. If you suddenly tilted a spinning planet, the orbits of its close-in satellites would gradually also tilt to follow the planet's equator, and soon (geologically speaking) they'd be in the equatorial plane again. This is no doubt why even Uranus, lying on its side at nearly 90° to its orbit, has its nearby satellites in the plane of its equator.

In fact, *really* close-in satellites are limited by irregularities in the planet itself. Real planets have mountains and valleys, denser rock and lighter rock, and all these make a planet's gravity vary slightly from place to place. This is why, for example, a close-in satellite of the Moon is unstable; such variations soon would change the orbit enough that it would collide with the ground. In fact, it's been suggested that some of the ancient, huge craters on the Moon were made by short-lived lunar satellites, back when the Earth and Moon were still forming.

These variations also make mapping the Moon from close orbit less straightforward than it seems, because perturbations (especially from the far side, where you know even less about the mass distribution) soon send your satellite crashing into the ground if you try to orbit too closely. So, for example, mapping or surveillance satellites can't be located arbitrarily close to a world, and that fact could be a plot element. By the way, on Earth such subtle variations in surface gravity are measured by geophysicists, especially in the oil business, to determine subsurface geologic structure.

## Tides

A tidal force simply results from the *difference* in gravity across an object. Consider (for example) the Moon orbiting the Earth: the gravitational attraction is in exact balance with the "centrifugal force" (page 81) of the orbital motion only at the center of mass of the Earth-Moon system. Parts of the Earth nearer the Moon feel an extra gravitational tug, and parts farther away feel an extra centrifugal force. The upshot is that a tidal force raises a symmetrical bulge that points both toward and away from the body causing the tide.

The tide, of course, is most familiar at the seashore, from the rise and fall of the sea. Ocean tides occur because the oceans bulge toward (and away) from the Moon. Water can bulge much more than solid rock because it's free to flow. But since the Earth is rotating, we see the sea level at the shore rise and fall as Earth spins through the bulge twice a day (figure 4, page 26). (Since the Sun also raises a tide, tides are more complicated than this. But that's the idea.)

---

### SCALING THE TIDES

The details of tidal forces are very complicated, as they vary in latitude and with the orientation of the tide-raising body. Fortunately, we don't need those details (see a reference such as Stacey in the Reference List if you're interested); we're only interested in how the overall magnitude of the tide-raising force changes with different distances and masses. (A physicist would say we're interested in the "scaling" of the tides.) In this way we can roughly compare the magnitude of the tidal effect with that of some familiar system, say the Moon on the Earth, or the Sun on Mercury.

The scaling goes as follows:

$$T = M/R^3,$$

where $M$ is the mass of the tide-raising body, $R$ the distance at which the tidal effect is to be measured, and $T$ the relative magnitude of the tides. (This equation assumes that R is much larger than the size of the bodies themselves.) To use this equation, measure M and R in terms of some familiar object. For example, to see how the tide-raising force compares with that of the Moon on the Earth, take M in terms of the Moon's mass and R in terms of the distance of the Moon from the Earth. A satellite with twice the mass of the Moon at half the distance, for example, would exert:

$$T = 2/(1/2)^3 = 2/(1/8) = 2 \times 8 = 16$$

times the tidal effect of the Moon.

Now, this doesn't mean tides will be sixteen times as high, because the tidal height also depends on such things as the viscosity of water (how easily it flows) and the friction with the sea floor—some of those details we said we'd ignore! But it gives an idea of how things will change. In particular, such a calculation gives a sense of how much tidal braking (page 27) has probably occurred.

You can see that the tide-raising force drops off as the *cube* of distance; that is, much more quickly than does gravity itself. This comes about because it depends on a *difference* in distance. For example, the Moon is only ~250,000 miles away. Since the Earth is ~8000 miles in diameter, you can be 8000 miles closer to the Moon on one side of the Earth than the other. That's a difference of 8000/250,000, or ~3%. However, the difference with the Sun, 93,000,000 miles away, is only 8000/93,000,000, or ~0.009%. This is why the lunar tide is so much stronger—the Moon is a *lot* closer. For Earth, the lunar tide is something like two-thirds of the total, the solar tide only about one-third.

Because they also distort a planet or moon from a spherical shape, tides provide another lever for gravitational perturbations. Furthermore, it's a lever that depends very strongly on how far away the tide-raising body is. Even more important, tides generally *change*, because the direction and/or distance of the tide-raising body (or bodies) generally changes. Two planets that always kept the same face to each other, for example, would be distorted by their tides, but that's all. The tides wouldn't stress the planets, and an ocean wouldn't slosh up and down because it wouldn't be rotating through the tidal bulge.

Tidal effects dominate how the eccentricity of a close-in satellite orbit changes. For a satellite revolving in the same direction as its primary rotates (a "prograde" satellite), tidal perturbations would increase the eccentricity if nothing else happened. In effect, the orbit's always getting a push at its closest point in the direction that tends to add energy to the orbit. Because the tidal force drops off so quickly, most of the effects occur when the satellite's closest. In fact, though, tides nearly always cause orbits to become more

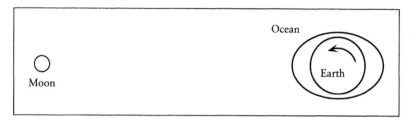

**FIG. 4** Tides in the Oceans.
The Moon raises a symmetric tidal bulge on the oceans, which are free to
flow. As the Earth rotates through this bulge, we see sea level rise and fall
twice a day. Ocean and bulge are *not* to scale.

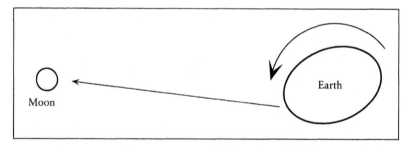

**FIG. 5** Braking of the Earth's Rotation by the Moon.
The Earth's rotation carries the tidal bulge slightly out of alignment with the
Moon, so that the Moon pulls back on it. Similarly, the bulge pulls forward on
the Moon, which adds energy to the Moon's orbit and so causes it to move
gradually away from the Earth. Drawing *not* to scale.

circular (that is, less eccentric). This is because the satellite's orbital energy gets dissipated into heat. The tidal bulge gets bigger and smaller as the satellite comes into pericentron and apocentron; that flexes the satellite, and friction turns some of that flexing into heat.

If the satellite has a backward or "retrograde" orbit, though, tidal effects always circularize the orbit. Neptune's large moon Triton is a spectacular example; it has a close-in, retrograde orbit that's indistinguishable from a perfect circle. This also means an enormous amount of energy has been dissipated, enough to melt Triton several times over.

## Tidal Braking

Tidal braking is the slowing of rotation by tidal action. It's why the Moon now keeps the same face toward Earth, in a so-called *tidal lock*. The Moon's rotation was braked long ago. And the Moon, of course, is returning the compliment: It's braking the Earth's rotation. If things go to completion, the Moon's retreat will halt when the Earth always keeps one face toward the Moon. Earth and Moon will then face each other permanently, slowly rotating like a couple in a country-western dance. Pluto and its large satellite Charon are in this position right now.

How does this happen? A planet's rotation tends to carry the tidal bulge forward so that it's no longer lined up with the satellite. The satellite pulls back on the bulge with its gravity and thus slows the planet down (figure 5, previous page). Similarly, the bulge pulls forward on the moon, adding energy to its orbit and thus causing it to move farther from the primary. The Moon is moving away from the Earth about one-and-one-half inches per year. Thus, tidal braking also moves "spin" (angular momentum, technically) from the rotation of worlds around their axes to their revolution in their orbits. The Moon's orbit gets bigger as the Earth's spin slows down. The changes have been slow over most of geologic time; it seems that even four billion years ago, only six hundred million years after the Earth and the Solar System formed, the Moon was already half as far away as it is now (and thus looked twice as big in the sky; see page 136), and the day was about ten hours long.

Tidal evolution of orbits means, though, that catastrophic changes can come very late in a planetary system's history. After billions of years of slow, steady changes, a threshold is crossed; and suddenly one satellite can collide with another, or be broken up by passing within Roche's limit, or tumble chaotically in its orbit, or whatever. As we'll see, such abrupt changes have happened in the Solar System in the geologic past, and they will happen again in the future—and they have been little exploited as settings for stories.

Obviously the tidal braking also dissipates energy. The rotational energy of the Earth is slowly being turned into heat as the Moon brakes it; and the speed at which energy is turned into heat by friction in the Earth (in the oceans, chiefly) is what determines how fast the Moon retreats. In fact, the braking is unusually strong right now because the tides are nearly in *resonance* (page 32) with the natural frequency at which the Earth's ocean "sloshes."

The Sun has similarly braked Mercury, but the lock is more complicated. Although for years Mercury was thought to keep the same face to the Sun, as the Moon does to the Earth, that's not true. It's instead a 3:2 lock; Mercury rotates three times for every two orbits (page 114). The lock is stabilized by Mercury's elliptical orbit, for reasons too involved to get into here. Such a lock, though, is likely to be critical in arranging interesting planets around small, dim stars, as described in detail later (page 138).

Things can go the other way, too, although "braking" is then a misnomer. If the pull goes the other way—if the bulge is pulling the satellite *ahead* in its orbit—it marches the satellite right back into the planet while the planet spins faster and faster! Obviously this is the situation if the direction of the satellite's orbit is retrograde, and Triton's fate will be to get dragged into destruction in a few hundred million years or so. But it happens even if the planet merely rotates more slowly than its satellite orbits.

For this reason things get even dicier with a third tide-raising body in the system. Mercury and Venus don't have satellites because, after their rotations were locked into a very slow rate by the Sun, the solar tides would then have caused any satellites to migrate back into the parent planet. In fact, one scientist has suggested that many of the (geologically) recent craters on Venus result from the decay of its satellites! In the far, far future this would also eventually happen to the Moon, once it succeeds in locking Earth's rotation, but by then the Sun will have long since burned out. This effect puts limits on how near their star "double planet" systems could orbit, though, as with a system around a small, red star (page 138).

## ROCHE'S LIMIT

This is the approximate point where a close-in satellite will be torn apart by tidal forces. It assumes the satellite is held together only by its own gravity; i.e., it has no mechanical strength. Thus it doesn't apply to, say, spacecraft in close orbits, which aren't held together just by their gravity.

For a satellite of density $\rho_s$ orbiting planet of radius $r$ and density $\rho_p$:

$$L = 2.44\ r\ \sqrt[3]{(\rho_p/\rho_s)}$$

For Earth and Moon this is about 2.89 r, or 18,400 km (between centers), which works out to 12,040 km from the Earth's surface.

### Many Bodies

Things also get much more complicated if more than two bodies are interacting gravitationally—which, of course, is the case in the real world. Only the two-body system can be solved exactly. Add a third body and no such solution exists. The system is, in general, chaotic in the dynamical sense.

Or rather, most solutions are chaotic. There are stable positions for a third body in a two-body system. To visualize them, imagine two equilateral triangles joined along one edge. If the primary and the secondary are at the vertexes at each end of the joined edges, then the stable points are at the isolated vertexes (figure 6, next page). As many of you already know, these are the Lagrange-4 and Lagrange-5 (L-4 and L-5, for short) points, named after the French physicist who discovered them mathematically in the eighteenth century.

So, another possibility is satellites at the L-4 and L-5 points. Jupiter has such companions at both points, the so-called Trojan asteroids. (So called because they're named after heroes in the Trojan War.) Over the last ten years or so, too, astronomers have searched off and on for debris at Earth's L-4 and L-5 ("Trojan") points, along its orbit around the Sun. (No luck so far.) And of course, the Trojan points in the Earth-Moon system were proposed as sites for space colonies back in the 1970s. Saturn's moon Tethys actually has natural L-4 and

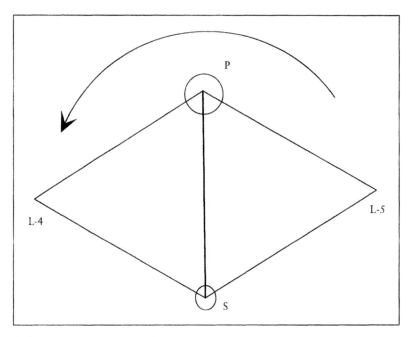

**FIG. 6** Position of Trojan Points L-4 and L-5.

The position of the Trojan points L-4 and L-5 are shown on the orbit of a secondary body *S* orbiting a primary *P*. Direction of orbital motion shown by arrow.

L-5 companions, and another moon, Dione, has an L-4 companion.

In a real solar system, which consists of more than just three bodies, the Trojan points themselves are not always stable. To a first approximation, for something at a Trojan point to remain there indefinitely the mass of the secondary must be less than about 4 percent of the primary. And the mass of the body at the Trojan point must be negligible. Otherwise, perturbations will cause the Trojan to wander away. As it is, even permanent Trojan bodies can wander quite a way from the exact L-4 or L-5 point. They actually orbit around the point. Some of the Trojan asteroids, for example, can at times be farther from their Lagrange point than the Earth is from the Sun.

Since all the planets have less than 4 percent the mass of the Sun, though, all their Trojan points should be stable. But so far only Jupiter is known to have Trojan companions.

Elsewhere, we can imagine Earthlike planets in a Trojan orbit with two stars. Poul Anderson used such a setting for his novel *Planet of No Return* (republished as *Question and Answer*). But because of that 4 percent secondary-to-primary limit, we really can't speak of two *stars*, because stars (at least those with Earthlike planets) don't vary in mass that much. For example, if the primary were the size of the Sun, the secondary could have at most only 4 percent of the Sun's mass, and that's not quite enough to light the nuclear fires. It would be an object between a planet and a star, a so-called "brown dwarf" (page 141).

Still, it would glow deep, dull red, from heat released by gravitational energy when it accreted. And in any case it could be seen easily from the night sky of the Earthlike planet, as it would reflect the primary's light. Like Venus and Mercury in our own System (page 110), it could never appear in the midnight sky; it would always be a morning or evening star (page 110). On the other hand, being so big it would be bright enough to be visible in full daylight. No doubt many legends would arise about this brilliant, unusual object—the Daystar. A bigger question would be whether an Earthlike planet could form in a Trojan position in the first place, but we don't know for sure it's impossible.

## Rings

Once thought to be unique to Saturn, ring systems have turned out to be de rigeur for giant planets, at least in our Solar System.

Saturn's are just the most spectacular. But they're still poorly understood, just because of their mathematical complexity. Of course, rings consists of millions of separate tiny satellites, each in its own orbit.

One problem with understanding rings has been what keeps them together. You can show they'll tend to be thin; as their orbits evolve, the particles tend to spread out into the same plane. But what keeps them from spreading out indefinitely until they disperse completely? Until recently the well-defined edges of, say, Saturn's rings were very hard to explain.

This problem was solved with the discovery of "shepherd moons" near the edges of the rings; like sheepdogs, they keep the rings in place, in a subtle manner. Take the outer "shepherd" as an example. The rings' gravity pulls back on the satellite, which removes energy from it; so it tends to drop into a lower orbit, at which point it moves faster! At the same time its gravity pulls ahead on the ring particles, pulling them into higher orbits so they slow down—and as the ring particles slow down and the satellite pulls ahead, the gravitational pull between them drops off rapidly. Thus, the satellite's gravity "massages" the edge of the rings, keeping the ring particles' orbits from spreading. This also means the shepherd moons must themselves be small enough to be affected by the mass of the rings.

The shepherds and rings are particular examples of *resonance*. This is a concept you find throughout dynamics, not just in the intricacies of gravity. An everyday example is pushing a child on a swing. We all know you have to time the pushes just right for the swing to swing. Or, as a physicist might say, the "forcing function" needs to be near the "resonant frequency" of the swing. More generally, a resonance happens when something gets pushed (or pulled) at about the frequency at which it would oscillate naturally—the "resonant frequency."

Could an Earthlike planet have rings, as in Poul Anderson's world Cleopatra, in *A World Called Cleopatra*? Possibly tidal perturbations would prevent this. An Earthlike planet is so close to its star, and its gravity, by comparison with Saturn's, is so modest that they wouldn't be stable geologically.

Maybe not, though. Or maybe rings could be formed by an unusual event and last for a "little while" geologically, but for a long time as the human race reckons it. Perhaps they could be the final result of a satellite's tidal decay, as it finally came within Roche's limit to be shattered into fragments. Or maybe a gigantic impact on a satellite could scatter some debris around the planet that could then settle into a ring system.

Rings would make for spectacular skies. To begin with, let's visualize their appearance during the summer in north temperate latitudes. During the day, a vast white arch, probably visibly subdivided into concentric arcs, would stretch high across the southern sky, pallid but plainly visible like the daytime Moon from the Earth. As the sun set, the arch would blaze with glory, intricate like a lacework with its multiple interior arcs. Shepherd moons would appear like brilliant pearls, but would slowly pace the edges of the rings. As nightfall encroached, though, a great black bite would be taken out of the arch to the east, where it fell within the planet's shadow, and as night wore on, the darkness would spread westward until it engulfed the entire arch. Only at this point could any but the very brightest stars appear; and no stars at all would appear in a black band across the sky, where the shadowed rings would block the view of the sky beyond. Toward dawn the process would be reversed; high in the east a brilliant arc would appear where the rings first caught the sunlight, and the brilliance would spread westward until the whole arch would glow just before dawn.

The position of the arch in the sky depends on the latitude; it will stand high in low latitudes, but lie toward the horizon as seen from the poles. Near the equator it will soar directly overhead, but it will always be nearly edge-on and thus difficult to see!

The rings would have massive climatic effects, too. To see why, consider how they're distributed around the planet. They're close: they'll lie within Roche's limit, and because of the dynamical reasons outlined above, they'll also lie in the plane of the planet's equator. Hence the rings will define a broad band in the sky some ninety degrees away from the *celestial pole*, the point in the sky around which the rest of the sky seems to rotate due to the planet's spin. (Polaris, the North Star, currently marks this point on Earth.) In the summer, when the planet's axis tilts toward its sun, the sun's path will pass north of the rings (for an observer in the northern hemisphere), and so the rings will have little effect. In wintertime, though, when the planet's axis tilts away from the sun, the sun's path will lie behind the rings; or in other words, the rings will cast a broad band of shadow across the temperate zone (figure 7, page

35). As seen from the ground, the sun would sparkle behind a diaphanous veil, a backlit, gauzy ribbon in which moving moonlets might be plainly visible. Obviously this will make the winters colder and darker.

Over the course of the seasons, then, the sun actually passes behind the rings, later to re-emerge as spring comes again. Imagine the implications for mythology and religion! Maybe the day the sun first comes out from behind the ring, on the way to summer, is a major festival.

## Resonances

Co-orbiting satellites are another weird example of a resonance. Saturn's tiny moons Janus and Epithemis nearly share an orbit; but one never passes the other. They're forever going faster and slower in the orbit, approaching as though to pass a baton in a relay, only to drop back before getting close enough to touch. As seen from Saturn, they'd get closer, slow down, and then separate again as though they'd "bounced off" each other. Things would look even more bizarre from one of the moons themselves; you'd see the other moon approaching, but you'd slow down and it would speed up as you got closer, until finally it would flee out of sight. Then the whole pattern would repeat half an orbit later—but you'd have to go around to the other side of the satellite to watch it again.

The interaction is like that between a ring and a shepherd; as the satellite in the slightly lower orbit approaches, moving more quickly because it's nearer the primary, the gravity from the satellite ahead pulls it into a slightly higher orbit where it slows down. Similarly, the satellite ahead, pulled from behind, drops into a lower orbit where it can move more quickly. And this interchange happens over and over.

The co-orbiters in Saturn's system are stable, and perhaps co-orbiting planets occur somewhere, though I don't know that anyone's looked at the dynamics. Two Earthlike worlds, forever chasing each other around a star, is not a setting anyone's used, so far as I know!

Other resonances happen when orbital periods are multiples of each other. Consider two orbiting satellites, one with a period twice that of the other. Every second orbit, the lower satellite (the one with the shorter period) gets a tug from the outer satellite, always from the same direction.

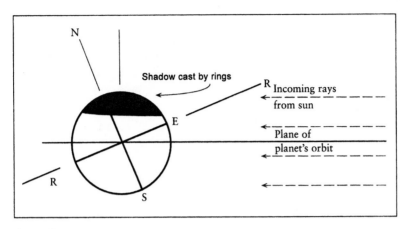

**FIG. 7** Effect of Rings on Surface Environment.
The effect of rings on the surface environment of a planet is illustrated for a hypothetical planet shown at northern hemisphere winter. The rings $R$ must lie in the plane of the planet's equator $E$ and must lie within Roche's limit (~2.44 planetary radii). ($N$ and $S$ mark the positions of the north and south poles.) As seen from the surface, the position of the rings in the sky will never change and will depend on latitude. From the poles, the rings will lie low in the sky; from the equator, the rings will be directly overhead but edge-on. Note that the temperate zone (and the pole, if the axial tilt is great enough) lie in the rings' shadow during the winter; this will make winter both colder and darker.

At first glance such an orbital resonance seems unstable; that extra gravitational pull at exactly the same time on every other orbit (or every third, or so) should perturb it right out of the resonance.

This happens, but a more detailed analysis shows that the perturbations tend to be self-canceling. That is, when the orbits go slightly out of resonance, then perturbations tend to bring them back into resonance, and so on. Thus the orbits oscillate around the resonance configuration. And if you have more than three bodies, resonances can get involved indeed. The Jovian moons Io, Europa and Ganymede are currently trapped into an intricate resonance whose stability remained unexplained for over three centuries, until 1979. Io's massive volcanism is maintained by this resonance (page 117).

In fact, the Solar System contains quite a number of resonances and near-resonances, and most must be quite stable. Evidently satellites can evolve into such configurations and stay there for a long time, as their orbits change from tidal evolution.

Such variations and complications give many possibilities for exotic settings that have been much less used in SF. Charles Sheffield's *Summertide* and Robert L. Forward's *Rocheworld* are both set on double *planets*, for example, in which the tidal distortion is important to the setting; it allows atmosphere to be exchanged between both worlds. Although such double planets are probably unstable because of the tidal braking from the parent star, as with satellites of Mercury and Venus, they give the flavor of the possible settings. Moreover, although detailed calculations of such scenarios are beyond the scope of this book, from this information you can come up with possibilities that, say, a friendly graduate student could work with to determine their limits and reasonableness.

# CHAPTER 3

# Making a Planet

N ow let's look briefly at how planets and stars form. We think we understand, in a very general way, how this happens, but it's a complicated and (so far as we can tell) somewhat haphazard process. Although broad limits exist, it seems that much of the details of a planetary system—the sizes of the planets, the compositions of their atmospheres, their rotation rates and obliquities, even their very distribution—do not seem to be inevitable. Instead they reflect vagaries in the formation of the particular planetary system. This strong element of historic contingency gives us a lots of options for storytelling.

## ELEMENTARY CONSIDERATIONS

Let's start with the composition of a planet. Is something as exotic as, say, a planet of gold reasonable? With ninety-odd chemical elements, it seems there'd be scope for variation here!

There is, but there are also some major constraints. Even though there are about ninety chemical elements, they have *extremely* different abundances; and *that* largely determines what planets (and stars) are made of. Obviously it's easier to make a world out of common elements rather than rare ones.

First, light elements are in general much more common than heavy elements. About 92 percent of the atoms in the Universe are hydrogen, and helium makes up most of the remaining 8 percent. All heavier elements are just impurity. As stars are mostly hydrogen and helium, their composition thus reflects the Universe. Since normal stars—those on the Main Sequence (page 133)—get their energy by fusing hydrogen into helium, there's lots of hydrogen for fuel!

Those "impurities" vary quite a bit, too. Carbon-12 ($^{12}$C) and oxygen-16 ($^{16}$O) are the most abundant heavy nuclei. Both have exceptionally stable nuclei and are readily synthesized by nuclear processes. Even so, they're a *very* distant third after hydrogen and helium. Next come nitrogen-14 ($^{14}$N) and neon-20 ($^{20}$Ne). Hence, one reason that the CHON (carbon-hydrogen-oxygen-nitrogen; see page 104) elements work so well as the basis of life is simply that they're abundant. By contrast, for example, the light elements lithium, beryllium, and boron are extremely rare. They have delicate nuclei that are easily broken up by stellar nuclear reactions. One implication of *this* is that alternative biochemistries based on boron will be very difficult to arrange. From its chemical properties, boron-based life seems vaguely possible, but it will be difficult to gather enough together to try.

After nitrogen and neon come sulfur (S), silicon (Si), magnesium (Mg), iron (Fe), with calcium (Ca), sodium (Na), aluminum (Al) and nickel (Ni) less abundant still. Finally, iron-56 has the most stable nucleus (page 144). This means that all elements heavier than iron—gold, zirconium, tungsten, uranium, iodine, europium, etc.—are very rare indeed, and in general the heavier, the rarer. Don't expect planets of gold or platinum!

---

### WHAT MAKES A CHEMICAL ELEMENT?

The chemical elements make up most of the matter in the Universe, including planets and stars, so we'll have occasion to talk about them a lot! Here's a quick review. The elements basically reflect different kinds of atoms. An atom has a positively charged *nucleus* that consists of positively charged *protons* and neutral *neutrons*. It's held together by nuclear forces. This nucleus is orbited by negative *electrons*, whose number is determined by the protons. Under some circumstances atoms can lose or gain one or more electrons. Such electrically charged atoms are called *ions*.

The chemical properties of the atom come from the interactions of these circling electrons (the "electron cloud") with other atoms. In this way atoms can bond together to form *molecules.* (Chemical bonds result from electrical forces among the atoms, as mediated by quantum mechanics, but we don't need those details! All we need to know is that atoms link together to form molecules according to specific rules that differ for each element.)

Each element has a different number of protons, and thus a different number of circling electrons. Indeed, it's this difference that make elements distinct. This number is called the *atomic number*. Carbon has an atomic number of 6; oxygen's is 8, gold's is 79; iron's is 26; and so on. Hydrogen is number 1.

All elements have one or two-letter abbreviations. Most are obvious: C for carbon, O for oxygen, Ca for calcium, Dy for dysprosium, and so forth. Note that the abbreviation is always capitalized, but the name of the element itself never is. A few elements take their abbreviations from the Latin name; e.g., iron (Fe, from ferrum); gold (Au, from aurum); copper (Cu, from cuprum), and so forth. As most such elements have been known since antiquity, most languages already have different names for them; thus using the Latin name was a useful international compromise. As a memory crutch you may put the atomic number in front as a subscript; e.g., $_8O$.

The formulas for molecules are written out by stringing together the chemical symbols for each element in the molecule, with the number of atoms of the element (if more than one) as a following subscript, e.g.: $H_2O$, two hydrogens and one oxygen; $CO_2$, one carbon and two oxygens, and so on.

Finally, nuclei themselves come in different varieties. Nuclei with different numbers of neutrons but the same number of protons are called *isotopes*, and the *mass number* is the sum of the protons and neutrons. It's also approximately the *atomic weight*. Because they have the same number of protons, the chemistry of isotopes is nearly identical (there are very small differences due to the different mass). Most elements have more than one naturally occurring isotope; e.g., oxygen has three ($^{16}O$, $^{17}O$, $^{18}O$, all with 8 protons but 8, 9 and 10 neutrons, respectively), iron has four ($^{54}Fe$, $^{56}Fe$, $^{57}Fe$, and $^{58}Fe$), nitrogen has two ($^{14}N$ and $^{15}N$), and so on. (Note that the mass number is written as a front superscript. Formerly it was written as a following superscript, e.g., $O^{16}$, but that's now obsolete.)

Certain combinations of neutrons and protons are unstable.
Such a nucleus will spontaneously change to a lower-energy
state with the release of energy and is called *radioactive*. (*Stable* nuclei are not radioactive.) Radioactive nuclei change, or
*decay*, exponentially at a constant rate that's characteristic of
the particular nucleus. This decay rate is commonly expressed as a *half-life*, the time for half of an initial quantity of
radioactive nuclei to decay. Most radioactive nuclei have half-lives that are very short compared with geologic time, and so
they don't occur in bodies such as planets. A few long-lived
nuclei do exist, however, and the energy they release on decaying is extremely important in powering planetary processes over geologic time (page 55). Finally, *all* nuclei are
radioactive if they have more than 83 protons (bismuth); that's
why there are only ~90 naturally existing elements.

## Forging the Elements

Nucleosynthesis, the synthesis of nuclei, is the collection of processes by which the elements got formed. Hydrogen and helium
are nearly all primordial, from the Big Bang thought to have formed
the Universe. However, since no stable isotopes have mass numbers of five or eight, primordial nucleosynthesis didn't build significantly beyond helium ($^4$He).

Nearly all heavier elements are built up in stars. And as you
might expect, stars make some elements more easily than others.
The reason an element is rare or common depends on nuclear
physics, on how easily it's synthesized in stars. The Main Sequence
(page 133) isn't important for nucleosynthesis, though, because
such stars only fuse hydrogen to helium. Stars beyond the Main
Sequence, which build up helium into even heavier elements, are
element forges.

*Very* massive stars are especially important in nucleosynthesis,
for there's another problem: it's not enough to make heavy elements; they also must get back out into the interstellar medium,
where they can later be incorporated into new stars (and planets)!

Stellar winds from red giants (page 144) help some, as do planetary nebulas (page 145) and ordinary novas (page 151). Even
though their contributions are all light elements, mostly things like

carbon, nitrogen, oxygen and neon, they may be locally important for making unusual worlds.

But the main nucleosynthetic factories are supernovas, the gigantic explosions of dying massive stars (page 145). Not only does the explosion spread lots of newly forged elements back into interstellar space, but the ferocious blizzard of nucleons loosed by the explosion piles more particles onto seed nuclei to build heavier nuclei. Nearly all the elements heavier than iron, which *take* energy to make, are made this way.

Where the supernova really shines (so to speak) is in the so-called "r-process." "R" is for "rapid," and it means neutrons are added *rapidly*—before the nucleus has a chance to decay into something more stable. This is the *only* way to make nuclei heavier than lead ($_{82}$Pb) and bismuth ($_{83}$Bi). All elements heavier than bismuth are alpha-radioactive, that is, they fly apart again by throwing off alpha particles ($^4$He nuclei). And the elements just heavier than bismuth are very short-lived indeed. Imagine adding a neutron to $^{209}$Bi, for example. You get $^{210}$Bi, which rapidly (with a half-life of about ten weeks) decays back to $^{206}$Pb.

So you're right back where you started—at a lead or bismuth isotope.

However, certain isotopes of thorium ($_{90}$Th) and uranium ($_{92}$U) have half-lives of billions of years. Even though these atoms are unstable, therefore, they can persist over geologic time. In fact, they're very important as power sources for keeping Earthlike planets habitable (page 55).

The only way to make these heavy nuclei is with the r-process. And the only place to do that is a supernova explosion. So when we break down uranium atoms for energy in a nuclear reactor, we're using energy stored in a supernova explosion billions of years ago.

## THE COLLAPSE OF A GMC

Star formation starts with the gravitational collapse of part of a GMC, a giant molecular cloud (not General Motors Corporation), and planets are at least an occasional by-product of this process. Such clouds are common in spiral galaxies like our Milky Way (page 151). They're vast agglomerations of gas and some dust that, although still a far better vacuum than anything we can make on Earth, are denser than the usual interstellar gas. They're dense enough, in fact, that lots of the atoms in them are combined into molecules, from which they get their name. As you'd expect, the hydrogen-gas molecule, $H_2$, is most abundant, simply because of the sheer abundance of hydrogen. Hydrogen doesn't show up well spectroscopically (page 70), though. A molecule that *does* show up well is CO (carbon monoxide), and it's been used to map these clouds in our Galaxy. Obviously, too, to make interesting planets such a cloud must be young enough that supernovas have placed heavy elements back into the interstellar medium.

A GMC starts to clump just from getting cold. Because the outside of the cloud shades the inside from starlight, the inside cools, just as a cloud shadow cools the ground on Earth. Of course, by everyday standards the cloud's pretty cold already! Starlight didn't warm it very much. But the shaded cloud cools from a balmy $-200°C$ or so to maybe $-250°C$—and that's a big difference.

Why? Because the pressure of the cloud gas is what keeps gravity from pulling it together. Pressure results from the gas molecules colliding as they rush around. But as a gas cools, its molecules move more slowly and hit less hard, and thus, its pressure lessens. So gravity can clump the cooler parts in tighter.

Still, such a clump can't yet quite fall together under its own gravity. It needs a push, just like a snowball that needs a little shove to start rolling. What kind of push? One possibility is a density wave, like you get along a Slinky spring when you push it in and out at one end. The spiral arms in spiral galaxies are now thought to be such waves. They're vast and sluggish, obviously, but they could still work. Another possibility is the shock wave from a nearby supernova. Some meteorites show evidence of a nearby supernova that blew just before the Solar System formed. Or maybe instead a nova or planetary nebula gave the push.

A nearby supernova or other exploding star would not be an odd coincidence, either. GMCs spawn a few very massive stars. As such stars have very short lifetimes (page 135), they go supernova quickly, before the overall cloud has changed much (on geologic timescales—say ten million years or so.) So while the cloud is still spawning new stars, the most massive first-formed stars are already starting to pop off within it.

In fact, it seems such explosions eventually blow the GMC apart before much of it has condensed into stars. Only a few percent of the cloud's mass ends up in stars; the rest becomes redispersed, perhaps to reaccumulate elsewhere. That's why galaxies like the Milky Way still have gas and dust to make new stars, billions of years after the galaxies themselves formed.

Now, as the clump collapses it starts to spin faster. "Spin" (angular momentum, formally) is "conserved," as physicists say. Just as with energy, you can move it around but you can't create or destroy it. The classic (and good) example from physics texts is the spinning figure skater who pulls in her arms to spin faster. So even though the cloud may have been spinning extremely slowly to start with, as it shrinks it must spin faster.

The amount of angular momentum is critical. If the cloud has too much, at some point it will spin fast enough to split up into multiple clouds, and you'll end up with a multiple star system. They seem to be less likely places for planets (page 148).

If there's too little spin, though, the nebula will all collapse into a single slowly spinning star—and again there will be no planets.

So, just like Goldilocks's porridge, the cloud needs to be just right: It needs enough angular momentum that everything doesn't end up in the star, but not so much that several stars form. In such a case you end up with a single star surrounded by a thick, disk-shaped nebula; an "accretion disk." This leftover nebula is what spawns planets. Perhaps 25 percent of stars end up this way. And as it collapses, the cloud heats up, from its released gravitational energy. It forms a "protosun" in the center that's hot even before the nuclear fires begin.

## THE TITIUS-BODE LAW

In the eighteenth century, Johann Titius noted that the planets are spaced roughly exponentially farther apart the farther they are from the Sun. The rule was subsequently popularized by Johann Bode. It goes as follows: take the successive powers of two (0, 1, 2, 4, 8, 16, etc.), multiply by 0.3, and add 0.4. The result is the successive planetary distances in AU, including the mean position of the asteroids. The fit is not bad for most of the planets, but the law breaks down for Neptune and fails completely for Pluto.

A lot of shouting has ensued over the years about the significance of the Titius-Bode progression. The most recent thinking is that it simply results from the gravity gradient away from the central star; that is, it's a tidal effect. The tides limit the width of the zone over which material could be gathered together efficiently into a planet. Regular satellite systems around the gas-giant planets (page 110) show similar logarithmic spacing, and probably other planetary systems will too.

Now, in our own Solar System we have two fundamentally different types of planets: big, gassy and Jupiter-like versus small, rocky and (relatively) Earthlike. It's not likely that these two types are unique to our Solar System, but they seem to reflect very different planet-formation processes. What happened?

The point where the nebula becomes cool enough that water can condense into ice—we'll call it the Ice Line—seems critical. The gas giants form beyond this distance. Water is a common substance in the Universe, and where it freezes out you deposit a lot of solid matter in the nebula. This seems to lead to a gravitational runaway: that matter clots under its own gravity to make a protoplanet core; then the core's gravity becomes great enough to gather in additional material from the surrounding nebula, which increases its gravity, which lets it gather in *more* matter, etc. Jupiter probably formed where ice first was able to condense. This may indicate, too, that the Ice Line is the site of the biggest planet.

Some close double stars may have formed this way, too. If the protoplanet core gets big enough, the nuclear fires will turn on, and suddenly you've got a small star rather than a planet. *Very* close binary stars, separated by less than a few astronomical units or so, have nearly circular orbits, just like planets—and that suggests they may have formed much like planets. Most multiple star systems have very elliptical orbits.

Gas-giant protoplanets also seem to spawn a small-scale version of the accretion disk around themselves, from which in turn their regular satellite system (page 110) forms. Because the heat of the protoplanet "cooks out" the nearer satellites, the inner ones are rockier and the outer ones icier, as with Jupiter's large satellites from Io out to Callisto.

But what about the rocky planets? To us, anyway, they're a lot more interesting than gas giants!

Well, first, they formed closer to the Sun, where it's warmer, and things like ice—much less hydrogen and helium—never condensed out. Only refractory (high-melting-point) stuff like rock and metal could condense, so even though it made up a tiny proportion of the original nebula, it was all that was left! In fact, as you might guess, the intense heating from the hot new star sets the inner limit of planet formation. That heating determines the distance where even the refractories can condense out.

So, we can see already that the innermost planets of hot stars are farther away from their sun. *Very* hot stars may have no planets at all for this reason. Hot stars also should have more rocky planets and fewer gas giants—maybe, indeed, none at all—simply because the Ice Line's going to be much farther from the central star. (With no Jupiter to clear things out early on (page 46), such a system may also have a bigger problem with ongoing impacts.) In fact, such stars should have fewer planets overall, simply because they're more massive. This comes from the fact that the cloud will have only so much angular momentum: If it had had too much to start with, it would have split up. So if the central star is massive, there won't be much nebula left over to make planets.

The outer limit of planet formation is set by two things. The first is the density of the nebula: How much planet-stuff is available? The nebula will be thinner out there. The second is the time available to accrete it. Processes in the outer nebula are very leisurely, because orbital velocities are low, from Kepler's Third Law. The material may not be able to coalesce before the nebula blows away as the star ignites. It's been estimated, for example, that Uranus and Neptune took three-hundred million years to grow, versus maybe a million years for Jupiter. This also is presumably why the Ice Line is the site of the biggest planet. Although ice must have condensed out farther as well, accretion just doesn't work so well out there. This suggests, too, that small stars also have small planetary systems. Faraway planets would grow much too leisurely indeed; there wouldn't be time to grow much of a planet before the nebula blows away.

## FOR HEALTHY GROWING PLANETS . . .

It appears that the first step in accretion is for grains of dust to chemically precipitate out of the disk around the forming star. In close, where the nebula is hot, these grains will consist of metal and rock; out farther, they'll be mostly ices. The grains then accrete into asteroid-sized bodies called *planetesimals*, and *these* in turn accrete into planets.

The step where you accrete planetesimals into planets is a critical one, however. For this to work, the planetesimals have to touch very gently indeed; otherwise they don't stick but shatter. They're still much too small to have any significant gravity to help hold them together.

Now, to touch so gently means the planetesimals must be in nearly circular, concentric orbits. In this way they can come together tangentially at very slow speeds. Things do hit *hard* later on, though. It's now pretty clear that *late* accretion—that is, accretion after the planets had largely formed—was a lot more violent than scientists originally thought. In fact, our Solar System was a pretty dangerous place for a few hundred million years after the planets had mostly accreted. Large leftover pieces, even some aborted planets, were careening around in unstable orbits. Nothing forced planets to accrete in geologically stable orbits! So, some exceedingly large collisions resulted. The formation of the Moon was one consequence (page 113), as was the loss of much of Mercury's rocky mantle (page 114). The planets we see today are probably just the leftovers that lucked into geologically stable orbits.

Jupiter didn't help, either. Once Jupiter accreted, its gravity also started stirring up the orbits of whatever planetesimals and half-grown planets were left. One effect was that the orbits became more elliptical. Thus their orbits started crossing each other—and when they hit under those circumstances, they hit *hard*. They don't accrete. Others got thrown out of the embryonic System completely. The present asteroids are the handful of leftover planetesimals that stumbled into stable orbits—all that's left, instead of the planet that might have grown there had Jupiter not grown first. In fact, Mars may be a shrunken world because Jupiter perturbed away most of the planetesimals that would have fed it. A major reason for thinking binary stars don't have planets is that another star would be even better than Jupiter at scattering planet-pieces before they could form planets (page 148).

So you might think that a planetary system with no gas giants, as around a hot star, would be a better bet for real estate. Possibly, though, Jupiter did a useful service to the biosphere by scattering away most of the planetesimals early in Solar System history. With few such objects left, huge impacts on planets like the Earth are rare later in Solar System history.

These careening leftovers caused the *late heavy bombardment*. This bombardment made the gigantic craters on the Moon, the so-called "basins," hundreds of kilometers across. On the Moon, the basins are generally filled with dark basalt lava that outlines roughly circular plains (Galileo's misnamed "seas") such as Mare Imbrium, Mare Crisium, and so on. [The basalt is not related to the impacts. It consists of "flood" basalt (page 56) flows erupted much later that filled in the basins because they were low-lying areas.] The Caloris Basin on Mercury and the Hellas Basin on Mars are similar features.

Opposite such basins, on the other side of the planet, we often see a weird, churned-up landscape. Such "antipodal chaotic terranes" result from the gigantic seismic waves generated by the impact. They travel out from the site of the collision; but they all come back together again exactly 180° away. So getting as far away from the impact as possible is *not* the thing to do; 90° away would be safer, although it's still not exactly safe.

The heavy bombardment obviously had profound effects—even on the Earth, although here the actual scars have long since been erased by erosion and plate tectonics. For one thing, the bombardment may have jump-started *plate tectonics* (page 59). You probably needed such a big nudge to get the crustal overturn, now so characteristic of Earth, going in the first place. On Mars, the Tharsis Ridge, site of several huge "hot-spot" volcanoes (page 56), is opposite Hellas, so perhaps these volcanoes were localized by the gigantic impact.

Another result is that the planets' initial spin rates and axial tilts are a crapshoot. They result from the vagaries of the last few really big impacts. For example, it had traditionally been thought that Venus spins slowly because, being close to the Sun, her original spin got braked by the solar tide. But maybe instead she *always* spun slowly. Of course, both the obliquity and rotation rate are subject to later change from perturbations and tidal braking.

The bombardment also affected the atmosphere, in contradictory ways. On large planets like Earth and Venus, the bombardment may have brought in atmosphere (page 96). It probably contained many comet-like bodies, rich in ices and other "volatiles," and the gravity of Venus and Earth is large enough that they'll keep such volatiles even if they come screaming in at ten or twenty kilometers a second. On the other hand, the bombardment may have splashed atmosphere off on smaller worlds, leaving Mars (for example) thin and dry. And the Moon-forming mega-impact on Earth certainly vaporized any volatiles that had accumulated beforehand.

This aura of crapshoot is nice for realistic world-building. It means there is lots of room for variation in planet formation: There's nothing inevitable about satellites, obliquity, eccentricity, distance or even the volatile content.

Even now, impact still occasionally happens in the Solar System, with catastrophic consequences for the biosphere, if an object hits the Earth. This, however, is one scenario that is certainly not under-utilized as an SF plot device!

## STIRRING THE INGREDIENTS

Stir together a planet-sized mass of rock and metal—seasoned with a little air and water, for a planet like the Earth—and simmer it for a few eons. What happens? As the forming planet heats up, partly from the heat released by natural radioactivity, and partly just from released gravitational energy, the elements react with each other and segregate (fractionate) according to their physical and chemical properties. And such chemical processing, especially when continued over geologic time, is vital for world-building. Even a fairly rare element can end up common in a planetary environment if its chemical properties are such that natural processes tend to concentrate it.

Let's look at this in more detail. Geochemists talk about four basic classes of chemical elements, depending on their behavior: *lithophile* (Greek, "rock-loving"), *chalcophile* ("sulfur-loving"), *siderophile* ("iron-loving"), and *volatile* (or *atmophile*, "air-loving").

Volatiles are all the low-melting point, low-boiling point things that are liquids or gases even at room temperature. Hydrogen and helium obviously make up most of them, but they also include the other noble gases: neon, argon and others, which do not form chemical compounds. Nitrogen is also largely volatile, both because it's a gas and because it combines with hydrogen to make ammonia ($NH_3$). Carbon and oxygen are also partly volatile, because they make gaseous compounds such as methane ($CH_4$), carbon dioxide and water vapor.

In the inner Solar System where the rocky planets formed, conditions were always too hot for the volatile elements to condense out in a big way. Neon, for example, is extremely rare on the Earth (page 96); although it's a common element, it just got blown out of the inner System early on. And of course, the fact that hydrogen and helium are gases even at very low temperatures is what lets nature separate out the much smaller amounts of heavy elements from them.

The other categories are more interesting, at least for us solid-world chauvinists, because they're solids at room temperature.

Lithophile elements make up rocks, just as you might expect from the name. Or alternatively: Lithophiles are all the elements that react enthusiastically with oxygen and so follow it. We could even call these elements "oxyphile" instead. (Rocks are made up of *minerals*, naturally occurring chemical compounds; nearly all common minerals are oxides or *silicates*, which are complex compounds of a silicon-oxygen "backbone" with other elements.) Lithophiles include silicon, magnesium, calcium, aluminum, sodium, potassium and many rarer metals. Some of the rare lithophile elements, such as uranium, are familiar, whereas others, like the so-called "rare earth elements," are hardly household words. As we saw, though, oxygen itself is also partly volatile, because it makes a low-boiling-point compound with hydrogen: water! So some of the oxygen gets lost with the volatiles.

Chalcophile elements follow sulfur, which although much rarer than oxygen is still more abundant than many metallic elements. Chalcophiles include metals like mercury, lead and zinc, and also the other "chalcogenides" (elements like sulfur) such as selenium and tellurium. As with oxygen, though, the chalcogenides themselves are also partly volatile, because they make gaseous compounds like hydrogen sulfide ($H_2S$).

Finally, siderophile elements follow metallic iron. After all the reactions with oxygen and sulfur are done, there's still iron left over. Because iron has the most stable nucleus, it's also pretty abundant as heavy elements go. This metallic iron dissolves other metals that don't react as readily with oxygen or sulfur, and so were left over: cobalt, nickel and copper, and also precious metals such as gold, iridium and platinum. Precious metals are especially unreactive, so it's not surprising they're left over.

Of course, these classes aren't hard and fast; nothing ever is. I mentioned how sulfur and oxygen both have some volatile character, for example. Iron too is multifaced: It has both lithophile and chalcophile character, even though it gave its name to the siderophile elements. Iron's partial lithophile character has a major implication for Earthlike worlds, as I'll discuss below. But nonetheless, the classes are useful. Think of them as general tendencies for different elements.

Now let's look at what this means for planet fractionation. For one thing, the metal sinks to form a massive iron *core*, while the rock floats on top, like oil and vinegar in a jar of salad dressing. And elements that "prefer" the metal—the siderophiles—sink with it into the core. For example, nickel is a relatively common element, being right there in that abundance peak with iron, and it's a relatively common element in the Earth *as a whole*. But nickel is siderophile, so virtually all the Earth's nickel is sitting 6000 kilometers below us, in the core, where it doesn't do us much good. That's why nickel is a strategic metal. (Strategic metals have important military uses but are extremely rare.)

The lithophiles floating on top of the core form a thick rocky *mantle*. Later a thin *crust* forms atop the mantle over geologic time, as the planet continues to further differentiate by such processes as lava formation and plate tectonics. You can think of the crust as "sweated out" of the mantle as the planet continues to stew while its internal heat slowly escapes.

The ongoing stirring of a planet by volcanism and tectonics also enriches planetary crusts in *lots* of rare elements—all those elements for which the crust is a more chemically favorable environment. So a planet, because of its internal heat, is a giant chemical fractionating plant that can (given time) separate rare elements out of a vast volume of common rock.

Two of the elements that tend to get sweated out are uranium and thorium. A common misconception (Frederik Pohl made this error in *Jem*, for example) is that uranium and thorium end up in the core, because they're heavy elements. Not so; they're also extremely reactive elements, and they react enthusiastically with oxygen. So they end up with the lithophile fraction; that is, with the rocks. In fact, they get enriched in the crust.

## Resources and Toxins

Nonetheless, many resources on an Earthlike planet are difficult to finagle, because such things as copper and tin are *already* rare on Earth. Their ores are highly anomalous concentrations from unusual geologic processes to begin with. Iron, however, is an exception (page 55).

Local toxicity of, say, the soil is occasionally used as plot element, as in Poul Anderson's Dathyna in *Satan's World* and Cleopatra in *A World Called Cleopatra*. Typically some (unspecified) element is said to be more concentrated than usual on Earth. This isn't unreasonable, as it certainly happens locally on Earth. Selenium, for example, gets concentrated to the point of toxicity in some soils in the Southwest United States.

Obviously such soil toxicity could, say, crimp colonization efforts. It could also foster conflict among the colonists, as it's likely the toxicity isn't uniformly spread. Imagine, for example, the reactions of colonists who'd been assigned land in the toxic zone—particularly if they'd paid for the privilege of emigrating!

A better idea, though, might be nutrient deficiency, and in particular potassium deficiency. Earth's crust is highly enriched in potassium, and this enrichment stems directly from plate tectonics (page 59). Without active tectonics, potassium would be a trace element in the crust—and since it's a critical nutrient element for Earth life, that could be awkward. This could be an important plot element in, say, a story in which humans are attempting to colonize a planet with less active tectonics than the Earth's.

## SOME ELEMENTARY VARIATIONS

The vagaries of chemical fractionation within a planet lead to interesting world-building variations. But what about changing the very element mix that makes up the nebula? This may happen occasionally through those *non*-supernova sources of elements: planetary nebulas, ordinary novas and giant stellar winds.

### The Cueball World

First, none of these processes makes much in the way of elements heavier than iron—after all, that takes energy. In particular they don't make any heavy r-process nuclei: thorium and uranium. And that's a problem.

The reason is that a habitable planet needs a certain amount of tectonics—mountain-building activity—to keep the crust stirred up. For one thing, nutrient elements are always settling out on the seafloor, as biologic material—dead critters, waste, shells and so on—sinks to the bottom. Phosphorus especially, which is critical to Earthly life, tends to plate out on the seafloor. On an active Earth, though, with the plates shifting, mountains rising, and volcanoes popping off, the nutrients don't stay buried. Such tectonic activity is also necessary to maintain the atmosphere with the carbonate-silicate cycle (page 68).

However, the slow decay of long-lived, natural radioactive elements, especially uranium and thorium, furnishes much of the energy to drive the tectonic activity. Without enough such elements to start with, volcanoes will congeal, seafloor spreading will stop, and the tectonic plates grind to a halt. Erosion alone will rule. Before too long—a few tens of millions of years, maybe—the planet will look like a cueball, a wet cueball. It will appear flat and featureless, with worldwide seas of almost uniform depth, with the continents ground down and the abyssal basins filled in. Quartz sand—durable, chemically stable and abundant—will blanket great tracts of the seafloor.

It's a different sort of aged world, not desiccated but leveled, and dying as its biosphere starves. This will be Earth's fate in a few billion years, if nothing else intervenes. But maybe lots of Earthlike planets have prematurely aged in this fashion.

## **"Carbonosis"**

Such non-supernova element factories also make a lot more carbon and nitrogen than oxygen. And that has a subtle effect indeed: It leads to iron depletion in the crust. In turn, iron's abundance has profound significance for whether a technical culture can arise, because—alone of the common crustal elements—iron can be smelted into metal with very primitive technology. Magnesium and aluminum are also abundant in the crust, but they're very difficult to extract. You can't do it with charcoal and a bellows, the way you can smelt iron!

To be sure, it's more difficult to smelt iron than copper or tin, but iron is a *lot* more common (fourth most common in the crust; see page 55). All the Bronze Age empires crashed with the discovery of iron, because weapons suddenly became cheap. (Bronze is an alloy of copper and tin.) Suddenly, every foot warrior could have his very own weaponry—and the fact that the iron weapons were not only cheaper but better than bronze just hastened the Bronze Age collapse. In contrast to tin and copper ores, too, the source could not be monopolized, because iron ores are abundant. Of course, cheap iron later was useful for lots besides weapons—plows, nails, fasteners, wheels—and it led directly to the steel technology on which so much of the modern world is based. Steels are simply iron alloys in which the proportion of dissolved carbon is low, and to which other metals have been added in controlled amounts.

So an Iron Age would be stillborn if for some reason iron were rare on the surface of a planet, and no such democratization of metalworking technology would occur. In a number of stories, Poul Anderson has proposed that iron would be rare on older planets than the Earth, because heavy elements would have been rarer when those planets formed. This may not work, though, because even though there won't be as much iron and other heavy elements as there is today, you won't notice. Even now, most of the Universe is still hydrogen and helium, but it all gets blown away when you build a solid planet.

Nonetheless, if first-generation supernovas don't build up iron as efficiently, as it seems might be the case, Anderson's idea might work. However, a way to *guarantee* an iron-depleted crust is to start with a nebula a bit richer in carbon, say, because of the contributions of a planetary nebula. Although the details are complicated, the reason, basically, is that all the leftover oxygen combines with the extra carbon instead of with any iron. Hence, virtually all the iron ends up in the siderophile or chalcophile fraction—and so *all* the iron ends up in the core. Although overall such a planet has as much iron as the Earth, none is in the crust where it's accessible. Iron on such a planet would be like the siderophile metals cobalt and nickel on the Earth; it could hardly lead to an Iron Age!

# CHAPTER 4

# The Earth

Because of the "plate-tectonics revolution" since the 1960s, we now have a much better idea of what makes our Earth the way it is. It takes more than just the right distance from the Sun, the right size, the right star, etc., to make a planet Earthlike! *Lots* of things make an Earth, and as the ecologists remind us, they're all interconnected. But, since we have to start somewhere, I'll begin by describing aspects of the Earth, along with possible variations that might lead to interesting worlds. Some of the most exotic possibilities I'll return to in more detail toward the end of the book. But remember, even though this book is condemned to a doggedly linear presentation just by the constraint of language, you can't, say, just dissect out the "atmosphere" without worrying about the energy the planet receives from its sun, the temperature, the tectonic processes, crustal reactions, etc. Planets are complicated! (That's their glory.)

As we saw, Earth is layered like an onion, with the outermost layer being the crust. Earth's crust comes in two basic types, oceanic and continental. Although both reflect material that has chemically separated out of the underlying mantle, like the froth on fermenting beer, they differ greatly in their origin and properties. Oceanic crust, which underlies the ocean basins, is continually made and destroyed as part of *plate tectonics* (page 59). Continental crust, however, remains at the surface of the Earth once it's made. Because it has low density, it won't sink any more than will a balloon. It's just swept around over geologic time. Most continental crust formed early in Earth's history, but small amounts continue to be made even today because of Earth's ongoing activity. Both types of crust are very thin; continental crust averages thirty-five to forty kilometers in thickness, oceanic crust only about five kilometers. Thus the crust, for all its importance as the surface we live on, forms an extremely small fraction of the Earth as a whole.

Just eight elements make up more than ninety-nine of every one hundred atoms in the continental crust. They are, in order: oxygen, silicon, aluminum, iron, magnesium, sodium, calcium, and potassium. Silicon and oxygen alone account for something like eighty atoms out of every one hundred in the crust.

The crust floats on the mantle, which forms by far the greatest proportion of the Earth. In part mantle rock is denser because its composition is different. It's much richer in iron and magnesium. Under the great pressures deep in the Earth, however, new, denser minerals also become stable, as the atoms are squeezed more closely together.

[I should mention that the crust is different from the *lithosphere*. In *plate tectonics* (page 59), the lithosphere is the outer, rigid part of the Earth that makes up the plates. The crust is only the topmost part of the lithosphere; most of the lithosphere is mantle.]

As we saw, below the mantle lies a dense core made of iron alloy. Despite its depth, though, the core is not irrelevant to the surface. For one thing, by raising Earth's density as a whole, it boosts the surface gravity (page 11). It's also the source of Earth's magnetic field. Finally, as we saw it's relevant for resources, but in a negative sense. When the core formed, it took lots of useful metals with it! Such strategic metals as nickel and cobalt are rare on the Earth's surface because most of the Earth's allotment of them sank into the core.

## POWERING A PLANET

An interesting planet like Earth is continually churned by geologic processes. Ongoing heat escape drives all this activity. In part this is leftover heat from the Earth's accretion (page 48). Because rock is a poor conductor of heat, it traps heat within, like a blanket. In part, too, the heat's maintained by the decay of long-lived radioactive elements, mainly potassium-40, thorium-232, uranium-235 and uranium-238, which keep generating new heat inside the Earth.

### Volcanism

So, as rock gets deeper, it gets hotter; and under the right circumstances it can melt. Most rocks at depth are *not* molten. Even though they're hot enough to melt under surface conditions, the tremendous surrounding pressure keeps them solid. If molten rock does form, though, it tends to rise because it's buoyant; like a balloon, it weighs less than the solid rock around it.

Volcanism is a major cause of the ongoing chemical fractionation in an active planet. It's also a major cause of planetary cooling, because once a melt forms, a lot of heat escapes. And that in turn tends to shut off the volcanism! So, volcanism is episodic. It requires locally unusual conditions. Eruptions can be big, too. Volcanic eruptions far, far larger than anything modern humans have dealt with have tormented the biosphere, and in the (relatively) recent geologic past at that. "Mother" Earth is an oxymoron!

*Lava* is a rock melt ("magma") that breaches the surface. They're unusual; most magmas cool at depth, within the crust. Lavas come in different varieties which mostly differ in their content of *silica* (silicon dioxide). And *that* greatly affects their viscosity, or "stickiness." The higher in silica, the stickier. The lavas from Mt. St. Helens are a good example of viscous lava.

And the stickier, the more explosive. Lavas on an Earthlike planet contain lots of water, which escapes as very hot steam when the lava's erupted. Since gases can't escape easily from viscous lava, they tend to explode.

Some kinds of volcanism seem to occur on any rocky planet. One of these is "hot spot" volcanism. These are caused by a thin plume of hot rock rising from *very* deep in the mantle. Examples include the Hawaiian Islands (and many other island chains), Yellowstone, and so on. A Mars example is the giant volcano Olympus Mons. (The Hawaiian Islands are strung out in a line because the lithospheric plate they punch through keeps moving. So all the lava doesn't pile up in one place. Since Mars doesn't have a moving lithosphere, though, the lava *does* all pile up, so Olympus Mons is much bigger than any of the Hawaiian Islands.) Hot spot volcanoes erupt basalt, an extremely common type of lava that's almost black when it cools. It's very fluid when it's hot, about like heavy engine oil.

Possibly related to hot spots are flood basalts. They've occurred a number of times in Earth's history, and also elsewhere, such as on the Moon (page 47). "Flood" basalt means just that—an eruption so large it floods a vast tract of land with fluid, molten rock. Southeastern Washington State and adjacent Oregon are covered with dozens of basalt lava flows hundreds of square miles in extent, the so-called Columbia River Basalts. Literally cubic miles of molten rock gushed out at the surface, from fissures in extreme western Idaho, and spilled hundreds of miles across Oregon and Washington. Many flows even continued out the valley of the Columbia River through the Cascade Range, past the site of modern Portland, and into the Pacific—there to build up huge pods of rock embedded in the offshore sediments.

This was catastrophic indeed. Imagine covering hundreds of square miles with molten rock at 1000°C, all within a week or so. There must have been vast effects far beyond the puddled lava itself: forest and prairie fires raging beyond the advancing lava, disruption of river drainages . . . in fact, for a brief time the entire Columbia River must have billowed up into an immense cloud of steam, as its course was blocked by the lava. Weather patterns would also have been skewed. A column of hot air would have boiled up above the hot lava, and to replace it, high winds would rush in from all sides. That would have caused a firestorm around the flow.

And then that miles-wide, barren expanse of bleak black rock, soilless and hard; how long did it take to reseed? Surely hundreds of years, as winds gradually blew dirt in so new plants could take root. And after a few tens to hundred thousand years, the whole thing happened *again*, when the next flood basalt erupted.

These eruptions are only about fifteen million years old, too. Since the dinosaurs became extinct about sixty-five million years ago, such eruptions are hardly a phenomenon restricted to a youthful, active Earth! They also demonstrate the resilience of the biosphere. Despite a calamity on the scale of a local nuclear war, the biosphere survived, and even recolonized the cooled basalt surfaces quickly, within a few thousands to tens of thousands of years. Earth is a capricious mother, but life is a more tenacious offspring than it's sometimes given credit for!

Flood basalts may sometimes have had a role in major extinctions, though. A huge set of flood basalts in India, the Deccan basalts, erupted around the time the dinosaurs went extinct, and worldwide fallout from these eruptions has been proposed as an alternative explanation of the extinction.

It's even been suggested that flood basalts could result from a major meteorite impact. Again, rock kilometers deep in the Earth is hot enough to melt, but is kept solid by the pressure of the surrounding rock. Take that pressure off by digging a *big* hole in the ground, though, and the rock would melt. The crater left by a major impact is a good way to dig a big hole in a hurry. Still, even if this happens sometimes, it can't account for all flood basalts: Too many keep erupting in the same general area, over too long a period of time. Most must reflect ongoing processes deep in the Earth.

Other Earth volcanism is specifically related to *plate tectonics*, such as in *volcanic arcs* (page 60), and also in "extensional" settings, where the continental crust is being stretched like taffy. Some such eruptions are the most catastrophic known, far worse than flood basalts. They're giant "ignimbrite" (from Latin for "fire-cloud"; stress the second syllable) eruptions. Ignimbrites are igneous rocks formed from molten rock particles dispersed in hot gas. When the particles settle out, they're still hot enough to stick together, to form rocks as solid as lava flows. Because the particles weld when they settle, another name for ignimbrites is "welded tuffs."

Ignimbrites are erupted as bits of molten rock dispersed in superheated gas, rather like the froth on a soda. The gas-plus-suspended-particles mixture acts just like a debris blow, flowing as a separate fluid over the ground surface. Such a hot debris flow is called a "nuee ardente" (French for "glowing cloud"; pronounced, very approximately, "noo-AY ar-DAHN"). We've seen small-scale *nuees ardentes* from some modern eruptions. For example, the town of St. Pierre on the island of Martinique was obliterated by a *nuee ardente* in 1902, a setting used by Steven Utley in "The Glowing Cloud."

*Nuees ardentes* are *hot*. By comparison, the Mt. St. Helens ash-cloud, even near the mountain, was little more than a dust storm. Near the mountain, Mt. St. Helens ash, which was just powdered rock, was suspended in gas at a few hundred degrees centigrade— plenty hot enough to scald animal life, to be sure—but to *weld* silicate grains together requires temperatures on the order of 1000°C! So a typical *nuee ardente*, where it deposits welded tuff, is several times as hot as the Mt. St. Helens cloud. By the way, the gas from a volcanic eruption consists mostly of $H_2O$—very hot to *extremely* hot steam. Steam, even at "just" 300°C, will set wood on fire.

Now, in the western U.S., in Nevada and extending into California, Arizona and Utah, are tens to hundreds of vast ignimbrite sheets, each the result of a single gigantic eruption. Some of these ignimbrites cover hundreds of square miles—and that, of course, is just where they're preserved, where the rock was still hot enough to weld when it settled out! Hot ash, but not hot enough to weld, must originally have extended for hundreds of miles farther from the original eruption. Since it didn't weld, though, it was easily eroded away.

*Nuees ardentes* so big they covered hundreds of square miles with welded tuff are so large—so beyond current and historical experience—as to be almost inconceivable. J. Hoover Mackin, a geologist describing some of these eruptions in the *American Journal of Science*, wrote in 1960:

> Tertiary eruptions of the Great Basin would compare with those of modern times as the explosion of a hydrogen bomb with the bursting of a firecracker.

People don't usually write like that in a technical journal!

And like the flood basalts, these eruptions were not a youthful exuberance of a hot young Earth. These ignimbrites in this area range from perhaps forty million to less than one million years old—and for comparison, the dinosaurs went extinct about sixty-five million years ago.

Such big eruptions have never been treated in sf, to my knowledge. It's common to call a planet vaguely "geologically unstable," but with no details supplied. A threat of such gigantic eruptions, or, say, the immediate aftermath of one, could make such "instability" very real. It would be another of those vivid details that can animate a story, and could also be a fruitful source of plot conflicts.

## PLATE TECTONICS

*Tectonics* is the geologist's name for all processes that raise the land. In fact, an active planet such as the Earth is a giant, inefficient heat engine, converting some of its heat flow into mechanical movement via excruciatingly slow *convection*, like a very sluggish version of the heat-driven circulation in the atmosphere (page 81).

*Plate tectonics* is the dominant style of Earthly tectonics. So far as we know, it's unique to the Earth in the solar system, but presumably it's present on most if not all Earthlike planets. Rigid "plates" make up the "lithosphere," which consists of upper mantle and crust. They cover the Earth like a cracked eggshell, with the edges jostling incessantly.

New plates form at *spreading centers* such as at the mid-Atlantic ridge and other mid-ocean ridges. They move away symmetrically from the ridge, at rates of several centimeters per year. For comparison, this is the same rate at which fingernails grow. Upwelling magma at the center forms the new plates and also makes the ridges sites of major volcanism.

The plates collide at *convergent boundaries*, the sites of most tectonic activity: earthquakes, mountain building, and certain kinds of volcanism. One kind is a *subduction zone*, where the plates are consumed by diving back into the mantle. They're generally marked by an oceanic trench. Partial melting of the downgoing plate also generates a *volcanic arc* in back of the trench. Island arcs with their parallel oceanic trenches offshore, such as Japan with the Japanese trench, are typical fingerprints of subduction zones. The volcanic arc may, however, lie atop a continent, as with the Andes Mountains behind the Peru-Chile trench, along the west coast of South America.

Major mountain building occurs at continent-continent collisions. Because continental rock is too buoyant to subduct, it just pushes up and deforms like the snow in front of a plow, to make a massive mountain range. The Himalayas, for example, were raised by the collision of India and Asia. How high can such mountains get? Foldbelt mountains like the Himalaya float on the Earth the way an iceberg floats at sea. They're buoyed up by a "root" of less dense continental rock below, a principle called "isostasy." So, to make the mountain higher the root must be deeper, and at a depth of about one hundred kilometers (under Earthlike gravity), the low-density minerals in the root become unstable. This in turn implies that mountains can't be much higher than about ten kilometers, except maybe for geologically brief times. If you need more exact calculations, isostasy is described in geophysics texts, such as Stacey in the Reference List. (A massive mountain range also tries to slide away on low-angle fractures, or "faults," that develop near its base. For all these reasons, the enormous mountain in Rick Shelley and Lee Goodloe's "Because It's There" is undoubtedly extremely short-lived, if it's possible at all! But at least the authors implied reasons why the mountain could be anomalous.)

The plates slide over a weaker layer deeper in the mantle, the *asthenosphere*, named from the Greek word for "weak." The asthenosphere is probably convecting; even though at ordinary timescales this "flowing" rock is perfectly solid, over geologic time it acts as an extremely viscous liquid. The plates are also not completely rigid, and deform somewhat internally. This means that earthquakes can occasionally occur far from plate boundaries, as with the enormous New Madrid quakes in Missouri in 1812.

## THE ELECTROMAGNETIC SPECTRUM

We'll have many occasions to talk about radiant energy, the energy put out by a hot object such as a star, so it will be convenient to review some fundamentals. All such energy falls into the *electromagnetic spectrum*, a suite of different kinds of radiant energy that, despite their great diversity, differ only in wavelength. They're called "electromagnetic" because they consist of varying electric and magnetic fields. For all electromagnetic radiation, the shorter its wavelength, the higher its energy.

The electromagnetic spectrum includes visible light as a very small part, extending from wavelengths of ~400 nm (violet) to 760 nm (red). (1 nanometer (nm) = 1 billionth of a meter = 10 Ångstrom units.) Infrared (IR) radiation is invisible light with wavelengths longer than red. It's often called "heat" radiation because you can feel it but not see it, as with a barely turned on stove burner. Ultraviolet (UV) light is invisible light with wavelengths shorter than violet. The electromagnetic spectrum also includes radio waves (very long wavelengths, feet to miles), microwave radiation (wavelengths between IR and radio), X rays (very short wavelengths, less than 1 nm), and gamma rays (extremely short wavelengths, typically output during radioactive decay). (See figure 8, next page.)

## WATER AND AIR: THE VOLATILES

Volatiles make up atmospheres and oceans. They're a mere film on the surface, but they have profound effects. Try to stop breathing if you're not convinced! In fact, to us surface chauvinists, they're the important part, because they're what makes the surface of a planet habitable.

Contrast Earth's "twin" Venus, the next planet inward in our planetary system. It's Earth-sized, but a less hospitable world is

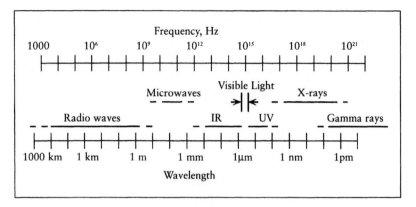

**FIG. 8** The Electromagnetic Spectrum.

The wavelengths corresponding to various sorts of radiant energy are labeled; in most cases the boundaries are gradational. The units of wavelength are km, kilometer (1000 meters); m, meter; mm, millimeter (one thousandth of a meter); μ m, micrometer (one millionth of a meter); nm, nanometer (one billionth of a meter); pm, picometer (one trillionth of a meter). Frequency is measured in hertz (Hz), or cycles per second. For electromagnetic radiation, wavelength and frequency are related by the equation $f = c/\omega$, where $f$ is the frequency in hertz, $c$ is the speed of light (in meters per second; $c = 300,000$ m/s), and $\omega$ is the wavelength in meters.

hard to imagine. It has a crushingly thick carbon dioxide ($CO_2$) atmosphere almost one hundred times as heavy as Earth's, permanent clouds of sulfuric acid droplets containing the only water (it's utterly dry otherwise), and a greenhouse effect (page 67) from the clouds and thick atmosphere maintaining surface temperatures over 400°C (750°F). How did this staggering contrast between two grossly similar worlds come about? As we'll see later, understanding *that* yields major insights into what determines a planetary environment.

Not only does Earth's modern atmosphere support life, it's also largely a *product* of life. The oxygen we breathe is a product of photosynthesis by green plants, which use the energy of sunlight to make oxygen and sugars from water and carbon dioxide. Most of the trace gases in our atmosphere also are products of living things. Even the nitrogen that makes up most of our air results mostly from decay bacteria, and at least the minor constituents in the ocean are strongly affected by biological activity.

## THE ATMOSPHERE

The atmosphere is an envelope of gas around the planet that's held down by gravity. The weight of that gas is *pressure*. It's equal to the mass of the overlying atmosphere times *g*, the gravitational acceleration (page 10). Pressure is measured in a variety of units. Most obvious is the *atmosphere* (atm)! It equals 1.01 *bars*, the traditional metric unit, or 760 mm of mercury (Hg), or 14.7 pounds per square inch (psi). The modern metric unit is the *pascal* (Pa): 100,000 ($10^5$) pascals is 1 bar, or $10^6$ pascals = 1 megapascal (MPa) = 10 bars. For our purposes, the atm will be most convenient.

Real atmospheres are typically mixtures of gases, and sometimes we need to know how much pressure is due to each constituent. The *partial pressure* is the contribution to the total pressure of a particular gas constituent. It's simply the total pressure times the percentage that the constituent makes up. For example, the partial pressure of oxygen in our atmosphere is 0.21 atm, or (0.21) × 14.7 ~3.1 psi. Thus, spacecraft using pure oxygen atmospheres can be simpler and lighter because they need to hold in a much smaller pressure. This was a major reason for using such atmospheres back in the 1960s.

In a gas, individual molecules are moving freely. Indeed, they're in violent motion, caroming off each other like tiny billiard balls. If they're going too fast (faster than *escape velocity*, see page 12), the molecules will escape into space from the outer edge of the atmosphere. In fact, a certain percentage will *always* exceed escape velocity, and if that percentage is too high, the atmosphere will leak away in a geologically short time. Thus, a planet needs enough gravity to hold an atmosphere, and that means it can't be too small.

The outer atmosphere temperature is also important, because gas molecules travel faster with increasing temperature. This means that the hotter the outer atmosphere (the "exosphere") is, the greater the gravity must be. Thus, worlds nearer their sun must be larger to hold atmospheres equivalent to those around cooler worlds.

Atmosphere composition also matters. Lighter molecules move faster at the same temperature. So, for the same surface gravity, a planet can hold on to certain molecules but can't keep others. The light gases escape while the heavy gases stay. For example, hydrogen and helium, the lightest gases, escape from Earth's atmosphere. The geologic stability of an atmosphere is thus set by a balance of gravity vs. temperature vs. composition (figure 9, next page).

Composition and pressure are not completely free parameters otherwise, either. They're modified by lots of things, such as chemical reaction with the surface of the planet, life (as noted!), and *photodissociation* (page 71) at the outer edge of the atmosphere. The atmosphere will also change over geologic time: the Sun changes, life evolves and lighter gases are lost.

In fact, it's not enough to have enough gravity just to hold down the air; the planet has to be big enough to *buffer* the air. That is, the air has to interact with crustal rocks over time, as in the carbonate/silicate cycle (page 68). For such interaction to take place, moreover, the planet must be large enough to keep its crust stirred up. Too small, and the planet loses its internal heat too fast, and it runs down too soon. Mars is an example (page 115).

If you want to have your atmosphere hospitable for Earth life, that puts stringent limits on its composition. Earth's atmosphere contains, roughly, 21 percent oxygen, 78 percent nitrogen, and 1 percent argon, with other gases present in trace amounts. To be breathable, the atmosphere must have a partial pressure of least 0.16 atm oxygen ($O_2$), but no more than 0.5. To prevent nitrogen narcosis, a "drunkenness" resulting from nitrogen gas dissolved in

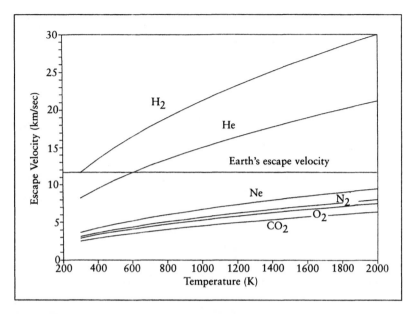

**FIG. 9** Escape of Gases From a Gravity Field.

Vertical axis is escape velocity; horizontal axis is the temperature of the gas in kelvins. The curves for various gases reflect one-sixth of the mean velocity of the gas molecules at that temperature. (If a larger percentage of molecules has velocity greater than this, the gas will escape in a geologically short time.) Earth cannot keep hydrogen ($H_2$) or helium (He) over geologic time, as the temperature of the outer atmosphere, where escape occurs, is ~1500 K. However, the Earth can retain oxygen ($O_2$), nitrogen ($N_2$), carbon dioxide ($CO_2$) and neon (Ne) indefinitely. The outer atmosphere temperature is substantially higher (over 1000 kelvins!) than the sea level value because of interaction with very high-energy ultraviolet light put out by the Sun. However, the gas at that altitude is so extremely tenuous that its actual content of heat is nearly negligible.

the tissues that divers call "rapture of the deep," the partial pressure of nitrogen ($N_2$) also must be less than ~3 atm.

Probably most stringent is $CO_2$ toxicity. The $CO_2$ partial pressure *must* be less than 0.02 atm for humans to breathe indefinitely, and it should be less than 0.005 atm to avoid physiological stresses. Poul Anderson used this in *Orbit Unlimited*; the $CO_2$ level was so high on the planet Rustum that the lowlands were uninhabitable, except by a little boy whose tolerance was unusually high, and whose rescue was therefore difficult. The value of 0.09 atm $CO_2$ that Harry Turtledove quotes for Minerva, in *A World of Difference*, obviously falls in the marginal range.

Other Earth life, however, is not so demanding as humans and other large mammals. Many plants can survive, indeed thrive, in low oxygen/high $CO_2$ conditions. This means that Earth plants will grow in many atmospheres that humans can't breathe. This can be a fruitful source of plot elements, as in Anderson's novel.

## ALBEDO AND PLANETARY TEMPERATURE

A planet's temperature obviously depends on how much radiant energy it receives from the star it orbits. But it also depends on two other factors. The simplest is the reflectivity, or *albedo*, which determines how much energy the planet absorbs. Albedo is expressed as a number between 0 (perfect absorber) to 1 (perfect reflector). Earth's albedo is ~0.3. The temperature of an *airless* planet warmed by a star and radiating as a *blackbody* (defined on page 127) is:

$$T = 374 \ (1 - A) \ I^{\frac{1}{4}}$$

where A is the albedo, I is the total amount of incident light (where the Sun = 1, and including invisible wavelengths such as infrared), and T is the temperature in kelvins. The planet is also assumed to be rotating rapidly enough to even out the heating. This predicts an average temperature for Earth of 255 K = $-18°C$, compared with the actual mean temperature of ~288 K = 15°C. Obviously this equation is useful only for rough calculation!

The temperature of a planet with an atmosphere is substantially modified by the *greenhouse effect*. This can be taken into account with a "fudge factor" in the above relation:

$$T = 374 \ G \ (1 - A) \ I^{\frac{1}{4}}$$

where G is the greenhouse correction. It's ~1.1 for an Earth-like planet, which lets you roughly estimate your planet's temperature.

## The Greenhouse Effect

Broadly, an atmosphere acts like a blanket around a planet, holding heat in and raising the temperature. This is called the *greenhouse effect*. It arises because an atmosphere is not equally transparent at all wavelengths. Certain gases, although transparent to visible light, are nearly opaque to *infrared* wavelengths (see sidebar above). Thus, sunlight can travel though the atmosphere to heat the ground; but the infrared radiation radiated by that warmed ground can't escape freely, because it's absorbed by those gases. So, the atmosphere gets warmer from the trapped energy (see sidebar above for a rough calculation).

Carbon dioxide ($CO_2$) is the most notorious greenhouse gas because its concentration has increased over the last century-and-a-half from the increased burning of fossil fuels. Trace atmospheric constituents of both natural and artificial origin, such as methane ($CH_4$), ammonia ($NH_3$), and chlorofluorinated hydrocarbons (CFCs) such as Freon, are even more effective greenhouse gases, although present at vastly lower concentrations. But although carbon dioxide is the most famous greenhouse gas, it's not the most important. The major greenhouse gas on Earth, and presumably on similar planets, is simply water vapor.

Water vapor's an unusual greenhouse gas, too. On a planet, like Earth, that has extensive bodies of liquid water on the surface, its concentration is not a free parameter. The amount of water vapor in the atmosphere is fundamentally fixed by the mean temperature, through an "equilibrium" with liquid water: At a given temperature, a liquid must have certain partial pressure of vapor over it, and that partial pressure increases with temperature. So the higher the temperature, the more water evaporates, and the higher the water vapor content in the air. Conversely, the water vapor content drops as the atmosphere cools, by liquid water condensing out (e.g., into clouds).

Now consider what happens on an ocean planet if you raise the temperature. More water vapor evaporates, so that the vapor content of the atmosphere is higher. Thus the greenhouse effect increases, so that *more* water evaporates, so that the temperature rises yet more. . . . It's a positive feedback.

In fact, this "amplifier effect" of water vapor makes the other greenhouse gases much more effective. You don't have to add nearly as much, say, $CO_2$ as you might think to get a certain amount of warming. Now, the positive feedback is mitigated a bit by such things as cloud formation. As water vapor becomes more abundant, clouds form more easily, and since they reflect sunlight well they tend to cool things off. But if temperatures get too high, this amplification can get out of control—as we'll see in the case of Venus.

## The Carbonate-Silicate Cycle

What controls atmosphere thickness and composition? Evidently there's no direct relation with the size of the planet, as shown by the contrast between Venus and Earth! They're instead controlled by a host of processes acting over geologic time.

Reaction with the crust and ocean is one of these. One of the most important processes is the *carbonate-silicate cycle*, or the "inorganic carbon" cycle, which ultimately regulates the $CO_2$ content of the atmosphere. The organic carbon cycle is more familiar: Plants take up $CO_2$ and release oxygen ($O_2$) by photosynthesis, using the energy of sunlight; then animals breathe the $O_2$ to oxidize food and re-release $CO_2$. But $CO_2$ also participates in an *inorganic* cycle, and—at least in terms of the quantities involved—this cycle is by far the more important. It acts as "Earth's thermostat" by maintaining habitable temperatures over geologic time.

It works as follows. Virtually all Earth's carbon is locked in the crust in limestone, which consists mostly of calcium carbonate ($CaCO_3$). Thus, nearly all Earth's $CO_2$ is in its crust. If you cooked out Earth's crust—say, by putting the planet in a giant limekiln— you'd end up with a thick $CO_2$ atmosphere like Venus's.

Now, $CaCO_3$ precipitates easily from water solution if enough dissolved calcium is present, and if the water contains some dissolved $CO_2$. Since calcium is one of the most abundant elements in the Earth's crust, it's always present at least somewhere. Furthermore, the more $CO_2$ in the air, the more gets dissolved in water exposed to that air. So, if too much atmospheric $CO_2$ accumulates so that things get too warm, efficient weathering under the warm conditions releases lots of calcium, which sooner or later brings the $CO_2$ level down. Since solutions of $CO_2$ in water are mildly acidic (carbonic acid), the effectiveness of weathering also increases as $CO_2$ levels increase.

Hence over geologic time the carbonate cycle tends to keep Earth at a constant temperature. For the thermostat to work, though, an Earthlike planet probably requires surface water, so that limestone forms easily. It also must be geologically active. Processes must continually be raising raw new rock for weathering, and crustal rocks must be cycled so $CO_2$ can be "baked out" to emerge again in volcanic gases. Thus, for an Earthlike planet to *stay* Earthlike, it needs to be big enough, and retain enough internal heat, to support active tectonics. Mars has probably frozen up because it wasn't quite big enough (page 115). This requirement puts a different, and probably more stringent, limit on how small an Earthlike planet can be. It's not just a matter of being big enough to hold an atmosphere; it has to maintain that atmosphere!

This also means that humanity's current enhancement of $CO_2$ levels, and hence of any greenhouse effect, by the burning of fossil fuels is geologically ephemeral. Over the next few tens of thousands of years all the extra $CO_2$ will be extracted into new limestone. But it might be awkward in the interim!

The carbonate cycle is now mostly mediated biologically. Although calcium carbonate forms easily without the activities of living things, in fact most modern limestones are accumulations of biological debris: reefs, shells and so on, all cemented with inorganically precipitated carbonate. Lots of critters have "discovered" that calcium carbonate makes a dandy skeleton.

The carbonate cycle also guards against excess surface water acidity—this is why lakes in limestone country are virtually unaffected by acid rain, by the way. The soda-water seas of some SF stories are unlikely; you'd have to shield them from all calcium, and it's a *common* element. So, in the presence of rock and water, there's only so much carbon dioxide you can have in the atmosphere. In retrospect, many of the old "soda-water Venus" models were naive for just this reason.

## The Gases of Life

Obviously oxygen's a product of plants. But it's not so well known that nitrogen is just as much a product of life. Without decay bacteria constantly breaking down nitrogen-bearing molecules, it would all eventually end up as nitrates in the soil or sea. Hal Clement's *The Nitrogen Fix* describes an Earth on which this has happened, due to a collapse of the nitrogen cycle. A host of other trace gases in the atmosphere also result from biological processes; methane, for example, results from fermentation in wetlands and in the guts of herbivores. $CO_2$ itself obviously has a biological role as a raw material for photosynthesis. In fact, the only atmospheric constituents *without* a biological role are the noble gases, which do not form chemical compounds.

The result is that the Earth's atmosphere is a mishmash of gases that is far out of simple chemical equilibrium. Even a trace of methane, for example, should not exist in an oxygen-rich atmosphere; it is the active ingredient of natural gas and reacts easily with free oxygen. This composition is maintained dynamically by living things, ultimately with the energy of the Sun, and would rapidly vanish without them. So, a life-bearing planet should be obvious from far away; indeed, as soon as an atmospheric composition can be measured by *spectroscopy*. (Because different atoms absorb different wavelengths of light, the light reflected by an object can contain a great deal of information about the composition of that object.) By the middle of the next century, gigantic, Moon-based or space-based telescopes may even be able to identify potential life-worlds around the nearer stars—an element too little used in SF stories!

Why, on Earth, is the relative concentration of nitrogen to oxygen about four to one, and the total pressure about one atmosphere? Again, it seems to result from feedback loops, and not all are subtle or biological. One of the simplest is flammability; things *burn*. This puts a strong upper limit on oxygen abundance; at oxygen concentrations of 30 percent or more even wet vegetation burns enthusiastically. The high oxygen partial pressures in Anderson's planet Starkad (in *Ensign Flandry*) probably can't occur; things simply get too flammable. Organic chlorine compounds inhibit flames; if such high-pressure worlds exist, maybe the local flora has evolved such compounds as fire retardants.

Nonetheless, the controls on the proportions of gases in our atmosphere are poorly understood. Within the broad zones of "reasonableness" outlined above, this gives you a lot of flexibility in designing an atmosphere to fit the needs of your story. And no doubt atmospheres wildly different from Earth's are possible, as I'll discuss in the last chapter.

## Photodissociation: The Monster That Ate an Ocean

Another process, whose importance was almost totally unrealized B.S. (before spaceflight), is *photodissociation*, "dissociation by light." Solar ultraviolet light breaks up molecules at the outer edge of the atmosphere. This causes a loss of hydrogen-bearing compounds such as water, because the light hydrogen atoms can then escape.

On the Earth, the atmosphere gets cold enough to freeze out most water before it gets high enough to be destroyed—the so-called "cold trap." But without a cold trap, it's easy to destroy an ocean's worth of water in a fraction of geologic time. As we'll see below, that had major consequences for the history of Venus.

Another consequence of photodissociation is that the traditional "early reducing atmosphere" of ammonia ($NH_3$) and methane ($CH_4$) most probably never existed (page 95), as those molecules are just broken up too easily by solar UV.

## Venus Vs. Earth: The Runaway Greenhouse

Small changes can have big effects. This is as true for planets as people, as shown by that contrast between Venus and Earth. Many scientists think the stark contrast between modern Venus and modern Earth results from a chilling scenario: the "runaway greenhouse." Recall that water vapor is the most important greenhouse gas, and the water vapor content goes up with rising temperatures, which leads to a positive feedback. Although this feedback damps out on Earth, it wouldn't if temperatures were a bit higher, about 10 percent according to some estimates. Temperatures would soar and the oceans boil.

This is the "runaway greenhouse," and it may be what happened to Venus early in its history, simply because Venus was always a bit warmer than Earth from being closer to the Sun.

Once the greenhouse runs away, any cold trap in the upper atmosphere breaks down, so all the planet's water gets photodissociated geologically quickly. Then without oceans the carbonate-silicate cycle also can't function, and thus the $CO_2$ all stays in the atmosphere rather than forming limestone. In fact, the $CO_2$ may all get baked out of limestones after the temperature soars: The planet became a giant limekiln. The greenhouse effect from a steam atmosphere, if Venus's oceans boiled, would lead to surface temperatures hot enough to melt rock! We're thus left with modern Venus: a hellish dry world with a crushing $CO_2$ atmosphere.

Now, it's recently been suggested that the greenhouse didn't ever quite run away. Venus's atmosphere may simply have become too warm to sustain a cold trap. Then, once the water all got photodissociated away the $CO_2$ just accumulated in the atmosphere. In any case, though, Venus probably started out a lot more Earthlike, maybe even with oceans. Perhaps the runaway effect was finally triggered by inexorably rising temperatures: When first formed, the Sun was probably about 30 percent less luminous than today, but its luminosity has slowly increased over geologic time (page 135). Or perhaps simply photodissociation finally clobbered all the water.

All this has major implications for SF world-building. For one thing, habitable zones around stars may be thinner than we've thought (as presented in the classic book *Habitable Planets for Man* by Stephen H. Dole, for example). Venus was not all *that* much hotter than Earth to begin with; but it was hotter enough that it lost all its water to photodissociation—even if the greenhouse never quite ran away. This again underscores how "interconnected" a planet is.

For another implication, consider the early threshold of greenhouse runaway as a story setting on an otherwise Earthlike planet. Although it won't happen overnight, because of the large amount of energy needed to boil an ocean, the timescale might be a few hundred years. A different flavor of disaster novel. . . .

Another variation might be the "hot dryworld"; a world with minimal water in small, shallow and saline seas; or maybe no seas at all, just playas or salt pans amid sere deserts. Perhaps this could occur from a "not-quite-Venus" desiccation scenario. A steam atmosphere results from greenhouse runaway, but unlike Venus there's little carbon dioxide to keep the greenhouse effect going without the steam. So after most of the water vapor dissociates, temperatures cool off again, maybe to livable temperatures. [Although with no oceans to moderate the temperatures (page 84), even the "livable" climate will be extreme, frigid nights alternating with searing days.] Thin, nearly vanished oceans; vast basins dusted whitely with salt, the ghosts of vanished seas . . . it sounds a bit like Frank Herbert's Arrakis in *Dune*, doesn't it?

Yet another possibility is the aged dryworld, a planet that's lost all its water over geologic time. This has a nostalgic echo of Percival Lowell. One of his almost-forgotten notions was "desertification": Over time a planet inevitably loses its water to space. Indeed, Lowell postulated the traditional dying civilization on Mars, frantically meting out the last of its water through a vast canal network as its planet desiccated. Of course, the "dying Mars" scenario took on a life of its own, chiefly through the works of Edgar Rice Burroughs and later Robert A. Heinlein. But authors from H.G. Wells (*The Time Machine*) to Arthur C. Clarke ("Exile of the Eons"; *The City and the Stars*) have used this setting for a "superannuated Earth," effectively evoking an oppressive sense of age, decay and loss.

On Earth, losing water by photodissociation takes a long time, because of the atmospheric cold trap. A different world might age prematurely, though. For example, the cold trap may be less effective on a warmer planet. A star somewhat hotter than the Sun (spectral type F, see page 129) might be even more effective, not so much because of its greater heat but because such a star outputs a greater proportion of UV light, which would make photodissociation more efficient. Poul Anderson has used this as a background element in a number of stories, such as the planet Dathyna in *Satan's World* and Aeneas in *The Rebel Worlds*.

A possible problem with dryworlds, at least in extreme cases, is that the desiccation will ultimately shut down plate tectonics, as plate tectonics needs oceans (page 81). Without tectonic activity, the continents will wear down, and essential nutrient elements (e.g., phosphorus) will wind up buried and useless. The carbonate cycle will also shut down, with the result that the climate could go permanently out of the habitable region; the planet will either bake or freeze. The latter case seems to have happened on Mars (page 115). Planetary processes are interconnected!

These examples also suggest the possibilities of differing volatile contents for creating interesting worlds (chapter eight).

## Atmosphere Structure

Let's consider the thickness of the atmosphere. It has some unexpected consequences as well. First, the thicker the atmosphere (or the lower the gravity), the easier flight is. The difficulty of flight depends primarily on two things: the density of the air, and $g$, the gravitational acceleration at the surface. Poul Anderson has again explored some of the possibilities here. On the planet Diomedes (in *The Man Who Counts*), a thick atmosphere made a flying species easily possible. Other effects of the atmosphere provided striking plot details; e.g., because sound travels better in a denser medium, the humans' hearing was much more sensitive than the aliens', with the result they could often overhear the aliens' discussions. Storms were also more intense because of the greater mass of moving air.

His Ythrians (*People of the Wind, Earth Book of Stormgate*), on the other hand, were adapted to nearly Earth-normal conditions. For this reason they needed a huge food intake and extraordinarily effective metabolism, because of the huge energy requirements for a large flying animal in an Earthlike atmosphere. This in turn had major implications for their psychology and social structures. (On Earth, human-powered flight is just barely possible, but only with athletes in exceptional physical shape and wearing enormous, cumbersome, extremely light wings.)

If the gravity is low enough and the air thick enough, however, even humans might be able to fly with simple equipment, just as Icarus did in legend. With a third of the gravity—about the same as Mars—and air twice as thick, for example, flight would be six times as easy, or as easy as in a Moon colony. (The Moon has a surface gravity about one-sixth that of Earth.) Although this has been used as a background detail in many stories set within Moon colonies, it's been little used in a planetary environment.

---

## THE UPWARD THINNING OF AN ATMOSPHERE

As anyone who has driven up a mountain knows, the air thins with altitude, gradually dropping off to the vacuum of space. This thinning occurs at an approximately exponential rate:

$$p = p_0 \exp(-gh/H)$$

where $p$ is the pressure at an altitude $h$, $p_0$ is sea-level pressure, $g$ is the gravitational pull in terms of Earth (i.e., Earth = 1), and $H$ is the *scale height*. The scale height basically measures how fast the atmosphere tapers off: The larger it is, the more slowly the atmosphere thins. On Earth the scale height is about 7400 meters. [The "exp" function is the exponential function, which is the number $e$ (approximately 2.71828 . . .) raised to the power represented here by the value of $-gh/H$. Spreadsheet programs and many modern calculators have the exp function built in. If your calculator does not have exp specifically, it is the inverse of the ln—natural logarithm—function.] Because the scale height increases with increasing temperature, the relation above is exactly correct only if the atmosphere is the same temperature throughout, but it nonetheless is useful for estimates.

The scale height also depends on composition. The heavier the gases in the atmosphere, the smaller the scale height, and so the pressure drops off more quickly. To be quantitative, the scale height is proportional to the average atomic weight of the atmosphere:

$$H_p = H \times (A_e/A_p)$$

where $H_p$ and $A_p$ are the scale height and mean atmospheric atomic weight, respectively, of the planet's atmosphere.

The average atomic weight of the Earth's atmosphere is roughly:

$$A_e = 0.78 \times 28 + 0.21 \times 32 + 0.01 \times 40 \sim 29$$

i.e., the percentage of nitrogen (78%) times the atomic weight of nitrogen gas ($N_2 = 28$), plus the corresponding values for oxygen and argon. Other constituents are too rare to matter.

If you don't have a calculator, it may be easier to remember the height over which the pressure falls by one-half:

$$h(1/2) = H \text{ (ln 2) } \sim 5100 \text{ m for Earth,}$$

where ln $2 = 0.693147$ . . . is the natural logarithm of two. (The natural logarithm function is also built into spreadsheet programs and many pocket calculators.)

You can use these relationships to estimate how high humans could climb. Mt. BIT in Shelley and Goodloe's "Because It's There," for example, stood over 68,000 feet (~20,800 m) above the sea level on a world with 1.2 times the gravity of Earth. Assuming the same sea level pressure as on Earth, the pressure at the summit was therefore:

$$P = P_0 \times \exp[ -1.2 \times (20,800/7400) ] = (1) \times \exp( -3.37 ) \sim 0.035,$$

or only ~3.5% of its sea level value. Hence a human on this mountain would need not only breathing apparatus but a pressure suit, and that fact drove much of the story background.

For another example, you can estimate the pressure at the bottom of the Mediterranean basin if the sea dried up (page 100), a popular setting for SF. Taking the maximum depth as 3000 meters below sea level:

$$P = P_0 \times \exp( -gh/H ) = \exp - (-3000/7400) \sim 1.6,$$

so that the air is over half again as thick as sea level. Winds will be stronger, and the whole area will be oppressively hot—both gritty details for the story setting. Note that since we're dealing with an elevation below sea level, it must be entered as negative.

Atmosphere structure also has some striking, and at first glance counterintuitive, consequences for world-building. For one thing, because atmosphere density falls off more slowly with height on smaller worlds, smaller planets have proportionately more massive atmospheres for the same surface pressure, and the atmosphere is thicker! To see why, note that pressure is weight per area, so with low gravity, you need more mass to get the same weight. One effect of this more massive atmosphere is that it's an even better shield against meteorites, cosmic rays and solar-wind particles. Such a world is also likely to be even more favorable for flyers than the low gravity would suggest.

Conversely, the atmosphere thins more quickly with height on a higher-gravity world. Again, Shelley and Goodloe used this in their novella. The greater size of their world rationalized greater activity, as it would likely contain a greater complement of internal heat. This in turn might make taller mountains possible, although certainly the higher gravity would make raising mountains more difficult. More importantly, the environment atop the mountain peak could get spacelike, as the atmosphere thinned more rapidly with height than on Earth. Thus the characters advanced—on foot—from an ordinary Earthlike shirtsleeve environment to conditions requiring pressure suits, and in which they needed to worry about such typically spacelike disasters as a giant solar flare. In turn, the higher gravity furnished vivid background details: Rocks fell faster, climbers fatigued more and the whole endeavor was made more dangerous.

The different thicknesses of atmosphere also have an unexpected effect on the greenhouse effect. A greenhouse effect depends on the *amount* of air, not its pressure! So a large planet has a *smaller* greenhouse effect for the same total pressure—the opposite of what one might naively expect. This is good if the planet is close to its sun, and so in danger of overheating. It's not so good if the planet is far away. A problem with Turtledove's Minerva, which was postulated to be a planet larger than Earth in the orbit of Mars, is that it needs a large greenhouse effect—which is not what you expect with a larger planet, other things being equal.

Conversely, of course, small planets have a larger greenhouse effect for the same pressure, but again, the planet also needs to be big enough to support ongoing tectonic activity, to maintain the atmosphere (page 69). Mars probably dried out and froze up because it couldn't (page 115).

## The Ozone Layer

High in Earth's upper stratosphere is a thin zone rich in *ozone*, a highly active (and toxic) form of oxygen with three atoms per molecule ($O_3$) instead of the usual two. This is the now-famous ozone layer. Ozone absorbs high-energy UV light strongly and thus shields Earth's surface from these wavelengths. This is extremely important for life on land (and in shallow water), because such wavelengths are energetic enough to break up the biomolecules making up living cells. (This is why UV is used in sterilizing lamps.) Indeed, the ozone layer makes the land and shallows habitable. Some equivalent of an ozone layer is probably necessary on a life-bearing planet, at least around a star that puts out as much UV as the Sun. Also, oxygen must be present in the atmosphere if ozone is to exist, because the ozone forms by the breakup of ordinary oxygen molecules ($O_2$) into single oxygen atoms, followed by the reaction of a single oxygen atom with another $O_2$ molecule to form $O_3$.

## THE OCEAN

The ocean, of course, is an extensive body of liquid water covering some three-fourths of the Earth's surface, and an ocean is probably typical of most Earthlike planets, at least at some point in their history. The dissolved salts in Earth's modern ocean make up an average salinity of about 3.5 percent by weight. Most of the dissolved material is just table salt, sodium chloride (NaCl), but magnesium sulfate and magnesium chloride, as well as a host of minor constituents, are also present. In dissolving, the salts break up into *ions*, positively and negatively charged atoms. The metals become positive and the non-metals negative. In particular, the chlorine becomes the *chloride ion* ($Cl^-$), which is extremely stable in water solution. In fact, much of the Earth's chlorine is chloride in the oceans; it's been concentrated out of the entire planet by geologic processes. *That* fact has striking world-building significance I'll return to in the last chapter.

The salinity of the ocean seems to change little over geologic time. (It's not true that our blood reflects the salinity of the ancient seas! That's a long-outdated idea, before the extreme antiquity of the oceans was understood.) Salinity fluctuates a bit from tectonic vagaries, as salt is sequestered by evaporation in, say, rift valleys, or salt deposits are redissolved on exposure and erosion. But such variations seem minor. In fact, since most of the water and most of the chlorine on an Earthlike planet end up in its oceans, the overall salinity is set by their ratio. That ratio might vary a lot, too, because the volatiles make up a very small proportion of a planet, and how much chlorine, say, you get is probably a crapshoot. Thus, the salinity of its seas is probably as characteristic of a planet as its orbit or its surface gravity. Among other things, too, sea salinity can affect climate. For example, the saltier the ocean, the less freely water evaporates from it—and that can decrease the greenhouse effect. If oceans start out very salty, a "greenhouse runaway" (page 71) could be more difficult to arrange.

Obviously having an ocean requires enough water! Much of

Earth's is on the surface, although a significant amount gets recycled into the mantle by plate tectonics—a fact with *lots* of other implications (pages 68, 81). An ocean also requires the right temperature range; it can't all freeze or boil. To some degree, once oceans are present the carbonate cycle acts as a thermostat to *keep* the temperature in the liquid range. Still, oceans are possible only over a certain range of distances from a star, the so-called "habitable zone."

Liquid water also needs enough pressure. Liquid vaporizes without an atmosphere to hold it down. Water boils in vacuum even at room temperature. This in turn implies that an ocean planet must be big enough to hold an atmosphere. Contrast our Moon! Obviously it lies in the habitable zone, as its mean distance from the Sun is the same as Earth's. But it's far too small to keep an atmosphere or ocean.

## The Ocean Basins

If you graph height with respect to sea level for the entire Earth, you will find most values fall around two preferred positions; the abyssal depths (about $-3800$ m) and the average continental height (about 800 m). This demonstrates the continents are not just random high spots but real features of the crust. Continents ride high above the mean surface of the Earth for the same reason ships ride high above the water surface: They're buoyant. Again, continental crust is different from oceanic crust. It's made of lighter rock, richer in elements that don't fit well into the dense iron-magnesium silicates of the mantle, and thus have tended to get sweated out of the Earth over time. So, if you have a planet richer in such material, you'll get more, or bigger, continents.

Moreover, it's probably not just happenstance that the amount of water on the Earth just slightly overfills the basins between the continents. Plate tectonics pushes continental rock together over geologic time; then when the mound breaches the water surface, erosion becomes extremely effective and tends to level it off at about sea level.

Here's another idea: the "oceanworld." In contrast to the dryworld, this is a planet covered, or nearly so, by water. Arthur C. Clarke's Thalassa in *The Songs of Distant Earth* or Joan Slonczewski's Shora in *A Door Into Ocean* are examples. Although such a planet obviously can support life, technical intelligence seems unlikely, as fire and metal, the beginner's blocks of technology, are stillborn. Perhaps, as SF author and scientist David Brin has pointed out, lots of intelligent creatures are stuck on otherwise Earthlike planets with no land area. They'd either be confined to the sea themselves, or else there's too little land for a "critical mass" to have the technological breakthrough. After all, you probably need a *lot* of land—just an island or two won't do. In fact, the very diversity of environments on lots of land area may help spur intelligence. Slonczewski, however, suggested that biological science might thrive on such a world—not to mention other cultural endeavors!

In view of this, it's interesting that Earth itself has almost been an oceanworld, many times. The ocean basin volume does change somewhat through geologic time because of tectonic processes (page 99). When the basin volume is low, sea level stands high, and we have a *marine transgression*: shallow seas cover most of the continents. Such are very common in the geologic record. Right now sea level stands unusually low: We're in a *regression*.

Although not completely an "oceanworld," the broad shallow seas and restricted land area of the Earth during transgressions obviously profoundly affected both climate and biological evolution. Had intelligence arisen at those times, it probably would have been stymied in developing a sophisticated technology. (Indeed, perhaps it did, but in the absence of technology left no fossil record. *There's* a story idea . . .) This is another underutilized setting, but Andre Norton's Hawaika (in *Key Out of Time*) and Ursula LeGuin's Earthsea trilogy have some of the flavor. This also shows the advantage of using the ancient Earth in designing a planet, an idea worth a chapter (chapter five) of its own.

## Plate Tectonics, Oceans and Life

So far as we know, life and plate tectonics are unique to the Earth, at least in our Solar System. It now looks as though these two unique Earthly phenomena are related. Life on Earth, of course, relies on liquid water: The oceans were vital in both the origin and evolution of living things. And oceans almost certainly are also vital to plate tectonics, because they lubricate the plates. When the plates subduct at oceanic trenches, they carry some seawater down into the mantle. There, it has a profound effect on that hot rock; it makes it flow much more easily, so that the plates can slide over it. It keeps the asthenosphere weak. Without such a mechanism to carry water back into the Earth, it would eventually all be outgassed by volcanic processes; then the asthenosphere would dry up, become rigid and plate tectonics would stop.

So it seems that without deep surface water, there's no plate tectonics. Obviously this is a potential problem for a dryworld (page 72).

## Climate and Weather

Climate is average weather. In turn, temperature and precipitation largely determine weather; and they in turn depend on latitudes, seasons, and topography—overall a wide set of variables. The polar regions are cold, even to (sometimes) supporting icecaps; deserts are concentrated along a midlatitude high-pressure belt; high mountains create deserts behind them by wringing the moisture out of air flowing over them; polar latitudes are strongly seasonal, while the seasons are barely perceptible in the tropics—the list goes on and on.

Weather fundamentally stems from the interaction of the ocean and atmosphere with heating by the Sun. This heating drives the circulation of the atmosphere and ocean, which in turn moves heat around and so tends to even out temperatures over the globe. The main mechanism driving circulation is *convection*: heated material expands, and being less dense, rises. Look at cooling coffee in a cup, or boiling teakettle; it's that simple! Convection in the atmosphere drives winds. In the oceans, it drives an "overturn," in which cold water sinks at the poles. This overturn moves nutrients as well as heat around. (Under other circumstances convection in the ocean can be quite different, as we'll see.)

---

### THE CORIOLIS EFFECT

Earth is spinning, and things at the surface appear to be subject to external forces because of that spin. The most familiar such "force" is the centrifugal effect, which appears as an outward force directly away from the center of rotation. A less familiar but equally important "force" is the Coriolis effect, which appears as a sideways force on something moving along lines of longitude (i.e., north or south). You can visualize this force as follows: consider an object on Earth's equator. Since it's moving along with the Earth, it shares the rotational velocity at the equator, some 900 miles/hour. As that object moves off the equator, though, the ground underneath is moving more slowly (obviously, at the poles there's no rotational velocity at all). So the object ends up with "excess" velocity that pulls it to one side—just as though a force were pushing to the side. In the northern hemisphere the force is to the right, whereas it's to the left in the southern hemisphere.

Thus the Coriolis effect twists large-scale flows into gyres. (To debunk some folklore, however, the Coriolis force does *not* affect water running down a drain! That's much too small-scale. Water spinning down the drain can spin either way, in either hemisphere, depending on the vagaries of its internal motions.) In the air this makes the giant, spiral "cyclonic" storms so familiar from satellite weather photos. Hurricanes are a spectacular example. In fact, they generally can't form within five degrees of the equator because there's not enough Coriolis force. For this reason Poul Anderson's planet Avalon was suggested to have especially violent storms because of its rapid rotation. A planet spinning twice as fast has twice the Coriolis effect, and other things being equal, storms will spiral twice as tightly. Other things won't quite be equal because of the friction of the air, but that will be a minor effect unless the air is thick indeed. Note also that the young Earth would have had more violent weather because of its swifter spin (page 27).

However, it does not follow that a very slowly rotating planet has gentler weather. Because it's much less evenly heated it might have violent weather indeed, from convective winds flowing between the day and night sides.

## Convection in the Atmosphere

It all starts with the warming of the Earth's surface by the Sun. The warm ground heats the air above, which rises, and cooler air flows in from the sides to compensate.

But of course there are *lots* of details. The Coriolis force (see sidebar above, page 81) twists the airflows into great spirals. The flows are also diverted by topography, and so the distribution of continents and oceans has an especially profound effect. The atmosphere also contains a "condensable phase"—water vapor. As water evaporates and condenses it greatly affects the atmosphere, by absorbing and removing heat, and by changing the albedo; white clouds obviously reflect sunlight very well!

From everyday experience we know that temperature generally decreases with altitude. Snow persists on mountain peaks long after it has vanished in the valleys below. Rising air cools because its expansion occurs at the expense of its internal heat. In theory, the drop-off of temperature with height should follow an "adiabatic" profile, in which the decrease of temperature exactly compensates for the expansion.

As you'd expect, though, in something as chaotic as an atmosphere, an adiabatic profile is often not present. In *inversions* a body of cold air stays stuck on the ground, typically in a valley or basin, because it's heavier. Breaking up the inversion requires heating the air from below again, or wind. Conversely, a "superadiabatic" profile, in which the air is abnormally warm at high altitudes, is often a factor in violent storms. Convection accelerates once it begins.

Particles—dust or cloud—can dramatically change the distribution of heat in the atmosphere, and thus its circulation. This can have a devastating effect on climate, especially if they're high in the atmosphere. Although the amount of incident sunlight is the same, it's absorbed not on the ground but high in the atmosphere. So the surface stays cold, and there's no convection! It's a permanent inversion. This is potentially most interesting for catastrophes that inject lots of dust into the upper atmosphere, as with the aftermath of a giant meteorite impact or volcanic eruption. The "nuclear winter," a cause célèbre about ten years ago, was just this scenario. Such a dust layer might be especially catastrophic on a dry world, because it would never rain out.

The other thing that makes weather complicated is that condensable phase, water vapor. If the vapor content exceeds a certain level, which depends on temperature, liquid water can condense out to form a cloud. As warmer air can hold more water vapor than cooler air (page 67), condensation happens upon cooling. Hence clouds commonly form high above the ground, at the point where the air has cooled enough. Or they can form where the air is cooled for other reasons, as in a fogbank at sea.

As evaporation absorbs heat whereas condensation releases it again, evaporation and condensation also move heat around. In fact, cloud formation can drive the further expansion and rising of air masses. This is another factor in storms. Warm surface seawater, with a temperature of at least 27°C (80°F), is "hurricane fuel," a fact used by John Barnes in *Mother of Storms*.

## Convection in the Ocean

In Earth's present-day ocean, the main circulation driver is the sinking of cold polar water. Surface seawater at the poles cools down almost to freezing and thus becomes denser. It sinks, and flows back toward the equator in the abyssal depths. This deep, frigid flow is compensated by a tendency of warm, surface equatorial water to flow back toward the poles. Thus, the modern ocean is dominated by cold water. Below a thin warm surface layer, the deep sea is almost freezing. The modern ocean is also oxygenated; cold water holds more gas in solution, so the deep ocean (again, with trifling exceptions) is oxygenated completely to the bottom. Thus oxygen-breathers can live on the sea floor to scavenge and burrow.

The surface flow gets substantially modified, of course. Prevailing winds establish currents by pushing surface water along, which the Coriolis force tends to force into spirals. Tides (page 155) also rearrange currents, especially near shore. Like the Coriolis force, though, they just stir up the surface. They don't force mixing between shallow and deep water the way convection does.

The enormous amount of water in the ocean also means it's very difficult to heat the Earth up quickly, or to cool it, once heated. Oceans are "heat banks": Not only does water have high "heat capacity," which means it takes a lot of energy to heat up, but it also takes a lot of energy to evaporate. This is relevant for disaster scenarios such as how quickly the oceans could boil in a "runaway greenhouse" (page 71) scenario. For example, it would take *all* the energy Earth receives from the Sun for about 650 years to boil our oceans.

Again, all flows in both atmosphere and ocean are profoundly modified by barriers; islands, seamounts and especially continents block and redirect currents of both air and water. This means that continental distribution has a profound effect on climate. And, since continents change their sizes and positions drastically over geologic time, this means Earth has been vastly different at times in its past.

## THE MAGNETIC FIELD AND MAGNETOSPHERE

As any Boy Scout learns, Earth has a magnetic field that's roughly aligned with its spin axis. This field is generated somehow in the liquid outer core by electrical currents. There's *lots* of controversy over what powers the geodynamo, but it seems to require (1) a rapidly rotating planet; and (2) an electrically conducting core. (Since the core consists of an iron alloy, it's an electrical conductor.) Venus probably has an iron core like the Earth's but rotates slowly; and it has no field. Mars rotates at about the same rate as Earth, but probably has a small core or none at all; and it also has no field.

Obviously a magnetic field is good for navigation, and so it may have a profound effect on both technological and social development. Consider Europe's Age of Exploration in the fifteenth and sixteenth centuries. How important this is, of course, depends on how difficult it is to navigate around the planet. Otherwise, although a few other living things use the field for navigation, it's not clear most life-forms directly need a magnetic field at all.

Indirect effects may be important, though. The magnetic field partly deflects the solar wind, a continuous stream of subatomic particles (mostly protons) streaming from the Sun. Some particles are trapped temporarily by the magnetic field, in the Van Allen radiation belts. Others are funneled onto the magnetic poles, where they interact spectacularly with the atmosphere to form *auroras*, in which the highly rarefied outer atmosphere lights up like a neon tube. Without the magnetic field, auroras would be everywhere. Of course, if the Sun's output remained the same they'd be less intense, because they'd be spread over the entire Earth. This probably also would inhibit radio communication.

Auroras might be especially intense with a hotter star, as it would put out more high-energy particles. Poul Anderson used this to good effect in his Nebula-winning "The Queen of Air and Darkness." The ethereal light supported the mood by maintaining a sense of mystery with an undertone of menace. The auroras also stymied radio communication, which was a plot necessity.

The magnetic field may also help protect the atmosphere over geologic time, as the solar wind impact can increase exosphere temperature and so increase atmosphere loss. This could be especially effective with a hotter star than the Sun, with its hotter and denser solar wind. This may be another reason planets are dryer around hotter stars.

The magnetic field may also help protect the Earth from solar tantrums, such as a solar megaflare: a great burst of heat, light, and high-energy-charged particles from the Sun. Larry Niven's classic story "Inconstant Moon" used this idea—the flare crisped the daytime side of the Earth. Ben Bova wrote an entire novel (*Test of Fire*) using this scenario, with the added wrinkle that the flare triggered a nuclear war because it was (reasonably) misinterpreted as a nuclear attack.

A flare so hot as to burn vegetation—not to mention glassify surface rocks—isn't very likely, because we see no evidence of such a thing in the geologic record. A thin layer formed by a glassed-over desert, such as the cooked Sahara sands in Bova's novel, would make a distinctive horizon indeed in the sedimentary record. Of course, things might be different with another star, less stable than the Sun. Poul Anderson used this as background in *Satan's World*.

A megaflare could cause major havoc even if it didn't completely cook the dayside, though. For one thing, it might cause a mass extinction by killing off lots of critters with hard radiation, such as secondary X rays created when multiple trillions of high-energy protons slam into atmospheric atoms. Even lesser flares might heighten the mutation rate by spraying Earth with subatomic particles. Of course, *one* low-level flare probably wouldn't have much effect. You'd have to keep irradiating the biosphere for at least a few years. So we'd now be talking about an ongoing series of flares, presumably from unusual solar activity.

Heightened levels of ionizing radiation from such activity might drastically affect the biosphere even if none of it reaches the Earth's surface, by destroying the ozone layer. (High-energy radiation is often called "ionizing" radiation because it has enough energy to tear electrons off atoms—that is, to make ions.) As the radiation is absorbed in the upper atmosphere, it will break up oxygen ($O_2$) and nitrogen ($N_2$) molecules into free atoms. Some of these will then combine into nitrogen oxides, which are extremely good at causing ozone destruction. Before man-made chlorine compounds got into the upper atmosphere, low levels of natural nitrogen oxides were the main ozone-destroying agent.

Finally, every once in a while the Earth's magnetic poles reverse—the south pole becomes the north pole, and conversely. The Earth doesn't turn over; all that happens is the main field dies away briefly (geologically speaking!—it seems to take about 10,000 years); and when it builds up again, it can just as easily have the opposite polarity. Such "geomagnetic reversals" don't seem to be correlated with extinctions. They're just too common and just not that big a deal. Navigation would be awkward, though. And a megaflare could especially cause havoc if it happened to hit during a geomagnetic reversal, because then the intensity of the magnetic field is maybe only 10 percent of normal.

## THE COLORS OF A PLANET

What makes color? Most simply, if a substance absorbs some wavelengths in the visible region, the wavelengths reflected make up the color we see. Common rocks owe their color largely to a single element: iron. All those pallid greens, deep blacks, light tans, pale oranges and bright reds come from iron in different chemical states. Metallurgists and ceramicists refer to such things as calcium oxide, magnesium oxide and so on as the "white oxides" for a reason! Iron compounds are colored because the atom has electrons in intermediate energy states where they can absorb visible light. Similar metals, such as manganese and copper, also make colored compounds, but they're a lot rarer on Earth. (That's why, though, ore minerals tend to be brightly colored.)

Organic compounds—those containing carbon linked to itself, such as biomolecules—are also commonly colored. Think of the green of chlorophyll (the pigment in plants), the red of hemoglobin (which colors blood), and so on. Great variety is possible here: consider the lurid hues of artificial dyes, all of which are organic compounds! Alien blood doesn't have to be red; alien leaves won't be green. In fact, organic compounds can be any color at all, because the absorption depends on subtleties of the chemical bonds between the carbon atoms. The colors aren't completely arbitrary, though, because they'll depend on what the organism is using the colored compound for. For photosynthesis, for example, the color has to be such that the right wavelengths are absorbed to run the biochemical mechanisms that carry out the photosynthesis.

What sets the color of the sky is another thing you can't find easily in textbooks. The blue of the cloudless sky results from scattering by the very molecules in the air. Long wavelengths (red) are scattered much less easily, but short-wavelength blue is scattered all over the sky. Obviously, then, the sky color depends on the available wavelengths—that is, on the color of the star. If the star is, say, red, the sky will look reddish, as there's no blue to scatter. With an orangish sun, the sky may look more greenish than blue. This effect will only appear under extreme cases, however, as even most "red" stars look white to the eye (page 129).

Scattering by dust may also be important. Big particles don't discriminate among wavelengths. That's why clouds are white, because the droplets in them are much bigger than a wavelength of light (white is a mixture of all wavelengths). Colored particles, though, absorb certain wavelengths, and that will tint the sky. Mars's pinkish sky comes from the extremely fine reddish dust raised off its surface by winds. The ocean's color reflects the sky: It's blue under blue skies, gray under gray. Water also weakly absorbs red light, which is why underwater scenes are greenish-blue.

Uranus and Neptune look bluish because methane ($CH_4$) in their atmospheres slightly absorbs red light. Don't expect methane to be a major constituent of an Earthlike atmosphere, though, because it reacts readily with oxygen—it's the main ingredient in natural gas! (And, anyway, like water methane is colorless except in great thicknesses.) In fact, the gases you'll find on Earthlike planets are colorless; that is, they don't absorb light in the visible region. Some could be important on some of the un-Earthly worlds described later, though. The chlorine on the chloroxygen world (page 155) would give the sky a greenish tint, and would make things at the surface hazy, how much so depending on the concentration. Nitrogen dioxide is brownish and in fact largely gives city smog its irritating hue; it would be a major constituent of the atmosphere of a nitroxy world (page 164).

## DAY AND NIGHT

A planet's rotation rate has other effects besides the profound influence on weather due to the Coriolis effect. If it rotates too fast, the planet will fly apart, just like an overspun tire or flywheel. This limit is about two hours for Earth. The reason, of course, is "centrifugal force." If the spin is too quick the outward force at the equator exceeds the gravitational pull. Even for the more modest rotational rates of real planets, the spin distorts the planet with an "equatorial bulge." This bulge provides a "handle" for gravitational perturbations (page 22) that have—on the Earth, and no doubt elsewhere—long-term consequences for climate.

Too slow a spin rate leads to different problems, or perhaps challenges. A rapidly spinning planet is easy to keep at a reasonable temperature, but as the rotation rate gets slower and slower, the day side tends to broil and the night side to freeze. You need to exchange heat—which, on very slowly rotating planets, would lead to *ferocious* winds—or heat needs to be stored in the daytime, to be released at night. (Warm, saline oceans, like those described above, might work.)

The ultimate slowness of rotation is once per revolution, so the Sun never rises and sets at all. Because of the extreme winds, such a world is not generally considered viable, as Stephen Dole originally suggested in the study *Planets for Man*. Poul Anderson, however, proposed such a habitable world, the planet Ikrananka in *The Trouble Twisters*. A sociological implication was the fatalism of the dominant planetary culture, due to the monotony of the endless, unchanging day. In *Prelude to Space*, Arthur C. Clarke suggested that Venus presented one face to the Sun, as Mercury was then thought to do, and the extreme winds blocked access from space! Although this proved not to be the case for Venus, the idea hasn't been used again, to my knowledge.

## SIDEREAL VS. SOLAR ROTATION PERIODS

The "sidereal" rotation period is the true rotation period of a body. The name comes from the Latin word for "star" and refers to the rotation period that would be measured from a very distant object, such as another star. That's not the relevant period if you're actually living on the surface of a planet, though. Then we want the *solar day*, which is simply the ordinary "day," the time between two successive sunrises.

Why do they differ? Well, for a rapidly rotating planet like the Earth, they don't differ much. Earth's solar day is, of course, twenty-four hours, whereas its sidereal period is only about four minutes shorter. But the difference starts to matter when the rotation period is a significant fraction of the revolution period; i.e., of the year.

The reason is that the solar day depends on the revolution period around the sun, as well as on the sidereal period. As a planet moves along in its orbit, it must rotate a bit more (or a bit less, if its orbit is retrograde) to face its sun again (figure 10, page 92). Mathematically, the relation between solar and sidereal day is:

$$1/p' = 1/p - 1/P$$

where $p'$ is the time between sunrises (the solar day), $P$ is the revolution period (year length), and $p$ is the sidereal rotation period (the "sidereal day"). (Be sure you use the same units for both $p$ and $P$!) Note that if $P$ is less than $p$, $p'$ comes out with a negative sign; this means the sun rises in the west. If the sidereal rotation period $p$ itself is "backward" (retrograde), take it as negative.

For example, here are the values for Venus:

$$p = -243.01 \text{ d (i.e., the rotation is retrograde)}$$
$$P = 224.7 \text{ d (length of Venusian year)}$$

So $1/p' = 1/(-243.01) - 1/(224.7) = -0.00857$, and therefore $p' = 1/(-0.00857) = -116.75$ days. Thus sunrise on Venus occurs at nearly four-month intervals, and the Sun rises in the west (because of the negative sign on $p'$).

Similarly, we can rearrange this equation to get the sidereal day if we know the solar day. For Earth, for example:

$$p' = 1 \text{ d (Mean solar day)}$$
$$P = 365.25 \text{ d (year)}$$

On solving for p, we find:

$$p = Pp'/(P + p') = 365.25 \times 1/(365.25 + 1)$$
$$= 0.9973 \text{ solar days, or } \sim 23 \text{ h } 56 \text{ min.}$$

Again, on a rapidly rotating planet, there's not much difference!

One final note: On any planet with a tilted axis, the proportion of day vs. night varies with the seasons, as we know from everyday experience. For planets with highly tilted axes the variations get extreme indeed, and the details require trigonometry that lies beyond the scope of this book. We can make some general observations, though. First, the Arctic and Antarctic circles will lie at a distance from each pole that corresponds to the axial tilt (e.g., 23.5° in the case of the Earth; see page 17). These, remember, mark the position at which the sun will not rise (or set) for at least one day during the year. So, only equator-ward of this point will the Sun always rise and set. Summer days will get longer and longer the closer to the Arctic (or Antarctic) circle, and conversely for winter days. The nearer the equator, on the other hand, the more nearly equal day and night, all through the year.

## A THOUGHT EXPERIMENT: THE ICE WORLD

Consider a world completely sheathed in ice, a bigger version of the Jovian moon Europa (page 117). Surely plate tectonics would still work. After all, ice should subduct, and it will hardly persist as ice in the subsurface! A naive calculation indicates that if the Earth were completely covered with ice, and no other effects intervened, the ice wouldn't melt, because the Earth's albedo would then be so high. Climatologists used to worry, therefore, about a "runaway glaciation," in which the Earth would freeze over permanently. On Earth, though, this wouldn't happen because of the carbonate cycle. With no oceans, carbon dioxide from volcanic activity would accumulate in the air, increasing the greenhouse effect until the ice melted again. Perhaps on a smaller, less active planet, though, such a runaway glaciation remains a possible disaster. Some recent models also suggest it can happen if the upper atmosphere gets cold enough to condense clouds of carbon dioxide ice, because of their high albedo.

In fact, it seems difficult to sheathe an Earth in ice, at least until it runs down permanently. In the early Archean, about 3.5 billion years ago, the Sun was considerably fainter (page 135), yet liquid

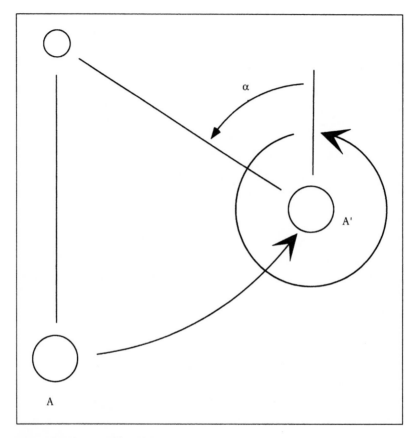

**FIG. 10** Solar vs. Sidereal Day.

The planet completes one rotation (sidereal period) during which it has moved along its orbit from A to A'. Hence it must rotate through the additional angle α to face its sun again. Since the solar day is, by definition, the time between successive appearances of the sun at the same position in the sky, the time needed to rotate through that additional angle accounts for the difference between the sidereal day and solar day.

water was evidently abundant on Earth's surface.

So is a tectonically active ice world intrinsically unstable? Let's see if we can rationalize it. To stabilize ice, we need to keep the $CO_2$ content down. Maybe we need very cold-tolerant photosynthetic vegetation. On Earth, increasing cold and ice cover limit vegetation growth. Vegetation that *thrives* under icy conditions might, however, keep the $CO_2$ from building up. Icehouse conditions would be further stabilized if things got cold enough for carbon dioxide crystals to condense in the stratosphere. None of this has happened on Earth, but maybe that's the point!

# CHAPTER 5

# The Ancient Earth

## THE PLANETS EARTH

Lots of stories have what I call the "Cenozoic Earth" syndrome. (The Cenozoic is the last sixty-five million years of Earth history, ever since the dinosaurs became extinct. It's either the "Age of Mammals" or the "Age of Grasses," depending on your prejudices.) A few exotic beasts consisting of rearrangements of some familiar elements (fur or maybe scales; horns or claws or even antennae), but complex, quadrupedal and warm-blooded, are trotting (loping, leaping, crawling) in an landscape of finagled grasses or trees: It's hardly "alien!" Our own Earth's been a lot weirder than that.

Now, this certainly works in the hands of a master. Andre Norton can evoke an alien world with a few such vivid details. Too often, though, this approach degenerates into a hodgepodge of ill-fitting elements. (For ideas about designing believable aliens, see Stanley Schmidt's book in this series.)

For what do we mean by "Earthlike," anyway? The Earth has been very different at different times in the geologic past, and some of those Earths are more alien than most authors' "alien" planets! Not only the life, but the very land itself alters as shifting plate motions shove the continents around like scum on a pond. So, we can use the ancient Earth for inspiration; and we'll have to remember that any other real planet will vary over geologic time too. Our Earth is *ancient*. It's the ultimate result of historical processes extending over literally billions of years, and there was nothing inevitable about the particular path its history took.

## DEEP TIME

"When dinosaurs walked and the Earth was young. . . ."

That's part of the problem right there. When the dinosaurs walked the Earth was already *old* and in its modern form. If the Earth were a 46.5 year old human (a scale of 1 year = 100 million years; the Earth is about 4.65 billion years old), the dinosaurs walked from about age forty-four through forty-six years. Even the "Cambrian explosion," the first appearance of hard-shelled life in the fossil record, didn't occur till after forty.

For some five-sixths of its history—almost four billion years— the Earth was a "scumworld," populated only by microbes; and for at least half that time there wasn't any oxygen in the atmosphere! Or at least enough to breathe. How come such a world has never figured in SF? There must be a lot of them out there!

## THE ANCIENT ATMOSPHERE

The original composition of the atmosphere was very different from today's. With no life, there was little free oxygen, and no ozone layer, either! But although Earth's primitive atmosphere wasn't oxidizing, its exact nature has been disputed. Until recently many textbooks presented as fact a composition of ammonia ($NH_3$) and methane ($CH_4$), a "traditional" idea proposed by the late Harold Urey, the pioneer of solar-system chemistry.

But such an atmosphere almost certainly never existed. Both molecules are too easily photodissociated (page 71). Furthermore, because both have very low freezing points, an upper-atmosphere cold trap, such as protects Earth's water vapor (page 71), isn't possible. These gases are also not chemically stable with common rocks and, sure enough, we see no evidence for them in the geologic record. Among other things, $NH_3$ reacts enthusiastically with water and we should see *some* indication of different marine chemistry. But we don't.

Alas, no primitive Earthlike but lifeless worlds, sterile oceans swathed with a reducing welkin, are awaiting biological seeding packages, as Larry Niven proposed in *World Out of Time*. Sterile worlds dominated by thinnish $CO_2$ atmospheres might be a different story, however. The primitive atmosphere was more likely a mixture of $CO_2$, $N_2$, water vapor and a whiff of other stuff. In fact, it probably contained toxic levels of $CO_2$ for humans, quite apart from its lack of oxygen: The greenhouse must have been more effective than today's, because the new-formed Sun was probably about 30 percent fainter than it is now (see page 135), yet Earth was never totally frozen over. The oldest rocks preserve evidence of liquid water.

At least Niven tried. Explorers in nearly all other SF arrive at a world at the same stage as Earth, despite the fact that the present oxygen-rich atmosphere reflects a much smaller percentage of our planet's history!

## Atmosphere Origin

By the early 1950s scientists realized Earth's present atmosphere couldn't be "primordial"; that is, left over from the condensation of the nebula that formed the Solar System. This follows because the noble gases, especially neon, are so rare in the atmosphere. The Earth can easily hold neon in its atmosphere (figure 9, page 65), and it's an abundant element, as heavy elements go. Neon in the Universe is half again as abundant as nitrogen, but on Earth less than one atom in ten billion is left. Like all the noble gases, neon stands aloof from chemical compounds, and freezes only at low temperatures. Presumably the circumstances under which the Earth formed were always too hot for neon to condense (page 44). It may be hard to get a world like Diomedes (in Anderson's *The Man Who Counts*), where neon is a major atmospheric component. But neon is *so* abundant; it's worth a try (page 154)!

So the Earth's atmosphere is secondary. Traditionally, it's been ascribed to "outgassing"; gases (and water) in chemical combination in rocks were eventually spewed out of volcanoes after the Earth stewed a little bit. This isn't a silly idea, as we see exactly this happening at modern volcanoes, although with the recognition of plate tectonics, we now realize that most volcanic gases are simply recycled seawater.

But another idea has become trendy recently: much of the atmosphere was brought in at the very last stage of planetary accretion in comet-like bodies containing ices and other volatile-rich material. These bodies formed at least part of the late heavy bombardment, which pocked the Moon and other inner planets with giant craters (page 42). Many represented material condensed farther out in the solar nebula, where it was cooler, and only later were they perturbed into orbits that caused collisions with the inner planets.

The difference isn't completely semantic. Even though material's thoroughly mixed into the planet either way, the extremely haphazard nature of late accretion makes it easy to vary the composition and mass of the volatiles greatly. Their composition is also completely unrelated to the main body of the planet. In fact, the violent vagaries of the late gigantic impacts probably boiled away all the previously acquired volatiles more than once, as when the Moon formed (page 113).

Thus volatile abundances should be a fruitful source of variety, particularly because compared with the mass of the planet as a whole they're just a wisp. Only 0.024 percent of Earth's mass is ocean, for example. The possibilities here are so varied that they're the subject of a chapter of their own (see chapter seven).

The about 1 percent of argon, another noble gas, in Earth's atmosphere is a product of Earth itself. It is almost entirely the isotope $^{40}Ar$, which is a decay product of radioactive potassium-40 ($^{40}K$), one of the main heat sources within the Earth (page 55), with a half-life of about 1.3 billion years. Of course, the fact we see so much $^{40}Ar$ in the atmosphere tells us significant outgassing of the Earth has occurred! We just don't know what else may have come out along with the argon.

Helium on Earth is also such a "radiogenic" gas. Alpha particles from the radioactive decay of heavy elements are simply helium atoms. For every atom of uranium-238 that bites the dust, for example, you get eight helium atoms. This is the source of the helium found in some natural gas wells; uranium and thorium often occur in sedimentary rocks, and the helium they produce gets trapped like any other natural gas. In fact, one modestly trendy oil-exploration technique is "helium sniffing": Since helium escapes its reservoir more easily than hydrocarbons, it can sometimes be detected at the surface.

Unfortunately, once in the atmosphere helium doesn't stick around; it is so light that, like hydrogen, it eventually escapes to space. Its residence time in Earth's atmosphere is only about a million years. This fact was used in Niven and Pournelle's *The Mote in God's Eye*; since Mote Prime had about 1 percent helium in its atmosphere, the expedition scientists eventually inferred a long-lived technical culture, since the helium couldn't have remained over geologic time. Presumably the helium was the waste product from hydrogen fusion.

## THE ARCHEAN EARTH

The "Archean" is the oldest period of Earth history, extending by definition from the oldest rocks preserved up to 2.5 billion years ago. It was substantially different from our modern world in ways besides the oxygen-free atmosphere described above. Because the Earth was hotter, heat flow was higher, so the crust was thinner, volcanism was hotter and more active, and continents drifted more swiftly. The continents were also smaller, but the amount of continental crust grew rapidly in the first billion years or so, as the crust separated out from volcanic activity. It was a scumworld, too: bacterial mats were the highest form of life. By the end of the Archean, mats of cyanobacteria ("blue-green algae") had begun to release free oxygen from photosynthesis, probably the most drastic change in Earth's environment ever. This, the first global air pollution, was a harbinger of the great changes living things would wreak.

The Archean is another underutilized setting. Arthur C. Clarke's Thalassa (in *The Songs of Distant Earth*) was a valiant attempt, but his timescales were off. He suggested that Thalassa was a near-oceanworld because the continents hadn't formed yet. However, Thalassa had an oxygen atmosphere and complex, multicelled life forms. On Earth, though, substantial protocontinents already existed in the early Archean while all life was still bacterial—and atmospheric oxygen lay over a billion years in the future!

## THE DANCE OF THE CONTINENTS

As I've noted, continental arrangement has an utterly profound effect on climate, because of the major effect of continental barriers on air and ocean current flow. And that arrangement is constantly changing. Plate tectonics is continually shoving the continents around, smashing them together to form mountain ranges, then splitting them apart again as the patterns of seafloor spreading shift. Because continental rock is too buoyant to subduct, the continents always remain on the surface—but the distribution of land and sea is ephemeral.

Every now and then most of the continents get gathered together, most recently as the "supercontinent" Pangea, which formed about two hundred and fifty million years ago (abbreviated "Ma") and started to split up maybe fifty million years later. Pangea, however, was only the latest aggregation in a long history. The next most recent supercontinent has been named "Rodinia" and seems to have broken up in the latest Proterozoic, by about six hundred and fifty Ma.

Supercontinents break up geologically quickly because they're unstable. They disrupt the outward flow of heat, like a giant blanket plastered onto the Earth. The trapped heat eventually (within a few tens of millions of years) causes a wholly new global pattern of rifting; the pattern of seafloor spreading is completely rearranged, and the supercontinent fragments.

They also aren't prime real estate. They have extreme climates because so much of the land is far from the moderating effect of the oceans; Siberia looks like Hawaii by comparison. Only the coastal fringe would be really habitable and have the prospect of providing the economic surplus for a civilization.

This might have major consequences for an intelligent species that arose then. For example, suppose all the supercontinent's coasts are accessible with primitive craft. No long ocean voyages would be needed to reach essentially all the usable land, and the interior would be so hostile there'd be little threat of barbarian invasion from that direction. Thus an empire that conquered all the coasts might rule forever, and it might accomplish that conquest with only, say, Roman Empire technology. The only threats would be internal; from a local revolt, say, or from a local governor who decided to try his hand at being a warlord. But nothing like the horse barbarians, which pressured Rome so heavily from out of the central Eurasian steppe as the Empire tottered, would exist.

Earth, by contrast, in this geologic era has land and sea widely distributed across latitudes, such that it's difficult to reach all lands without a fairly sophisticated technology. This ensures that lots of social experiments can first take place in geographic isolation.

Marine transgressions, mentioned in the last chapter, are another by-product of tectonic activity. Commonly, wide, warm, shallow, "epeiric" seas cover much of the continents. One way they probably happen is when seafloor spreading is more active than at present; the mid-ocean ridges swell and spill water onto the continents. This in turn is possibly related to "superplumes," when an enormous pulse of hot rock rises from deep in the mantle, like a mega-hot spot. This happened most recently in the late Cretaceous, about eighty Ma, when sea level stood some two hundred and fifty meters higher than at present. Thus, plate tectonics probably goes in fits and starts.

The dance of the continents also causes crises for life; a salinity crisis, for example. As I said, generally the salt content of seawater has varied little over geologic time. The oceans are large, and it's difficult to take enough salt out—or to add enough—to make any difference. It happened at least once, though, and pretty recently at that, during the "Messinian salinity crisis" about six Ma. Ever since the breakup of Pangea, a belt of shallow marine water—what geologists and paleontologists traditionally call the Tethys—had run along the southern margin of Eurasia, extending from Spain to the Himalayas.

Tethys came in for a squeeze, though, as fragments of Gondwanaland—India, Africa, Arabia and smaller slivers—eventually came shoving up from the south. Slowly those shallow marine environments got throttled off by the encroaching continental pieces, becoming saltier and saltier as free interchange with the open sea was closed off. The environmental deterioration clobbered the Tethyan fauna. The continental collisions also eventually raised the mountain belts along the southern Eurasian margin—the Alps, the Caucasus, the Himalayas and so on.

And so much salt was extracted into those basins that the salinity of the world ocean dropped by several parts per thousand—enough to stress organisms adapted to normal marine salinity. Eventually, too, the convergence closed off the Mediterranean basin completely for a while, and it dried up. This formed a more spectacular desert basin than anything we have now, and it's a popular SF setting.

A different crisis was the invasion of South America about five Ma, when the Central American land bridge from North to South America rose. Up to this point South America, like Australia, had been an isolated continental fragment. And also like Australia, South America had evolved a whole set of unique marsupial mammals, grazers and carnivores and herbivores. But with the rise of the land bridge, South America could be invaded by placental mammals from North America—and it was. Most of the marsupials lost out to this invasion. (Not all, though: The opossum went the other way and successfully invaded North America!)

A last example of a crisis is the Permo-Triassic extinction, which marks the boundary between the Paleozoic and Mesozoic Eras about two hundred and fifty Ma and is the most catastrophic known. More than ninety-five of then-extant species went extinct. There's a shopping list of possible causes. One is a salinity crisis. Another is ecological collapse; the formation of Pangea, in conjunction with sea level drop, both dried up shallow seas and put lots of previously separated creatures into conflict. Possibly an "oxygen crisis" happened too; oxidation of previously deposited organic matter and sulfides, exposed by the sea level drop, may have reduced atmospheric oxygen too much.

Such scenarios provide little-used settings for SF, a different flavor of background for your story.

## ICE AGES

Another effect of different continental configurations is to set the stage for a glacial epoch. Everyone's heard of the Ice Age (Ages, actually). The glaciers have chugged down from the pole several times in the very recent past, geologically. But in a real sense we're *still* in the Ice Age, because massive icecaps lie at or near both poles. All that's happened recently is that the caps got bigger. But Earth usually (geologically speaking) doesn't have polar ice at all.

Ice ages nonetheless happen once in a while. The oldest documented glacial features are about two and a half billion years old, and major glaciations happened in the late Precambrian (~700-800 Ma), Ordovician (~450 Ma), and the late Paleozoic (~250 Ma). Now that we know about continental drift, we can understand glacial ages in general: If the continents are so arranged that surface seawater can circulate freely between the equator and the poles, climate will be more equable over the globe and polar ice won't exist.

For example, the current Antarctic glaciation seems to have started—suddenly, as geologic events go—in the mid Cenozoic, ~35 Ma. Continental drift had separated Australia and Antarctica, and as Australia moved inexorably toward the equator, the circum-Antarctic current became established. Hence cold surface water could remain in the Antarctic and stay cold. Before, the currents were forced northward so they mixed with warmer water. Then, once the glaciers started forming, Antarctica was fully ice-covered, through a positive feedback. What you need to start a glacial age is not frigid winters but lots of snow—and cool summers. To make ice the snow needs to accumulate, and to do *that* it can't all melt over the summer. That sets up the positive feedback: Snow is white and thus raises the albedo, which tends to cool things yet more, so *more* snow accumulates. . . . Before long you've covered most of a continent with ice.

By contrast, when wide shallow seas cover much of the Earth, as during the Cretaceous period about eighty Ma, or when the continents are distributed along the equator, as in the Cambrian period about five hundred and twenty Ma, the surface water could circulate freely and global climate was much more equable.

The cause of the ice sheets' *recent* waxing and waning has been more problematic, though. It's now pretty much the conventional wisdom it's due to small, periodic variations in the Earth's orbit and axial tilt—the Milankovich variations. (Milankovich was the Serbian physicist who proposed this theory beginning back in the 1920s.) He showed that these variations cause small but consistent changes in the average amount of sunlight—"insolation"—that high latitudes receive over a year.

These variations come from perturbations (see page 22) by the other planets. A couple come from the "precession of the equinoxes," a slow change in the direction that the Earth's axis tilts. "Precession" is a wobble of the axis of something that's already spinning around, just like a wobbling top that's about to fall over. Over ~25,000 years, the Earth's axis makes such a complete wobble, and climatic periods of ~19,000 and ~23,000 years are associated with this precession. They're not exactly 25,000 years because of the way the precession period combines with other periods. Another cycle is in the Earth's obliquity, which varies from ~22° to ~25° over ~41,000 years. Both these cycles result mostly from the Moon. Finally, the eccentricity (see page 13) of the Earth's orbit also changes slightly, with a period of ~100,000 years.

The Milankovich variations were ignored for decades because at their most extreme they cause a change of a only few percent in the average intensity of sunlight. But as geologists and oceanographers got better dates on the glacial periods they found they fitted very well with the Milankovich cycles, in particular the 100,000-year eccentricity cycle. Climate is so finely balanced right now that even changes of a few percent in insolation have large effects, because of positive feedbacks like the one described above. It's still not clear, though, exactly how the 100,000-year cycle triggers an ice age.

The waxing and waning of glacial ice also causes sea level to vary over hundreds of meters, as massive amounts of water are locked into ice and then released again. Obviously this changes the shape of the continents. But there's a more subtle result: the intricate, convoluted shorelines we take as "normal" on the modern coastline. Look at the eastern seaboard of the U.S., for example, with its innumerable estuaries, offshore islands, bars and spits. They resulted from the rise in sea level about ~12,000 years ago when the glaciers melted. River mouths were drowned, and long shore currents began to build bars and spits across the inlets. Over time, the shoreline will smooth out, as the rivers fill in the estuaries from behind and the bars wall them off from the sea. Estuaries, of course, are highly productive ecosystems, but Mother Nature destroys wetlands too! She just takes a bit longer.

Oceanic circulation also turns out to be intimately related to ice ages. As I said, we're still in an "ice age" now, because large bodies of ice exist at each pole. And as described earlier (see page 84), the sinking of cold polar water drives the overturn of the modern ocean. Thus, except for a thin surface layer in the tropics, the modern ocean is cold clear through. It is also oxygenated clear through, because cold water can hold lots more air in solution than warm water.

When there's no cold water to sink, the warm equatorial surface water sinks instead. Sure, being warm, it tends to expand and thus decrease its density, but it has also lost water to the air from evaporation. That leaves salts behind, which makes the surface seawater a bit more saline; and the extra salinity is what makes it sink. We have a small modern analog of this situation: the Mediterranean. The Med doesn't receive enough water from the rivers draining into it to replenish evaporation, so its surface waters get saline enough to sink, and a warm saline current flows at depth out the Strait of Gibraltar. (The Med isn't becoming less saline overall, though, because the deficit is made up by surface seawater flowing back in from the Atlantic.)

Such "warm saline bottom water" is also oxygen-poor, since warm water holds little air in solution. Only anaerobic microbes can survive in such water, and so lots of organic matter accumulates in the sediment—a big difference from the modern seas! The black shales so abundant in parts of the geologic record result from such organic-rich deposition. A modern, small-scale model of such an ocean is the Black Sea. The Bosporus is much too shallow to allow deep circulation with the Med, and obviously the Black Sea receives no cold polar water to drive its circulation. So below a thin surface layer with a normal marine fauna, the Black Sea is anoxic. Such an

anoxic ocean, by the way, is called "euxinic," from the Greek word
for the Black Sea.

## LIFE!

Life is what makes an Earthlike planet so interesting, and what
we're usually looking for in exotic planetary settings! Although this
book is not concerned with designing life forms—see Stanley
Schmidt's volume in this series (*Aliens and Alien Societies*) for
that—we need to pay some attention to the basic biochemistry of
life, because it's so closely tied with its planetary environment.

All Earth life, from bacteria to human beings, is based on the
same fundamental biochemical architecture. It all uses the same
DNA to make the same protein building blocks; the diversity is
largely in how they're arranged. Earth life is primarily based on
four fundamental elements: carbon (C), hydrogen (H), oxygen (O),
and nitrogen (N)—sometimes abbreviated with the acronym
CHON. A few other elements are also vital in specific applications.
Phosphorus, for example, is fundamental to the basic energy trans-
fer reactions used in living cells. Of the CHON elements, carbon
forms the backbone. It's the only element that makes arbitrarily
complex linkages to itself and so can build up extremely complex
molecules.

Earth life also requires liquid water. In fact, life in general probably needs a solvent that all its multitude of chemical reactions can
take place in. So let's first see why water works so well.

First, it's made of common elements—hydrogen and oxygen.
Hydrogen, of course, makes up most of the universe. Oxygen is
quite a bit rarer than that, but it's still a very common heavy element. It's so abundant because its most common isotope, $^{16}O$, is
exceptionally stable, so it gets made abundantly by nucleosynthesis
(see page 38). This quirk of nuclear physics makes water one of
the most abundant substances in the universe.

Water has unusual properties, too. Not only does it have a high
boiling point, but it also has a very long temperature range over
which it's liquid. This is convenient because planets vary in temperature from place to place—you don't want your ocean to boil at the
equator, even if it *does* freeze at the poles!

Water also is a near-universal solvent. It dissolves virtually anything, at least to some degree. This is just what you need for a
biochemical solvent. Not only can it expedite biochemical reactions

by making it easy to move things around—food and oxygen in, waste products out—but it provides a medium in which the chemical building blocks of life can move around.

Last, water *expands* when it freezes into ice. This is extremely unusual: Most liquids are less dense than the solids they melt from. Under very high pressures, water too is "normal": high-pressure forms of ice are denser than liquid water. Only "Ice I"—ordinary, low-pressure ice, the kind you find in your freezer—is less dense than the liquid. (In case you were going to ask, the high-density forms of ice—Ice II, Ice III, and so on—are stable only at extremely high pressures. They don't occur on the Earth, but probably occur deep within some of the icy worlds in the outer Solar System.)

This quirk is important in Earth's climate regulation. In the winter, the skin of ice that forms on oceans, lakes and other bodies of water keeps the water from freezing clear through. By insulating the water underneath, it makes it a "heat reservoir," because that unfrozen water can never get colder than freezing. It also lets critters needing liquid water, such as fish, survive even when the air temperature drops below freezing.

The basic information-carrying molecule of life is DNA, the famous double helix. It's basically a chain of "nucleotides," four different molecules that occur in two complementary pairs. This chain can split apart to duplicate itself, and it codes for *amino acids*, three nucleotide pairs per acid. Amino acids build up *proteins*. Although there are only about twenty amino acids, a staggering variety of proteins is possible because amino acids can be linked arbitrarily and indefinitely. Proteins are fundamental building blocks of the organism itself; they're structural (muscle, hair, skin), and also make *enzymes*, which are the catalysts that drive biochemical reactions, including those for building other biocompounds.

Living things trap part of the flow of energy from the Sun, mostly via photosynthesis by green plants. Basically, plants store solar energy in high-energy compounds that can be used as food by other organisms. Reacting these compounds with the oxygen the plants give off releases the stored energy again. This is why, say, $CO_2$ breathers aren't reasonable. Unlike oxygen, you can't react food with it to get energy. Indeed, life must exist in a flux of energy. Ultimately life on Earth merely temporarily diverts a bit of the continuous flow of heat from the Sun out to space. In doing so it maintains—and must maintain—an environment far out of simple chemical equilibrium.

## History of Life on Earth

The change in life forms over the history of the Earth is an obvious source of inspiration, one that's not exploited as well as it could be. Besides that, though, is the degree to which life has changed the Earth itself. Oxygen, of course, wrought profound changes when plants began to dump it into the atmosphere in large quantities, and as this example shows, life even precipitates its own crises once in a while. In this sense, the recent effects of human activities are merely part of a continuum with ancient roots.

The first living things (at least that we have records of) are primitive single-celled organisms: *prokaryotes*, the bacteria and cyanobacteria ("blue-green algae"). They're "primitive" in that they have simpler cells than higher organisms, and they reigned alone on Earth for over two billion years. Prokaryotes still dominate the modern Earth, though, and remain vital to maintaining Earth's habitability. "Advanced" life is merely a superstructure whose existence depends utterly on this prokaryotic base.

Prokaryotes also have an extraordinarily wide variety of "lifestyles" that make up ecosystems whose complexity does not suffer through being all made up of microbes. Some use other substances, instead of water, as bases for photosynthesis (organic molecules, hydrogen sulfide), and indeed these antedate the oxygen-releasing version that's so familiar. Others can feed off sulfide minerals such as pyrite, or use the sulfate dissolved in water to oxidize food, or convert complex organic molecules to methane, or break down nitrogenous molecules back to nitrous oxide ($N_2O$) or nitrogen gas ... the list goes on and on. And by no means are these pathways curiosities left over from a primitive Earth. Prokaryotes' ability to cycle a wide variety of chemical compounds is why they remain vital in keeping Earth Earthlike.

Some of these also suggest branch points for different biochemistries. Surely the particular pattern that Earth ended up with is not inevitable. One take-off might be the "chloroxygen world" (see page 155), in which certain organisms would "learn" to make chlorinated compounds from chloride in seawater, and ultimately to release free chlorine. For another, with no nitrogen-releasing bacteria the oxygen and nitrogen in the air will make nitrates. So a "nitrate cycle" might exist instead, as Hal Clement proposed in *The Nitrogen Fix*.

A staggering innovation that *did* occur, of course, was the "invention" of water-using photosynthesis by green plants, to trap solar energy directly. By about two billion years ago toxic, corrosive oxygen was pouring into the air, in the most catastrophic air pollution event ever. It may even have triggered the first recorded ice age, at the end of the Archean, because so much $CO_2$ was withdrawn from the atmosphere. Ultimately, however, it led to an equally staggering elaboration of the biosphere—after all, we now think of Earth as "green!" The rise of oxygen also established the ozone layer, which opened up the sea surface, and ultimately the land, to colonization by life.

The oxygen atmosphere was necessary, too, for the rise of the *eukaryotic* cell, an efficient oxygen-using cell, by about two billion years ago. In such cells the DNA is segregated into a separate nucleus, and they contain specialized within-cell "organelles" such as mitochondria (which carry out cellular respiration) and chloroplasts (which carry out photosynthesis). Such organelles may originally have been independent prokaryotic cells.

Although Earth remained a "scumworld" even with the appearance of eukaryotes, the stage had been set for the appearance of multicelled life forms: *metazoans.* Multicelled life probably requires an efficient oxygen-using cell, because you can't run a large, multicelled organism without a high-energy metabolism, and burning food with oxygen makes for one of the highest-energy metabolisms around.

Metazoans showed up geologically suddenly in the "Cambrian explosion" about 540 Ma. Body plans were rapidly elaborated in a very short geologic interval, and hard parts—shells and skeletons—appeared for the first time, which is why the Cambrian marks the beginning of the classic fossil record. But many body plan "experiments" did not survive, either, and the reasons may involve luck as much as "fitness." More of that contingent history. . . .

Anyway, though, for more than eighty percent of its history, Earth life was just microbes! The physical Earth was in its modern form when the trilobites crawled in the seas. Evidently organizing many cells to work together was a much more difficult step than life itself.

The land remained barren even a hundred million years after the Cambrian. Plants didn't begin to invade the continents until late Silurian and early Devonian time (~400 Ma), and animals didn't follow until even later. It's now extremely hard to visualize a pre-Devonian landscape, especially in a humid climate. We're so conditioned to jungles that what the land would look like if there's *nothing* to grow, no matter how much rain, stretches the imagination. Yet that was the case on Earth for almost four billion years; and for at least the few hundred million years of that time, the $O_2$ atmosphere was already in place.

How come so few SF stories describe such worlds? On an alien Earthlike world, explorers always seem to be hacking through jungles, rather than tramping across barren lands. If there *are* other Earthlike worlds, most will still be in the state of microbes-only, with scummy seas and empty continents. Surely there's an ethical consideration here too; an expedition to a scumworld would be extremely careful to avoid contamination, not so much from fear of diseases but so as not to overwhelm it with alien Earth bugs.

Relatively few animal body-plans have successfully invaded the land, too, and of these only vertebrates and arthropods are really successful. This has vast implications for the development of a technical species. Not only do you need land to develop fire and metal, you need the right sort of organism. Insects probably couldn't have managed! As Stephen Jay Gould has emphasized, obtaining creatures that could become intelligent may take a great deal of luck. Technical intelligence appeared in a geological eyeblink, but although in the long term it may prove an innovation as important as photosynthesis (and as destructive in the short term), it was not inevitable, either.

# CHAPTER 6

# The Other Planets

N ot only do we understand the Earth much better, we also understand the other planets much better. With the wealth of data from space probes, they're no longer just lights in the sky. They and their satellites are instead both a "reality check" and a source of inspiration for what can happen in the real universe. Of course, many data from the other planets have been discussed already, and those won't be repeated.

Planets come in two basic kinds (plus debris):

1. Jupiter-like ("jovian" or "gas giant") planets are rich in volatiles, especially hydrogen and its compounds, and helium. Thus, they reflect much more the average composition of the universe. They formed far from the parent star, where lots of volatile material could condense out. They also have many satellites, and typically, ring systems. They probably have no well-defined solid surfaces.
2. Terrestrial ("rocky") planets are made of high-boiling point ("refractory") material: rock and (in the core) iron-alloy metal. They have little in the way of volatiles. They're much smaller, are near the parent star, and have few satellites.

Finally, asteroids and comets are leftover pieces that never got accreted into planets. They range from pebbles to mountains in size, but there are vastly more of the small sizes. They're an ongoing source of debris for impacts.

This general distinction, no doubt, will probably occur in other planetary systems, although with multifarious differences in detail.

There may well be other types as well, such as brown dwarfs (see page 141).

Finally, satellites—bodies revolving around planets—are worlds in their own right, so they're worth a few words of their own. They're common, especially with large planets. As we saw (page 28), there are some limitations on their orbital stability, as when they are too close to the star, but intricate relations are nonetheless common. Planetary scientists generally speak of three general types of satellites: (1) *regular satellites*, which are like miniature solar systems. They're most characteristic of giant planets, and they tend to be bigger as the planet is bigger; (2) *outer satellites*, which are all very small and distant from the primary, and probably are captured asteroids; and (3) *anomalous satellites*, which include the Moon, Charon and Triton. These all stem from unusual circumstances: each is probably the result of a gigantic collision early in Solar System history!

## THE PLANETS IN THE SKY

You probably already know that the word "planet" comes from the Greek word for "wanderer." The planets are "wandering" stars, because they don't appear in the same position in the sky from night to night because of their own motions in their orbits around the Sun. Although a detailed explanation of the planets' motions lies beyond the scope of this book—check any astronomy text if you need that—a couple of basics are useful. First, planets with orbits inside the Earth's—the so-called *inferior* planets, Mercury and Venus—can never appear very far from the Sun in the sky, and so never can be seen too long after sunset. They can never appear at midnight, for example. They're always "morning" or "evening" stars. The maximum distance that Mercury can be from the Sun, its "maximum elongation," is roughly 20°, whereas Venus's is about 34°. "Elongation" is the angle between a planet and the Sun (figure 11, next page). The maximum elongation possible for an inferior planet occurs with an object in the same orbit as the planet itself; that is, in the Trojan position (see page 31). In this case it's 60° (figure 11, next page). For comparison, the distance from the horizon to the zenith is 90° and the diameters of the Sun and Moon are about 0.5° (see page 136).

Because they're illuminated at different angles as we see them from Earth, the inferior planets also show phases like the Moon's.

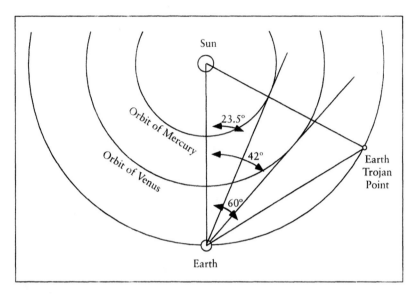

**FIG. 11** Maximum Elongation.
The maximum angular distance from the Sun in the sky ("maximum
elongation") of inferior planets is shown. Orbits are to scale except that
Mercury's orbit is shown as a circle rather than an ellipse, so its maximum
elongation is approximate. The size of the planets and Sun is *not* to scale. Note
that the maximum possible elongation of 60° occurs for a body in a Trojan
orbit.

The Moon's phases, of course, come about because the Sun shines on it from different angles as it orbits the Earth.

By contrast, a *superior* planet—one whose orbit lies outside the Earth's—can have any elongation, and so can appear at any time of day or night.

Of course, during the day *any* sort of planet typically can't be seen at all because it's overwhelmed by daylight. On Earth, Venus at its brightest can be seen in broad daylight, but only if you're looking exactly at it and the day is clear. (I've seen Venus on a pellucid Arizona day, so I'm not just repeating a textbook assertion here!) Such a "daystar," of course, might be much more prominent on another world, as with the Trojan planet, and it might have major mythological and sociological significance.

## THE OTHER ROCKY PLANETS: ABORTED EARTHS

These planets are not too "terrestrial" now, except that they're made of rock rather than gas.

### The Moon

OK, the Moon is not really a "planet," but it's a rocky world, and we know more about it than any other world except Earth itself. It also proves to be typical of more Solar System bodies than the Earth, in its preserved cratering record especially. It's small (only one eighty-first of the Earth's mass), so it can't hold an atmosphere. And although it had extensive volcanism in its early history, and was probably completely molten when it formed, it's now all cooled off and essentially dead. It's also completely dry—lunar rocks don't even contain a smidgen of water in combination, unlike Earth rocks. But because it's been inactive for the last few billion years, the Moon preserves an excellent record of the tremendous cratering that occurred in the infant Solar System, the so-called "late heavy bombardment" (page 47).

### Do We Need the Moon?

The Moon probably doesn't affect geology or climatology greatly. Tidal effects occur, to be sure, and there's some evidence earthquakes correlate with the position of the Moon, but any effect is weak. You *don't* need tides to release stress in the Earth; rocks fail just fine without it.

The tides are probably overrated as an evolutionary driver, too.

Not only do we still have the solar tide even without a moon, but influxes of water far up on the shoreline from major storms will occur in any case. In fact, sedimentologists even speak of "storm tides." Another outdated notion is that you need a large moon for "stripping away excess atmosphere." First, as we saw the problem with, say, Venus is not that she has too much air, but that the air didn't form limestone. The volatile budget on a rocky planet seems to be largely a crapshoot anyway (pages 47, 97).

Instead, where the Moon probably helped is by stabilizing the Earth's obliquity (see page 22). Hence the Moon is an angular momentum bank.

## Origin of the Moon

The now popular view is that a gigantic impact formed the Earth's Moon. Late in accretion, Earth was struck glancingly by a *large* object—a body about the size of Mars. The splash sprayed out lots of material; most escaped, but some stayed in an orbiting ring around the Earth. This later coalesced to form the Moon.

The model nicely accounts for the somewhat ill-defined geochemical kinship of the Earth and Moon, since some Earth rocks ended up in the debris ring that became the Moon. Supercomputer calculations also suggest this "worlds in collision" model is feasible. The mega-impact model also manages to finesse the problems in the classic hypotheses of lunar formation, problems that had gotten even worse after the Apollo missions.

This model also suggests our Moon results from a specific event. Earthlike planets don't *have* to have moons. On the other hand, though, with all that stuff careening around in the inner System, a mega-impact of some sort was all but inevitable. It now appears that late accretion was a very violent process indeed (page 46). So even though our Moon is unusual, being the only large satellite of a rocky planet, it's what the engineers call a "proof of concept": It shows it *can* happen!

And the size of the Moon seems to be happenstance. There seems to be no fundamental reason Earth and Moon couldn't be closer in size, and such a "double planet" has starred in a number of stories, most compellingly perhaps in the "shared worlds" Genji and Chujo designed by Poul Anderson for *Murasaki*. Of course, a large satellite—much less a full companion world—is likely to have profound social effects on a species that reaches the level where "culture" is relevant. The plurality of worlds would be demonstrated very early; Earth's Moon, by contrast, is just far enough away that it's not obviously another world to the naked eye. Perhaps it would goad early development of space flight. And, since such worlds would be tidally locked, there might be fundamental differences in the cultures of the moon-facing vs. away-facing hemispheres!

## Mercury

Mercury looks like an overgrown Moon but is much more dense; a mini-Earth in Moon's clothing, as one book put it. It's heavily cratered; as with the Moon, not much has happened since the end of the heavy bombardment. And, being so close to the Sun, there's only the merest wisp of atmosphere.

The high density results from a huge core: bigger than the Moon, according to even conservative estimates. Possibly, most of Mercury's crust and mantle were blasted off in another mega-collision early in Solar System history; and unlike Earth, Mercury was too small to get the debris back again, or even to keep it in an orbiting ring where it could later coalesce into a satellite.

Mercury's rotation has also been tidally braked by the Sun, but (unlike the Moon) with a 3:2 lock. Mercury orbits the Sun about once every 88 (Earth) days while spinning on its axis once every 59 days: the rotation period is exactly two-thirds of the revolution period. Hence at any point on the planet sunrise occurs every 178 days—exactly twice the year length (page 89). In other words, nights on Mercury are 88 Earth days long—almost three months!

Mercury also has a very eccentric orbit, more than any other planet's except Pluto. Thus, although Mercury's average distance from the Sun is 57.9 million kilometers, it varies by over 50 percent, from forty-six million kilometers at pericentron to almost seventy million kilometers at apocentron. So the total sunlight can vary by over 100 percent during the course of the three-month "day." The diameter of the Sun in the sky also changes by about 30 percent.

In fact, the same two places on the surface, the "hot poles," always get the maximum sunlight, almost eleven times what the Earth gets. The hot poles are two points on the equator, exactly 180° apart, for which high noon always comes exactly at pericentron. They swap places in alternate days: when it's noon at one, it's midnight at the other, and conversely during the next day-night cycle.

Things get even weirder when you consider that Mercury doesn't move along its orbit at a constant speed, because of Kepler's Second Law. The rotation rate around its axis, however, is constant. Hence, because of this mismatch the Sun's apparent speed across the sky will change. In fact, sometimes the Sun will actually go backward briefly in the sky, because the orbital motion overwhelms the rotation! From certain places on Mercury, then, the Sun can rise, then change its mind and set again before rising again. Such behavior certainly could provide local color for an Earthlike planet in a similar orbit.

## Venus

As we've seen, Venus is Earth-sized and Earth density but a false twin. All its $CO_2$ is in its atmosphere, instead of being locked safely away in limestone, while its intense greenhouse effect maintains surface temperatures hot enough to melt lead. What's more, Venus probably didn't start out all that much different from Earth, but landed in its present sorry state through having all its water photo-dissociated away, perhaps in a runaway greenhouse (page 71).

Venus is un-Earthlike in its rotation period, too. It rotates extremely slowly, and backward (retrograde) to boot, which leads to sunrise about every four months (page 89). The slow rotation is usually attributed to tidal braking (page 27), but it may be merely a vagary of the last few large impacts during late accretion (page 47).

## Mars

Mars is another disappointment. It's small, less dense than Earth, and cold. Perhaps it's shrunken because it was "starved" during accretion. Because of this, it's also much less active tectoni-cally than the Earth, although it's more active than the Moon. Evidently it lies below the "plate tectonic threshold"; its crust is too thick, too cold, and too strong to fragment into moving plates. In effect, its "lithosphere" consists of one extremely thick plate! Mars does, however, have some spectacular hotspot volcanoes such as Olympus Mons. They're far bigger than such mountains on Earth because the plate *wasn't* moving underneath, so the lava all piled up in one place.

Mars's smallness has had major effects for its atmosphere and for life. It's an extreme example of the cold and dry planet. Too small to have crustal cycling, it couldn't maintain its greenhouse with the carbonate cycle, so it froze up. The present atmosphere is very thin, and the pressure of $CO_2$ in it is set by the equilibrium pressure over solid $CO_2$ at the Martian poles. Thus adding more $CO_2$ to the Mars atmosphere doesn't raise the pressure—it just causes more $CO_2$ to freeze out.

Mars has also dried out. All water has either frozen out, or been lost to photodissociation—and the oxygen left behind has thoroughly oxidized the Martian surface. The pervasive rusty color is just that: rust, oxidized iron. Other oxides, unknown outside reagent bottles on Earth, also occur in the Martian soil. Mars thus shows that water photodissociation, over time, can lead to an extraordinarily oxidizing environment—a useful starting point for a number of possible worlds, as we'll see in the last chapter.

Because of its absence of plate tectonics, Mars has no continental crust like Earth's. This has an odd consequence: by Earth standards, the soil is highly depleted in potassium. As potassium is a critical nutrient, for Earth plant life especially, this poses a little-recognized problem for terraforming schemes. (Presumably if indigenous life had ever arisen it would be adapted to this scarcity.) This also shows how small differences in a planet's geologic processes might have unexpected effects on Earth life.

As it has no large moon, Mars also has extreme climatic excursions, because its obliquity varies a lot from perturbations (page 22). Although some have speculated that because of this Mars's climate has been much more clement at times, that hasn't been the case in the last few billion years, simply because of the loss of atmosphere. Moreover, the obliquity excursions are geologically short and probably would be traumatic for any biosphere more complex than microbes.

## THE GAS GIANTS (AND THEIR COMPANIONS)

### Jupiter and Saturn: Aborted Stars?

Rich in hydrogen and helium, with seething, deep atmospheres: these planets have little in common with an Earthlike world. But could they be sites for life even so? Many authors have postulated hydrogen breathers on jovian planets. This seems a long shot with present knowledge, though, as it turns out they have extremely turbulent, hot interiors. It seems hard to keep living things from being eventually carried down and cooked.

Their large satellites, worlds in themselves, seem more promising.

**Io.** Jupiter's innermost large satellite, Io, is one of the most interesting places in the Solar System. It has the highest rate of volcanism known, which is driven by tidal flexing. Because of the resonance with Jupiter's other satellites (page 36), Io is trapped into an eccentric orbit, so it's continually flexed, and the energy dissipated from that flexing shows up as heat in the interior.

Thus, Io maintains its high level of volcanism without radiogenic heating. This suggests an alternative power source for planets. Maybe somewhere a small, close-in planet of a dim star, probably in an elliptical orbit like Mercury's but subject to even larger tides, is kept habitable this way and so avoids the fate of Mars.

Io also shows how geologic processes can concentrate a relatively rare element, in this case sulfur. Sulfur dominates Io's surface, though it's just a veneer, only a few meters to maybe a couple hundred meters thick. Most of the volcanism involves it: Sulfur lavas splash and ooze across the surface, and sulfur-dioxide driven vapor eruptions spew material for hundreds of kilometers across the landscape. The sulfur must be melted by ordinary silicate lavas at depth, though; since Io's density is about like the Moon's, it can't be *all* sulfur. There must be a lot of rock below.

Io's sulfur got concentrated at the surface because all its other volatiles got blown away. Only sulfur, the heaviest of the lot, was left behind. Its volatile compound, sulfur dioxide, $SO_2$, also can't escape. Oxygen, although lighter than sulfur, tends to stick around because it's still relatively heavy. For this reason sulfur dioxide on Io is also immune to photodissociation loss. Even though UV light breaks up $SO_2$ easily enough, the sulfur and oxygen atoms hang around until they eventually combine again. It also looks as though sulfur dioxide on Io acts rather like water in Earthly volcanic processes. Most volcanic gas on Earth is just *very* hot steam (see page 58), which drives explosive eruptions by its expansion.

In fact, the existence of a sulfur-world like Io suggests some unusual planets indeed, which I'll elaborate on in the last chapter.

**Europa.** This, Jupiter's next large moon out, has less intense tidal heating. It's also Moon-sized, but is sheathed with a frozen ocean perhaps one hundred kilometers thick instead of sulfur, and as with Io, a rocky world lies below. A water layer—a "deep

ocean"—may underlie this ice cap, where heat diffusing out of the
rock below keeps it molten, and maybe it contains life. Although it
seems a long shot, because obviously there's no photosynthesis,
possibly life could use the heat leaking out of the interior as an
energy source, something like the deep-sea communities living in
oceanic rift zones on Earth. Perhaps, indeed, in the whole universe
liquid water may be far more common inside worlds than on them.
This isn't something that's come through in SF! Our Earth, with
its warm wisps of liquid water clinging to the outside, may be the
anomaly.

Liquid water also apparently erupts occasionally from this layer.
Europa's surface is very smooth, with none of the impact craters
we expect. Apparently the surface is covered by new ice often
enough to bury the impacts that occur.

The farther-out large satellites Ganymede and Callisto are "ice-
worlds," composed of ice with a fraction of rock. Goodloe and Oltion
used a thawed iceworld as a setting in their novella "Waterworld"
(page 145).

**Titan.** Saturn's Mercury-sized satellite Titan, the only known
satellite with a substantial atmosphere (surface pressure one and
a half times Earth's), is rich in the CHON elements. Like Earth's,
the atmosphere is composed dominantly of nitrogen, although presumably it's of very different origin. It's possibly left over from
Titan's formation, or alternatively came from ammonia photodissociation. Unlike Earth, though, the atmosphere has no free oxygen
and contains a frigid "organic smog." If life exists there it's very
different, as Titan is extremely cold. Liquid ethane ($C_2H_6$) lakes,
with a temperature below $-90°C$ and a density about half that of
water, have been proposed for the surface, and much of the underlying planet is solid ice, as with Ganymede or Callisto.

## Some Thoughts on Earthlike Satellites

An Earthlike world as a moon of a giant planet (or perhaps a
brown dwarf, page 141) has figured in a number of stories, such
as Poul Anderson's "The Longest Voyage." As with the "double
planet," the day would be very different, as the rotation period
would be synchronized with the revolution period around the primary.

Seasons might also be very different. Not only would they depend (as usual) on the tilt of the satellite's axis and the eccentricity

of the primary's orbit around the star, they would also depend on the tilt of the satellite's orbit around the primary. The orbital tilt could either cancel or reinforce the axial tilt—and either way, it would change systematically due to perturbations, analogously to the Milankovich variations.

For example, consider a primary with an axial tilt of forty degrees with respect to its orbit that has a distant, Earthlike satellite with a tilt of twenty-four degrees with respect to *its* orbit. Depending on the relative orientation of the tilts, then, the resulting tilt of the satellite with respect to the sun, which determines the seasons, can be anything from sixteen degrees ($40° - 24°$) to $64°$ ($40° + 24°$) (see figure 12, pages 120-121). We can call this value the "resultant tilt."

So far this doesn't seem too exotic. After all, seasons will be caused only by the resultant tilt, and the fact that it happens to be compounded of the tilt of the primary and the tilt of the Earthlike satellite seems irrelevant. However, the relative orientations of those tilts will *change* due to perturbations, so over time the resultant tilt will move though that entire range from $16°$ to $64°$. In particular, the axis of the satellite will wobble around due to precession, analogously to the precession of the equinoxes on the Earth. The satellite's precession is liable to be a lot faster than Earth's, though, because of the stronger gravitational perturbations it's subject to. Earth's axis completes one wobble about every twenty-five thousand years, but the timescale for precession of the axis of the satellite is likely to be only a few thousand years or less.

So, over a few millenia the resultant tilt will change from $16°$ to $64°$ and back again. That will cause an extraordinary change in the intensity of the seasons over a timescale that's short enough to have cultural effects. Maybe people remember legends of the Great Winters and Great Summers that occur when the resultant tilt is high, and contrast them with the Bland Years when seasonal changes are relatively mild. Perhaps, too, during those periods of high tilt, many cultures have to migrate out of high latitudes— which might lead to recurrent barbarian invasions of, say, civilizations that had arisen during the Bland Years. Lots of possibilities exist; and working out the effects of an exotic setting like this on individuals, cultures and societies is what world-building is all about!

The sky of the Earthlike satellite would also be very different. As Anderson notes, one side would be dominated by the looming

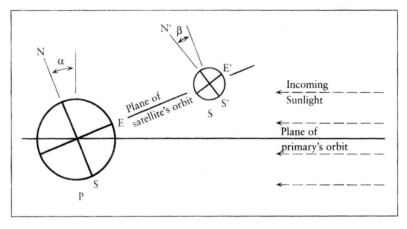

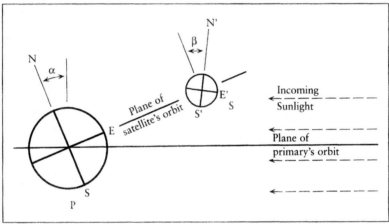

**FIG. 12a, b** Seasons.

Seasons on an Earthlike satellite $S$ orbiting a large primary $P$. $N$, $S$ and $E$ are the north pole, south pole and equator of the primary, respectively; $N'$, $S'$, and $E'$ are the north pole, south pole and equator of the satellite. The primary is tilted an angle $\alpha$ with respect to its orbit around the parent star. The satellite's orbit lies in the plane of the primary's equator, but its rotational axis is tilted by an angle $\beta$ with respect to *its* orbit. Thus the total inclination of the satellite with respect to the incident sunlight, which determines the intensity of seasons, is set by a combination of $\alpha$ and $\beta$. Two extreme cases are shown: (a) the tilt of the satellite is in the same direction as the tilt of the primary; hence the "resultant tilt" is $\alpha + \beta$, and so seasons on the satellite are more extreme; and (b) the tilt of the satellite is opposite the tilt of the primary, so that they tend to cancel; thus the resultant tilt is $\alpha - \beta$, and seasons are less pronounced. Obviously, all intermediate cases can also exist. Because the satellite's axis of rotation will be precessing, it will continually shift between case (a) and (b) over a few thousand years or less, and thus the intensity of seasons will vary greatly on an extremely rapid timescale, geologically speaking.

primary, vastly larger than the Moon from Earth, whereas the other side would have an empty sky. This might lead to striking social and cultural differences around the planet, as described for the "double planet" scenario.

Finally, such a situation might stabilize the orbit of a habitable planet in otherwise marginal stellar systems, by thwarting tidal braking by the parent star. More on this anon.

## Uranus and Neptune

These planets are the "outer leftovers" in our Solar System. They're richer in heavy elements than Jupiter and Saturn, but are still dominated by hydrogen and helium. The axial tilt of Uranus is unique in the Solar System, at least for a large planet: It lies on its side, probably as a result of a large impact late in accretion. The largest moon in its small regular satellite system is Miranda, which is only about five hundred kilometers in diameter. It seems to have gone through an extended melting event in the geologic past; the gravitational evolution of the Uranian system at one point put Miranda in a resonance that caused major tidal flexing, much as Io undergoes right now. Miranda may have been largely molten for a few hundred million years. As energy continued to be lost from its orbit, though, the orbit changed enough that the resonance lock was broken, and Miranda soon refroze.

As has been mentioned, Neptune's large moon Triton orbits backward, the only large satellite to do so. Current thinking is that Triton was originally a planetesimal that, when Neptune was nearly full-grown, collided head-on with an already formed satellite of Neptune's that was in an ordinary "prograde" orbit. The collision slowed Triton to the point it could be captured by Neptune's gravity.

The rest of the Neptune system supports some such scenario. Neptune has only one satellite (Nereid) farther out than Triton, and that satellite also has a weird orbit; although Nereid's orbit is pro-grade, it is extremely elliptical. By contrast, the Voyager flyby in 1989 discovered four new Neptunian satellites *inward* of Triton, and these satellites are all are "well behaved": They have nearly circular pro-grade orbits. They seem to be the ruins of Neptune's regular satellite system. Everything farther out seems to have been disrupted.

After its capture Triton initially would have been in a highly elliptical orbit, but over geologic time that orbit would have been "circularized" by tidal friction (see page 25). This would have dissipated an enormous amount of Triton's orbital energy as heat, enough to melt Triton completely several times over.

Models suggest Triton was a "waterworld," with oceans several hundred kilometers deep lying over a core of rock, for perhaps as long as half a billion years. Now, though, all that water has become solid ice. Any molten layer left inside must be very thin indeed. In fact, Triton now has the coldest surface known in the solar system (a mere thirty-eight kelvins). It is splashed with brilliant white nitrogen frost, which is replenished by liquid nitrogen geysers driven by solar heating during the local "summertime."

Triton and Miranda suggest an SF setting no one's used: the gradual refreezing of an iceworld that had been temporary (geologically speaking) melted by tidal friction. For a few hundred million years or so, a vast water ocean might lie incongruously far from the central star, in the cold outer reaches of a planetary system. That might be long enough for life to originate and flourish, especially if the iceworld had been "seeded" by, say, spores or microbes wafted off an Earthlike world closer in. No doubt, even in its heyday the ocean would be largely crusted over by an icecap, because of the intense cold right at the surface. Just as with Earth's polar oceans, though, such a cap would help insulate the water below and postpone its freezing.

A more interesting—if ultimately more tragic—scenario than the hypothetical deep-life below Europa's crust!

A last, interesting note is that since Neptune's orbit is nearly a perfect circle, the Solar System has not been significantly affected gravitationally since it was formed. Any perturbation, say by a near-passing star, would have made Neptune's orbit more elliptical.

## MORE ON SATELLITE MOTIONS

As with rotation (see page 89), the sidereal or "star" revolution period is the true period. It's the time it takes to complete one orbit around the planet. For watching from the planet's surface, though, we don't want the true revolution period. We want the time between moonrises, the *synodic* period. This depends on the rotation period of the planet as well as the satellite revolution period. The time between moonrises P' is given by:

$$1/P' = 1/p - 1/P$$

where $p$ is the sidereal rotation period of the planet and $P$ is the sidereal revolution period of the satellite. Note that this equation is virtually identical to the one for the solar day (see page 90).

For our own Moon, P is 27.321 d, and as we saw p is 0.9973 d, so $P' = 1.0351$ days, or about 24 hours, 50 minutes. Hence on average the Moon rises 50 minutes later each day.

This equation assumes the satellite is in a circular orbit, so that it moves along in its orbit at constant speed, and is in the same plane as the planet's equator. This is true or nearly so for most natural satellites, although the Moon's orbit is significantly elliptical. In natural systems, moreover, perturbations from the planet's equatorial bulge will force at least close-in satellites into the same plane as the equator in geologic time (page 23).

If P is smaller than p, the time between moonrises comes out as negative. This means the satellite rises and sets in the opposite sense to the rest of the sky. For Earth, for example, the satellite would rise in the west and set in the east. This is true for many artificial Earth satellites, as well as for Mars's (natural) satellite Phobos. If instead P is the same as p; i.e., the rotation and revolution periods match, the satellite neither rises nor sets but stays in the same place in the sky. This is the case for most communications satellites, which are typically placed in such a "geosynchronous" orbit. (This orbit is also sometimes called "Clarke" orbit, after Arthur C. Clarke, who first pointed out the value of this orbit for communication back in 1945.) Finally, if the satellite has retrograde revolution, like Triton, take P as negative.

One complication for a close-in satellite is eclipses, when the satellite passes into the planet's shadow as it goes behind it. They're unusual for a distant satellite like the Moon, but are virtually inevitable for close satellites. Most artificial satellites, for example, spend most of their nightside time in shadow. A solar eclipse, when the satellite just barely covers the parent star, is more unusual yet; but our own Moon shows it can happen once in a while!

The *month* is the time between successive appearances of the same *phase* of a satellite, say from full to full. To show the same phase the satellite must be in the same relative position with respect to the planet and the parent star. This bears the same relation to the sidereal month, the true revolution period, as does the solar day to the sidereal day, and is calculated the same way (see page 90). For Earth's Moon, for example, the length M of the month is given by:

$$1/M = 1/(27.321) - 1/(365.25)$$

or, M = 29.53 days.

Hence there are roughly 29½ days from full Moon to full Moon. Again this assumes a circular orbit, so it's approximate in the case of the Moon.

## Pluto and Beyond

Pluto and its satellite Charon form a unique double planet in the Solar System. They're small, extremely low density, and probably leftover planetesimals that collided glancingly enough to end up in orbit. It has recently been speculated that many more such planetesimals lie out beyond Pluto. Pluto and Charon merely lucked into a stable orbit closer in.

## Comets

Comets seem to be more leftover planet-stuff, the very low-boiling point material that got exiled to the fringes of the Solar System. Astronomers speak of two distant reservoirs, or "clouds" (another misnomer; they're inconceivably diffuse by everyday standards). The Kuiper Cloud extends from ~100 to ~10,000 AU, whereas the Oort Cloud extends from ~40,000 to ~60,000 AU. Some comet nuclei may orbit out to 100,000 AU. Beyond ~200,000 AU the galactic gravitational field exceeds that of the Sun, and anything thousands of AU distant is vulnerable to perturbations by passing stars. Such perturbations occasionally send a comet into the inner Solar System, where it can get trapped by a close planetary passage. In that case it will eventually hit a planet or get thrown out. The ices boil away in a geologically brief interval, and for a while the rock left behind can be an "asteroid" in an unusual orbit. Or, when the comet finally disaggregates completely, it can become a cloud of "buckshot," consisting of rocks traveling in parallel orbits. Such clouds cause meteor showers when they happen to run into the Earth.

# CHAPTER 7

# Stars and Suns

L et's now turn our attention from the planet itself to its sun. You need a candle to warm your planet! The parent star warms the planet, drives the weather, and provides the ultimate energy source for life. They also occur in a wide variety, and it's certainly not obvious that only stars exactly like our own Sun can support interesting planets.

## OF MASS AND TEMPERATURE

A star is approximately a *blackbody*, which is physicist-speak for something that shines solely because it's hot. "Shine" means output *electromagnetic radiation* (see page 61), and the radiation put out varies systematically with temperature. The equation, called the "Stefan-Boltzmann law," is:

$$I = \sigma T^4,$$

where $I$ is the intensity (per unit area; per square centimeter, say), $T$ the temperature (in kelvins), and $\sigma$ (Greek sigma) is the Stefan-Boltzmann constant. The important thing to see is that since the intensity increases at temperature to the fourth power, brightness increases *very* rapidly with temperature! Something shining at 2000 K, for example, is putting out sixteen times the energy for each square centimeter as something at 1000 K, because $2^4 = 16$. Something at 3000 K is eighty-one times as brilliant ($3^4 = 81$), and so on (figure 13, next page).

## COLOR AND SPECTRUM

If something is shining as a blackbody, its *temperature determines its color*, because not only does the intensity of the radiated electromagnetic energy change with temperature, so do its wavelengths.

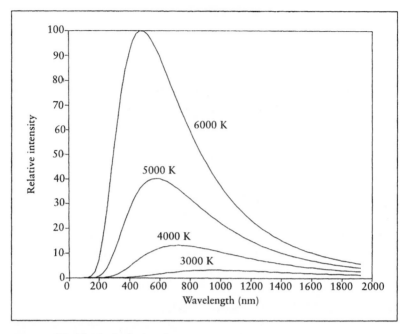

**FIG. 13** Blackbody Radiation Curves.

The vertical axis shows the relative intensity of radiation given off; the
horizontal axis shows the wavelength of the radiation in nanometers (visible
light ranges approximately from 400 to 700 nm). Labels on each curve are the
temperature in kelvins. The 6000 K curve approximates the Sun; the 3000 K
curve approximates a "red" dwarf star or a bright incandescent lamp such as
a projector bulb. Note that not only does the total amount of radiation put out
increase greatly with increasing temperature, but that the peak of the radiation
moves to shorter wavelengths.

The color tends from red toward blue with increasing temperature. Because of this, we often speak of "red stars" or "blue stars." These names, though, are largely misnomers in terms of what the eye would actually see. They just refer to the wavelength bias. Even a "cool" "red" star is extraordinarily bright and hot by everyday standards. A typical "red" dwarf, for example, which make up the bulk of the stars in the universe, has a temperature of about 3000 K, about the same as a filament in an ordinary incandescent light. The star's light won't look red at all, and the eye is sufficiently adaptable that scenes will look normal, just as things look perfectly normal by incandescent light on Earth. The temperature of something truly "red"—a charcoal fire or glowing stovetop, say—is more like 1000 K. Quite a few science fiction stories have spoken of the lurid light of a red sun: Robert L. Forward in *Rocheworld*, Poul Anderson in *Trader to the Stars*, and many others. But this "local color" is just not true! Obviously, when Jerry Oltion and Lee Goodloe talked about the "bloody light" of dawn from a red dwarf star, in their novella "Contact," the "star" was actually a brown dwarf. [To appear reddish the companion must be considerably cooler, and must be a so-called "brown dwarf" (page 141), a body that is not quite a star.]

Stars are also classified by *spectral type*, which is also due mostly to temperature. Different elements absorb (or emit) particular wavelengths of light, and these absorbed wavelengths show up as *spectral lines* superimposed on the blackbody background. (Obviously this also allows identification of those elements, by spectroscopy!) Furthermore, an element's spectral signature typically changes with temperature. At higher temperatures more atoms are ionized, because one or more of their electrons are knocked off by the increasingly violent collisions with other atoms. The upshot is that the spectrum of a star changes with temperature, and so the spectral type reflects temperature. From hottest to coolest, they are: O, B, A, F, G, K, M. (They're out of alphabetical order for historical reasons.) They're further subdivided by number; e.g., G5 is halfway between G0 and K0. The Sun is a type G2. Typical "effective temperatures" of the different spectral types are shown in table 2, page 178. (The effective temperature is the temperature of a perfect blackbody that puts out the same amount of radiation.)

## MAGNITUDES

The most casual look at the sky shows that stars have different brightnesses. These differences are expressed with a magnitude scale. In ancient times it was set up as a scale 1 through 6, with 1 being the brightest stars and 6 the faintest, barely visible on a clear, dark, moonless night. In modern times the scale was quantified by making each full magnitude change equal to $^5\sqrt{100}$, which is approximately 2.52. Thus a magnitude 1 star is 2.52 times as bright as a magnitude 2, a magnitude 2 star is 2.52 times as bright as a magnitude 3, a magnitude 1 is 6.35 ($2.52 \times 2.52$) times as bright as a magnitude 3, and so forth. Note that larger magnitudes are dimmer! The ancients did it backward, and modern astronomers have followed them.

The scale has also been extended using that factor of 2.52. Fainter objects have larger magnitudes: 7, 8, and so on, whereas brighter objects have zero and negative magnitudes (e.g., magnitude 0 is 2.52 times as bright as magnitude 1, etc.) The daytime Sun has a magnitude of about $-26.72$. It would be at the threshold of naked-eye visibility ($m = 6$) at a distance of 55.5 light-years.

### Absolute and Apparent Magnitudes

Obviously how bright a star appears in the sky depends on how far away it is, as well as how much light it actually puts out. The *apparent* magnitude is the magnitude of the star as actually seen in the sky, whereas the *absolute* magnitude is how the star would appear from a standard distance of ten parsecs. The magnitudes are related by the equation:

$$M = m + 5 - 5 \log p$$

where $M$ is the absolute magnitude, $m$ is the apparent magnitude, $p$ is the distance in parsecs, and "log" represents the common (base 10) logarithm. (This function is also present on most calculators and spreadsheets.)

For example, the absolute magnitude of the Sun is:

$$M = -26.72 + 5 - 5 \log ( 1/206264.8 ) = 4.85,$$

where $1/206264.8$ is the distance of the Sun in parsecs. Thus, from ten parsecs away the Sun would be a dim naked-eye star.

## LUMINOSITY

Luminosity is the total amount of radiant energy a star puts out. What we really need, for designing a planet, is the luminosity in terms of the Sun. Here's how to find it from the absolute magnitude, which in the case of a real star is what you look up in (or calculate from) a table. Set the luminosity of the Sun = 1; then the luminosity of the star is:

$$L_{star} = 2.52^{(4.85 - M)}$$

where M is the absolute magnitude of the star and 4.85 is the absolute magnitude of the Sun. For example, Tau Ceti has an apparent magnitude of 3.49 and a distance of 3.5 pc, so its absolute magnitude is:

$$M = 3.49 + 5 - 5 \log (3.5) = 5.77,$$

and its luminosity is:

$$L = 2.52^{(4.85 - 5.77)} = 0.43.$$

Hence Tau Ceti is less than half as bright as the Sun. For stars very different from the Sun, we have to correct the visual magnitude to the *bolometric* magnitude (page 132) before calculating the luminosity.

Once we know the brightness of its parent star, we next need to know how bright that star appears at the distance of the planet's orbit. The brightness of a light source falls off with distance, as we all know from everyday experience. This falloff follows an inverse-square law; that is, at twice the distance it's only ¼ as bright, and so on. The equation is:

$$I = L/R^2,$$

or,

$$R = \sqrt{L/I}$$

where *I* is the intensity of light (Earth = 1), *L* is the luminosity of the star (Sun = 1), and $R$ is the distance from the star (Earth's distance from the Sun = 1 = 1 AU). For example, to get the same amount of light Earth would need to be at a distance:

$$R = \sqrt{(0.43)}/1 = 0.65 \text{ AU}$$

from Tau Ceti.

## Bolometric vs. Visual Magnitudes: Or, Is a Heater a Lantern Too?

Not all a star's luminosity falls in visible light. At the "blue" end, much of the output is ultraviolet, whereas at the red end much is infrared. Thus a star can be much brighter in total luminosity than visibility, if a lot of its radiation falls in invisible wavelengths. Hence we must distinguish the *visual* magnitude, the brightness in visible light, from the *bolometric* magnitude, the brightness over all wavelengths. Obviously the bolometric magnitude is always larger, because *some* radiation is always invisible. For Sunlike stars, the difference is only a few percent—you don't need to worry about it.

The difference is large, though, for stars whose main output does not lie in the visible. For storytelling purposes, the most important of these are the long-lived "red" stars. A typical "red" dwarf has a bolometric luminosity about a thousandth or so that of the Sun, but their visible luminosity is a ten-thousandth or less. The reason is simply that so much of a "red" dwarf's output is infrared. But, those infrared wavelengths will help heat the planet up even though they're invisible—the same way a floor heater can heat a room without lighting it up. Thus you need to use the bolometric luminosity when designing a planet, because the total amount of heating the planet receives determines whether it's habitable. Again, electromagnetic radiation need not be visible to heat things up!

To get the bolometric magnitude, you look up a "bolometric correction" for the particular spectral type and add it to the magnitude (table 2, page 178). Unfortunately, there's no convenient formula for the bolometric correction, because it depends in detail on such things as the star's composition and structure.

We also can calculate how much of the total radiation is visible light from the bolometric correction. If $L_v$ is the luminosity in the visible region only, $L_b$ is the bolometric (total) luminosity, and $B$ is the bolometric correction, then

$$L_v/L_b = 2.52^B.$$

## The Hertzsprung-Russell (H-R) Diagram

Stars vary quite a bit in temperature (that is, in color or spectral type), but they vary *enormously* in luminosity. An obvious thing to do is graph temperature against luminosity to get the so-called *Hertzsprung-Russell (H-R) diagram*, named after the astronomers who first did so, around World War I (figure 14, next page).

**The Main Sequence.** Stars aren't scattered uniformly on such a graph but fall into distinct trends. In particular, something over 90 percent of stars fall into a zone running diagonally from upper left to lower right on the H-R diagram, the so-called *Main Sequence*. The Sun is a typical middling member. Nearly all stars spend most of their lifetime on the Main Sequence. It consists of stars that derive their energy by fusing hydrogen nuclei to helium:

$$4 \ ^1H \Rightarrow 1 \ ^4He + lots \text{ of energy}$$

This is often called "hydrogen burning," even though it's not really "burning" because it's a nuclear reaction.

A star's mass largely determines its position on the Main Sequence. The more massive it is, the hotter it burns, and the more luminous it is, because the more intense pressure at its core causes the nuclear reactions to proceed more quickly. This is an *extremely* strong effect, as can be seen from the *mass-luminosity law* for the Main Sequence:

$$L \sim M^{3.8} \text{ (or } M \sim L^{0.2632}),$$

where $L$ and $M$ are the luminosity and mass in terms of the Sun. This lets you calculate the mass of a star, given its luminosity (or vice versa). For example, since the luminosity of Tau Ceti is 0.43, its mass is $(0.43)^{(0.2632)} = 0.80$ of the Sun's.

The mass-luminosity law is approximate for a couple of reasons. First, the luminosity of a main-sequence star increases slightly over

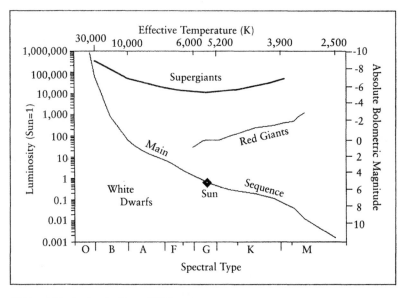

**FIG. 14** Hertzsprung-Russell Diagram.

This shows the distribution of stars with their luminosity and spectral type
(or, equivalently, color or temperature). Vertical axis on left shows luminosity
with respect to Sun; on right, as absolute *bolometric* magnitude (i.e., with *all*
output radiation taken into account, not just visible light). The lower horizontal
axis is the spectral type; the upper shows the effective temperature (the
temperature of a perfect blackbody outputting the same amount of radiation).
Note that stars fall into several distinct trends, of which the Main Sequence
is most important. It represents stars that derive their energy from fusing
hydrogen into helium. The Sun is a typical member; most stars in the Universe
are Main Sequence stars dimmer than the Sun. Red giants are bright stars,
not really "red," in which the hydrogen fuel in the core has been exhausted
(see text page 144); similarly, supergiant stars are aged, very massive stars.
Data on the diagram adapted and recalculated from Allen, Lang and Swihart
(see References).

its lifetime. The slow build-up of helium "ash" in its core boosts the core pressure and makes the star burn hotter. Our own Sun is generally thought to have steadily increased its luminosity by about 30 percent in the four and a half billion years since it was formed, a typical amount for a Main Sequence star like the Sun. A star's luminosity also depends somewhat on its heavy element (i.e., non-hydrogen-helium) composition. Both these effects are minor for our purposes, though.

Stars on the dim, low-mass, red end of the Main Sequence vastly outnumber those on the bright end. For every G star like the Sun, there are a dozen "red," type M dwarfs; and there is only one bright blue B star for every thousand or so Suns.

The brighter the star, the shorter its life (table 2, page 178). This again occurs because stars burn their fuel so much faster as they get a bit more massive. For example, a type A0, like Sirius, has a Main Sequence lifetime of a few hundred million years—barely time for planetary accretion to settle down—whereas a dim red dwarf like Proxima Centauri may last for a trillion years. A star of type F5, with a lifetime of about four billion years, is just long enough for multicellular life to evolve, assuming that Earth's timescale is typical.

Of course, knowing this constraint, one can rationalize a way around it. A plot element in Poul Anderson's "A Sun Invisible" was that the characters *knew* that the obvious, brilliant nearby star couldn't have habitable planets!

The corollary is that dim stars are very long-lived. Nonetheless, it's also been conventional wisdom that habitable planets are unlikely for stars redder than K5, for the reasons discussed on page 138. But again you can take such constraints as a point of departure (page 136).

The diameter of a star, which you need to find out how big it looks in its planet's sky, can be calculated from the temperature and luminosity. If the Sun's diameter is one:

$$D_{star} = T^2_{sun}/T^2_{star} \times \sqrt{L_{star}}$$

where $T_{sun}$ is the effective temperature of the Sun (5770 K), $T_{star}$ is the effective temperature of the star (table 2), and $L_{star}$ is the luminosity of the star. Be sure to use the bolometric magnitude when calculating the star's luminosity! The equation uses the Stefan-Boltzmann law and assumes the star is spherical; this will be in the

ballpark even for rapidly orbiting close binary stars, which tides
have bulged into distinct egg shapes. If you also want the star's
density, use the diameter to calculate the star's volume and then
calculate its mass from the mass-luminosity law. Dividing the volume by the mass yields density.

---

### THE SIZE IN THE SKY

What's the width (or "angular diameter," technically) of an
object in the sky? Obviously that depends on the size of the
body and how far away it is. From Earth, the diameter of both
the Moon and Sun is about half a degree. Even though their
sizes are very different, so are their distances from Earth, and
the differences cancel.

For small angles the size is roughly:

$$S = 57.3 \times D/R$$

where $S$ is the apparent size in degrees, $D$ is the diameter of
the object and $R$ its distance. For the Moon, for example, D
~ 2160 miles, R ~ 240,000 miles, and so:

$$S = 57.3 \times (2160/240,000) = 0.52°.$$

This equation gets progressively less accurate for apparent
sizes larger than ~20°. In that case you will need more sophisticated trigonometric calculations.

Size has several implications for the gritty environmental
details. First, a hot "blue" star will appear as a small but un-
bearably brilliant disk, and it probably will be too bright to
look anywhere near it in the sky. It will also cast very sharp
shadows. Conversely, a cool, "red" star will appear much
broader and be not nearly so brilliant. Lighting will also be
more diffuse as well as more yellowish.

---

### PUTTING IT TOGETHER: THE PLANET
### OF A SMALL RED STAR

Here's an extended example of designing an exotic but Earthlike
planet, one around a red dwarf star. We'll start with the star specifi-

cations and see what they imply for a planet. As I've noted, the alleged "lurid light" of a little "red" dwarf star is no reason for ignoring them. They're about as hot as a projector bulb!

Let's choose Ross 128, a nearby star that to my knowledge hasn't figured in any stories. From the *Catalog of Nearby Stars*, its visual magnitude is 11.1 and distance 3.3 pc, so its absolute visual magnitude is:

$$M = 11.1 + 5 - 5 \log (3.32) = 13.5$$

Since its spectral type is M4.5, the bolometric correction $B$ is approximately $-2.5$, so that its bolometric magnitude is:

$$13.5 + (-2.5) = 11.0$$

and its total luminosity is:

$$L = 2.52^{(4.85 - 11.0)} = 0.0034$$

or only 0.34 percent of the Sun. Furthermore, only about 10 percent of that is visible light, as we can calculate using the equation on page 133:

$$L_v/L_b = 2.52^B = 2.52^{(-2.5)} = 0.099.$$

Of course, this different wavelength mix will have subtle effects, too; with little UV, for example, photodissociation won't be a problem.

To keep things simple, let's now place a planet where it would need to be to get an Earthlike level of heating.

$$R = \sqrt{L/I} = \sqrt{0.0034/1} = 0.058 \text{ AU} \sim 8{,}700{,}000 \text{ km.}$$

Now we estimate the mass of the star from the mass-luminosity law:

$$M = (0.0034)^{(0.2632)} = 0.224$$

so the star still has over one-fifth the mass of the Sun. From Kepler's Third Law, then, the revolution period (year) is:

$P = \sqrt{[(0.058)^3 / (0.224)]} = 0.0297$ year, or 10 d, 20 h, 44 m, 5.5 s

—hardly more than a week!

We can now appreciate a better reason for ignoring the "red" stars: Even though a red dwarf star is vastly less luminous than the Sun, its mass is not all that much less. Thus, to get an Earthlike level of illumination, the planet must be proportionately far deeper in the star's gravity well.

And this means the planet's spin has been tidally locked. The tide-raising force is:

$F = M/D^3 = (0.224)/(0.058)^3 \sim 1130$ times the Sun on the Earth.

To compare with the Earth's effect on the Moon, we must express the Earth's mass in terms of the Sun (0.000 003), and the Moon's distance in AU (0.00257):

$F = 0.000\ 003 / (0.00257)^3 = 177.6,$

so the tidal effect of Ross 128 on its hypothetical planet is 1130/177.6 ~ 6.4 times that of the Earth on the Moon.

However, this need not be a show-stopper: Mercury's 3:2 tidal lock, instead of the Moon's 1:1, shows a possible alternative. What's necessary for the 3:2 rather than the 1:1 lock to be stable is a modestly elliptical orbit, which hardly seems unlikely for a near-in planet of another star. Robert L. Forward used just such a setup in *Timemaster*. Sure, this won't *always* happen, but it can happen for the sake of the story!

Another alternative for thwarting the tidal locking is to have the Earthlike planet be a satellite of a *brown dwarf* that in turn orbits the red dwarf (page 143). This might work because of the great mass of the brown dwarf. Unfortunately, however, a simple double-planet system with locked mutual rotation, such as the worlds Genji and Chujo in *Murasaki*, probably won't work, for the same reason that close-in planets such as Mercury and Venus don't have satellites. Tidal braking just causes the orbit to decay, so that the worlds eventually come within their mutual Roche limit and are destroyed. If the decay takes long enough geologically, though, it could be a plot element.

Of course, the "asynchronous" tidal lock still wouldn't help if the "solar day"—the time between sunrises (see page 90)—were around six months, as it is on Mercury! Day-night variations would just be too extreme. As we see, the revolution period (the "year") of our hypothetical planet is about ten days long. If we assume the planet's in a prograde 3:2 lock, like Mercury, the solar day works out to be exactly twice the year length—i.e., about twenty days.

That may be a bit long. Certainly it's going to exacerbate the day/night temperature changes. We could make the solar days shorter if the planet's in a 3:2 retrograde rotation. That is, the planet rotates in the opposite sense from the direction it revolves around its Sun, just as Venus does. Because this partly cancels the orbital motion, the solar day comes out much shorter (page 90). In fact it works out to be 40 percent of the year, or a bit more than four days. I don't know, however, whether the lock would remain stable under those circumstances.

To get the angular size at this distance, we now need the diameter of the star. Its effective temperature is about 3150 K, so:

$$D = (5770/3150)^2 \times \sqrt{(0.0034)} = 0.196 \text{ Sun} \sim 169,000 \text{ km},$$

so the star is only about one-fifth the diameter of the Sun. The diameter of the star seen from the planet is:

$$S = 57.3 \times (169,000/8,700,000) = 1.1°.$$

Thus, even though the star is smaller, the planet is so much closer that the apparent size in the sky is over double the Sun's. Obviously, then, area for area, the surface is dimmer than our Sun's. When you then consider that most of the radiation coming off each square centimeter of the star's surface is infrared, the sun is very dim indeed—at least by comparison with our Sun. You probably could look directly at it briefly, and you could probably see variations across its surface, such as sunspots. Still, you wouldn't want to stare at the star for any length of time, any more than you'd want to stare at a stage light. You won't get sunburned, either, any more than you can get a sunburn from an ordinary light bulb. The amount of UV Ross 128 puts off is inconsequential.

You won't notice that daylight is any dimmer, either, again just because of the adaptability of the human eye. Even though the visible light will be only a few percent that of daylight on Earth, that's still far more than you need to see clearly. Your pupils won't contract quite so much as they do in full sunlight on Earth, but you won't notice that.

One possible problem, though: many red dwarfs are "flare stars." For reasons that are still poorly understood, every now and then they shoot off a huge flare. This briefly increases their luminosity by as much as a hundred times—which could be awkward indeed for a habitable planet. Imagine a hundred suns briefly appearing in the sky! The planet will need a thick atmosphere and ocean to moderate such occasional pulses of heat. Cloud cover will help reflect any pulse of light, and the sheer thermal inertia of the ocean, with its resistance to rapid heating, will also moderate any untoward effects. Of course, such an atmosphere and ocean would also help to moderate the long days.

The native vegetation might look black to human eyes, the better to absorb all that infrared radiation. On the other hand, it might be brightly colored, just by accident. Since visible light makes up only a small part of the incident light, the local plant life may well not bother with it. After all, evolution tolerates much worse inefficiencies: Through an accident of evolution, Earthly plants reflect sunlight in the wavelength region, green, where it's most intense! You'd hardly predict *that* if you were trying to predict the color of Earthly vegetation. [Remember, the color of an object is set by the wavelengths it *reflects* (page 87). If plants absorbed green light, they wouldn't be green.]

Other bizarre effects would come about because of the markedly elliptical orbit necessary to stabilize the 3:2 tidal lock. Just as on Mercury, the sun will move unevenly across the sky. In fact, it can stop and back up briefly before continuing on, and so from a couple of longitudes on the planet, the sun will rise, "change its mind" and set again before rising. These effects will be even more extreme on the red-dwarf planet since its revolution period is so much shorter than Mercury's. If an indigenous civilization develops, these complexities may hinder their understanding of astronomy. It took long enough on Earth even with our simpler sky.

The elliptical orbit will make for perceptible changes in the size of the sun's disk over the course of a revolution period, too. If the eccentricity of the orbit is 0.206, the same as Mercury's, the disk will vary by over 30 percent in diameter during the course of a revolution period; that is, over about ten days. We can calculate this as follows: from page 13, the pericentron is $1 + 0.206 = 1.206$, while the apocentron is $1 - 0.206 = 0.794$, where as usual we take the mean distance of the planet as simply one. If the sun has diameter $d$, then (from the formula in the sidebar on page 136), its relative size in the sky changes from $d/1.206$ to $d/0.794$. (We don't need the actual diameter and distance because we're only interested in the relative *change* from maximum to minimum, not the angular diameter in degrees.) Thus, at its smallest, the sun has only $0.794/1.206 = 66\%$ of its diameter at its maximum.

Seasons will obviously be utterly different from Earth. It's hard to talk about a "season" when the "year" is only an Earth-week or so long, especially if it's longer than the local day! It doesn't seem likely there will be anything like a season at all, in terms of periodic variations of climate over a few months. And in any event, the variation in the amount of heating the red-dwarf planet receives will be dominated by the variations in distance from its sun during its elliptical orbit, not by its axial tilt. A large satellite like our Moon is also precluded by the stellar tides. The upshot is that weather and climate patterns will be utterly different.

All in all, then, such locales may be exotic but not utterly hostile.

And last, red dwarf stars have a huge advantage if you take the long view, because of their extremely long lives—over a trillion years, for some of the dimmest. That's fifty times the age of our Galaxy to this point. When all the bright stars have long since burned out, these stars will still be calmly shining, scarcely changed. If nothing else, they'll be retirement sites for long-lived civilizations. Humans can hope they're among them.

## BEYOND THE MAIN SEQUENCE

### Bigger and Smaller

Very hot, extremely massive stars are very rare. A star more than about one hundred times the mass of the Sun (the "Eddington limit") in theory can't even exist, because it would blow itself apart. Extremely massive stars are also *very* short lived, a few million years at most. They'd be great local color, though, as in Poul Anderson's "Supernova."

Very cool stars are more interesting. Not only are they exceedingly long-lived, but they grade into *brown dwarfs*. These are (so far hypothetical) objects much bigger than Jupiter, but still too small for the hydrogen-fusion fires to ignite in their core.

Are they stars or planets? That depends on your definition; of course, they don't put out energy from nuclear reactions, but they're still shining by light of their own! They would radiate energy for a long, long time, glowing dimly like dying coals in a campfire, just from their stored heat. An emerging definition seems to be that a brown dwarf forms like a star—that is, it forms directly from a collapsing giant molecular cloud (page 41)—but is too small to carry out hydrogen fusion in its core. By contrast, planets form out of matter that's lost at least some of its hydrogen and helium, because they're formed in a nebula that was "cooked out" by the nearness of a growing star.

Where's the cutoff for stardom, then? As we'll see it's a bit vague, but the limit for sustained hydrogen fusion seems to be about 8.5 percent of the Sun's mass, or about eighty-five Jupiter masses. There are a couple of complications, though.

For one thing, deuterium, heavy hydrogen ($^2H$) makes up about 0.002 percent of the hydrogen in the Universe, and it fuses much more easily than ordinary hydrogen. It's quite possible for an object to be big enough for the deuterium to fuse, but not big enough for ordinary hydrogen to fuse. The minimum mass for deuterium fusion is about 1.5 percent of a Sun. So an object of this size can shine like a "real" star for a bit—but it's a flash in the pan. The nuclear fires die away without causing anything else to happen, like lighter fluid flaming off wet wood. Even at best, a brown dwarf fuses deuterium for only about ten million years. It's not enough to make any difference in its ultimate evolution.

For the other complication, hydrogen burning doesn't start suddenly at a particular stellar mass. There's a transition region, from maybe 7 percent of a solar mass upward, where hydrogen can start slowly fusing. The extra energy so produced can delay the cooling of the brown dwarf for billions of years. Ultimately, however, even the fusion isn't great enough to keep the star from cooling off, and it collapses into brown-dwarfhood. For a large brown dwarf, though, this takes longer than the age of the Galaxy! So there's really no well-defined point at which an object becomes a "star" instead of a brown dwarf.

The exact mass of these threshold points, as well as the rate at which the brown dwarf cools, depends on how opaque the object is—its "opacity." The more opaque, the lower the mass limits, and the longer the cooling times, for an obvious reason: Just like a blanket, opaque gases keep the heat inside the star. Brown dwarfs are likely to have rather opaque atmospheres because they're cool enough to contain lots of molecules, which might even form clouds. They might even be dusty, with fine particles of iron metal or silicates precipitated out of the air like ice crystals in Earth's atmosphere.

By the way, even when brown dwarfs (and the very low-mass stars they grade imperceptibly into) fuse hydrogen, they don't "burn" hydrogen quite the way the Sun does. Instead of fusing four hydrogens into one helium $-4$, they only fuse three hydrogens to one helium $-3$, which has two protons but only one neutron. Conditions in the star's core aren't intense enough to go all the way to $^4$He.

A brown dwarf would be a good setting for an SF story, especially since it's likely the closest object to the Solar System is not another star but a brown dwarf. As I mentioned in chapter two, one possibility is a brown dwarf as part of a binary system, with an Earthlike planet at a Trojan (L-4 or L-5) point in the orbit.

A perhaps more interesting possibility is an Earthlike planet circling a brown dwarf, where the brown dwarf in turn circles another star. Poul Anderson suggested many years ago that such a situation could go a long way toward making Earthlike planets possible around a small red star, by thwarting the tidal locking. The Earthlike planet would, of course, be tidally locked to the brown dwarf. But just as the Sun rises and sets on the Moon as it goes around the Earth in its orbit, sunrise and sunset would occur on the Earthlike planet, even though the brown dwarf wouldn't change its position in the sky. This scenario assumes, of course, that the brown dwarf is itself not tidally locked by the star. Once that happens, the Earthlike planet's orbit will decay tidally, just as with the hypothetical satellites of Mercury and Venus. However, tidal locking of a massive, largely gaseous object like a brown dwarf should take a very long time indeed.

A brown dwarf is so massive that the orbital period of the Earthlike planet would be much shorter than a lunar month, too. For example, for a small brown dwarf with 1 percent of the Sun's mass, the one-day orbital period is at 631,000 kilometers—about the distance of Europa from Jupiter. From the planet, the dwarf would appear almost 11° across, twenty-two times the width of the Sun or full Moon: a vast ball perhaps glowing deep, dull red, with streamers and wisps of darker clouds and possibly storms and belts like Jupiter's.

In fact, at the upper end of the brown dwarf range, where they're transitional to small stars, the luminosity of the brown dwarf itself might make this scenario awkward. The dwarfs take so long to cool that even over a few billion years the luminosity doesn't change much. For example, a planet in a one-day orbit around a brown dwarf with 8 percent of the Sun's mass would receive more heat from the dwarf than it would from its Sun, assuming an Earthlike level of sunlight from the parent star!

On the other hand, of course, this could lead to some interesting variations. A planet in a one-day orbit around a brown dwarf with 7 percent of the Sun's mass, for example, would receive something like 6 percent as much heat from the dwarf as from its sun. That might lead to interesting climate effects: One hemisphere is permanently heated more than the other, at a low level to be sure, but even small changes can have large effects. And no doubt profound sociological effects, too! Consider the consequences for religion and legend if only one side of a world has a second, dim star, for example.

Alternatively, if the heating of the brown dwarf is significant, this could extend the habitable zone farther from the main star, as suggested by the planet Haven in Jerry Pournelle's *Warworld* series.

### When the Fuel Runs Out . . .

What happens when the hydrogen runs out (or starts to) on a Main-Sequence star? You eventually get a *red giant*. The star expands greatly, and although the outer surface cools, the luminosity nonetheless increases vastly because it's so much bigger. This will happen to the Sun in several billion years. Ultimately the helium accumulated in the core starts fusing to heavier elements, to carbon-12 and oxygen-16 initially. How far this fusion can go depends on the star's mass. It must stop at iron in any event, though, as iron (specifically, the nucleus $^{56}$Fe) is the most stable. Heavier nuclei *take* energy to make.

Nonetheless, helium fusion is not much of a new lease on life, because it doesn't last very long. It's a less energetic reaction, and the star is spending the energy more profligately. A star like the

Sun gains another hundred million years at most.

Hence you don't expect habitable planets around red giant stars! However, Lee Goodloe and Jerry Oltion rationalized just such a situation in their novella "Waterworld," a Mercury-sized planet consisting of just $H_2O$, a global ocean hundreds of miles deep. They suggested the planet was originally an "iceworld" like the Jovian moons Callisto or Ganymede that had thawed when the star expanded. They further hinted it been "seeded" by spores in deep freeze from an originally Earthlike planet farther in. This again shows how constraints are a point of departure.

When it's burned the last of its fuel, a red giant of small to middling size turns into a *planetary nebula*. This is a misnomer; it has nothing to do with planets! A planetary nebula is so called because it looks a bit like a planet through a telescope: It's a glowing disk of gas that's the outer shell blown off a red giant core. One familiar example is the Ring Nebula in the constellation Lyra. Our Sun will blow off a planetary nebula in about five billion years, after passing through its red giant phase. As we've seen, by changing the element composition of the interstellar gas, planetary nebulas can lead to some interesting world-building variations (page 52). The hot, incredibly dense, left-behind core is a *white dwarf*, no bigger than a small planet, but as massive as the Sun.

A large star ends more spectacularly, in a *supernova*, a gigantic explosion. When it finally runs out of nuclear fuel, after fusing as much as it can (up to iron), the star's gigantic, dense core abruptly collapses under its own gravity. It hits and rebounds, and *that* blows off the rest of the star with a violence that is almost inconceivable. For a brief while the star can outshine its entire galaxy.

The supernova may leave behind a *neutron star*, an "atomic nucleus" held together by gravity. It packs the mass of the Sun into a volume only a few miles across. A newly formed neutron star is spinning very rapidly—in less than a second—and sweeps a jet of particles around like a gigantic lawn sprinkler. If that jet should sweep across the Earth, we see a pulse of radio noise: a *pulsar*. In a *tour de force* of hard SF, Robert L. Forward has postulated life on a neutron star, in his novels *Dragon's Egg* and *Starquake*.

Alternatively, if it's too massive the supernova remnant becomes a black hole, a clot of mass in space so dense that not even light can escape.

A supernova is so catastrophic it could affect planets even several light years away. If the explosion were close enough, showers of subatomic particles—cosmic rays—streaming from the shattered star could stress the biosphere. Even if the radiation dose was too small to kill many living things outright, it could increase the mutation rate.

Poul Anderson treated this scenario fictionally in his story "Supernova" (republished as "Day of Burning"). In his story, the supernova was very close—just a few light-years away—so just shielding the planet from the sheer intensity of the radiation was a severe problem. He also suggested that the additional heat and light from the supernova would cause climatic disruption. Since he postulated a technical civilization on the planet, Anderson also noted that the nuclear "fallout" from the explosion—the intense rain of cosmic rays sprayed out—would present an extra hazard: Electronics are even more vulnerable to such things than are biosystems.

Anderson didn't mention destruction of the ozone layer, though, which in retrospect would be one of the major concerns in shielding a living planet. Obviously, the same mechanisms for destroying ozone will work whether the high-energy particles are coming from a planet's own star (page 86) or from a supernova.

In turn, this means a supernova doesn't have to be so close to have a severe impact on a biosphere. It's been calculated that even a supernova ten parsecs away—over thirty light years—could clobber enough ozone to cause a major extinction. (How bright would a supernova ten parsecs away be? Several hundred times the full Moon, assuming the peak luminosity of the supernova is about a billion times the Sun's. It would be *bright.*)

Supernovas, however, are a source of creation as well as destruction, as they're the main element factories in the universe (page 41).

## UNDER TWIN SUNS

Most stars are not single children, like our Sun. Something over 50 percent of all stars are twins, or triplets or even multiplets. That's a lot of story settings! Think of Isaac Asimov's classic "Nightfall," in which a planet in a multiple star system experienced darkness only every twenty-five hundred years or so—with catastrophic social consequences. But how realistic is a planet in a binary star system? Planets may be possible, at least in certain cases, although there are lots of potential problems. Let's look at some of them briefly.

The most important parameter for a planet is obvious: How far apart are the stars? If they're far enough apart, they're like two separate suns, and presumably each can have a family independently of the other. From one of the planetary systems, the other sun merely appears as a bright star.

How far is "far enough" apart? Anywhere from a hundred AU or so on up. The upper limit for the separation is set by gravitational perturbations from other nearby stars, which will disrupt the orbit if it's wider than a tenth of a light year or so—say more than about ten thousand AU.

We see many such widely separated binary stars. At such extreme separations, the orbital motion is tiny, so that it takes from thousands up to several million years for the stars to complete one orbit. How are they recognized as binary stars, then? One way is simple proximity in the sky—if they're close together, *and* at essentially the same distance, they must be binary. At very wide separations, your initial clue may be that the stars are traveling in parallel through the sky. Astronomers call these "common proper motion" (CPM) stars. ("Proper motion" is the "true" motion of the stars in the sky, which is due to a combination of their actual motion and the Solar System's. Proper motion is very small, but it causes the constellations to change slowly over centuries.)

Moderately wide pairs have been used as a setting in a number of stories. Poul Anderson's *Fire Time* tells of a world where the periodic (about once a century) approach of the second star causes an extremely hot season—Fire Time. In Brian W. Aldiss's *Helliconia* series, two stars have a highly elliptical orbit with a period of 2582 years, and an Earthlike planet orbits one star in 480 days. This superimposes a "Great Year" on the ordinary cycle of seasons: when the stars are near pericentron, a global summer lasting centuries ensues. In both cases, the settings are "exotic Earths," but the authors have worked them out in considerable detail.

Even farther away, say a tenth of a light year or so (about like Proxima from Alpha Centauri), the other member of a binary would be just a bright star. Though no doubt significant for mythology, it would have no effect on the other system (unless it became a supernova!). But if each member of the pair had its own planetary system with a habitable planet, that might spur early development of interstellar flight.

For closer binaries, say on the order of tens of AU, the stars start to impinge on each other, and arranging planetary systems becomes a bigger problem, as the gravitational effects from the second star will perturb any planetary orbits. Even so, approximate results from celestial mechanics suggest that planets could exist in stable orbits. In other words, there are zones around each star where planetary motion is "bounded"—that is, although the orbit might change from one revolution to the next, it will never get out of a ring-shaped zone around the star. Such a zone, of course, is necessary for the planet to be stable over geologic time!

Unfortunately, planets may not be able to form at moderate separations. The disk from which the planets would accrete (page 43) would be roiled too much so that you just end up with asteroid belts. Jupiter did a fine job of this in our system, and it's a lot smaller than another star (page 46).

This proximity problem is compounded with another: Most binary stars separated by more than ten AU or so have orbits that are markedly elliptical—they look like squashed footballs! So sometimes the stars are *much* closer than at other times. In these cases the average distance of the suns is irrelevant; the critical distance determining whether accretion will occur will be that closest approach. The gravity is *much* more effective then.

For an example, the average separation of the two main stars in Alpha Centauri is 24.3 AU, a bit more than the distance from the Sun to Uranus. However, their orbital eccentricity is 0.52. This means that they range from 35.6 AU apart—almost as far as Pluto is from the Sun to as close as 11.2 AU— about as far as from the Sun to Saturn. (In case you're wondering, Proxima Centauri, the third member of the system, has no effect—you couldn't even see it with the naked eye.)

For stars even closer, of course, there's an obvious problem with having planets: Even if they could accrete, there's no room left! Where are you going to fit an Earth if your suns are only one AU apart? We've seen that putting a planet in the L-4 or L-5 position might be possible, but only under unusual circumstances (page 31).

Finally, for suns that are *very* close, we may have some interesting possibilities indeed. If they're, say, within a tenth of an AU (fifteen million kilometers), we could truly have twin suns. An Earthlike planet could orbit *both*, as though around a single sun.

That could make for delightful sunrises!

There are some problems here, too, of course.

The accretion problems shouldn't be so bad, because from out where the planets would accrete, the suns look pretty much like a single gravity field. Gravitational perturbations should be a lot smaller.

But there are new problems. Such close stars interact a *lot*, and the closer they are, the more things that happen—things that will have major effects on a planetary system.

The first thing to consider is tidal effects. For two stars a few million kilometers apart the tidal bulge is huge. That's only a few star diameters apart, and both stars are stretched markedly into egg shapes. You should be able to see the distortion on cloudy days.

The stars also orbit quickly, in a matter of a few hours. Because of this, they're roiled much more than usual because they're forced to spin so fast. They have high sunspot activity, high flare activity, and their surfaces are seething much more than normal. Why is this? Stars have powerful magnetic fields internally, and these magnetic fields stir up the star-stuff profoundly when they're made to travel through it rapidly. Stars are made of plasma—ionized gas—and a plasma is an electrical conductor because of its ionization. (In a plasma, some electrons are detached from the atoms, so that you have a mixture of negatively charged electrons and positively charged ions.) It's just as though you were drawing copper wire through a magnetic field in a generator; you feel a resistance, and you're forcing an electric current to flow in the wire. Since their orbital motions force them to turn once every few hours, the magnetic fields are dragged around at a terrific rate.

By contrast, the Sun spins slowly, only about once a month, and its magnetic field doesn't get stirred very fast. Even so, the well-known eleven-year sunspot cycle results from the progressive twisting up of the Sun's magnetic field and its subsequent untwisting.

This magnetic resistance has another effect: It brakes the stars' orbital motion, and thus causes their mutual orbit to slowly decay. As I said, running stellar plasma through the magnetic field creates electric current, and that current drives intense "stellar winds"—flows of charged particles out from the stars. These winds steal energy from the orbit. For purists, gravitational waves, predicted by general relativity, also cause some braking, but that's less important.

In fact, the reason our Sun spins so slowly is that its rotation was braked long ago by its magnetic field working against the solar wind. But a close binary pair *can't* slow down; their own orbital motion forces them to keep turning quickly.

So when stars start out very close, they will get closer over geologic time through orbital decay. This seems like a catastrophic situation building; what happens when they get *too* close?

They merge, eventually. But a lot of fireworks happen first.

First, when the inner edge of a tidal bulge finally encounters the Roche limit, gas will start spilling off onto the other star. The larger star spills over first because it's less dense; or, in other words, since it takes up more space it's the first star to run up against the Roche limit. The gas doesn't fall straight in, however. It still has the orbital speed of the star it fell from, so it spirals in, falling in only as rapidly as that speed can be dissipated by friction. This spiraling gas makes an accretion disk of extremely hot gas embracing the smaller star like the rings of Saturn.

At this point the pair has become a "contact binary." Once the stars have gotten to this point, they greatly disrupt each other's evolution because they're exchanging mass. As the large star loses mass to the smaller, it burns more dimly, and it may even shrink to the point where it stops losing mass. Conversely, as the smaller star gains mass it swells and burns hotter; and eventually it will lose mass back to the original star. And so on, back and forth, as the orbit inexorably decays. This progressive decay is why few Main-Sequence stars are close binaries. The shuffling of mass back and forth, along with the steady orbital decay, is liable to take two initially main-sequence stars off the Main Sequence pretty quickly.

All this is significant for planets, at least for habitable planets. Once the system evolves into a contact binary, the hard radiation from the accretion disk is liable to fry the inner planetary system, and in any event the increased luminosity will disrupt—perhaps catastrophically—the climate on any Earthlike planets. In fact, as the orbit continues to dwindle, the ever-increasing speed of the revolving stars can throw gas right out of the system. It's a bit like taking an electric mixer out of the batter without turning it off first!

The novella "Contact," by Jerry Oltion and Lee Goodloe used such a setting as an unusual sort of disaster tale; the decaying orbit of a small red star around a Sunlike star destroyed an emerging civilization.

## Cataclysms and Contact

The contact binaries whose members are not on the Main Sequence are often called "cataclysmic binaries," for good reasons. You can get some very spectacular effects indeed from the mass spillover under those conditions! Classical novas, for example, are cataclysmic binaries. A nova is a star that briefly increases hundreds to thousands of times in brightness every few decades, only to subside back to its original brightness later. They consist of a white dwarf and a red giant. When the red giant expanded, it began spilling gas onto its white-dwarf companion. As the outer part of the red giant is still hydrogen, a layer of hydrogen slowly accumulates on the dead, but extremely dense and still very hot white dwarf.

Eventually the pressures build up to the point that the hydrogen layer detonates as a planet-sized hydrogen bomb. That's the nova outburst. After that, hydrogen begins accumulating again. . . .

X-ray stars are even more bizarre. Gas spills off a red giant orbiting a black hole to make a disk around the black hole. The black hole is so dense that gas falling into it is heated to extremely high temperatures, high enough to generate X rays.

Although neither are sites for habitable planets, they can be local color. They also can salt the local interstellar medium with different proportions of newly forged elements (page 51).

## GALAXIES

These are vast systems, containing anywhere from hundreds of millions to hundreds of billions of stars, that make up the Universe. They are in turn grouped into clusters of various sizes; the "Local Group," to which our Galaxy belongs, contains about twenty members. Galactic neighbors are typically separated by ten to one hundred times their diameter, so their proportional separation is not nearly so great as that of stars from stars, or even planets from planets.

Galaxies come in several types that have different implications for world-building. The types are distinguished by the amount of angular momentum they have. *Spiral* galaxies, like our own Milky Way, are lens-shaped, with a denser nucleus or core made of older, redder stars bulging in the center. The flat disk surrounding this nucleus contains the spiral arms that give them their name. The arms seem to be vast (and unbelievably tenuous, by everyday standards) waves in the exceedingly thin interstellar medium. They shine from the hot, young (and very short-lived) stars they've spawned. The Sun is a member of the Milky Way's disk population and lies about two-thirds of the distance from the galactic center. It orbits the core with revolution period of something like two hundred million years.

*Elliptical* galaxies resemble the disembodied central nucleus of a spiral galaxy. Their shapes range from spherical to lens-like, but with no disk. They range in size from the very smallest to the very largest galaxies known. They also have little or no star formation taking place now, as all the raw material has been used up.

*Irregular* galaxies are chaotic masses of stars, rich in interstellar gas and dust. The two Magellanic Clouds, which are visible from the southern hemisphere, are irregular galaxies. They're satellites of the Milky Way.

Finally, gravitational theory indicates that stars are always being expelled from galaxies, just by the vagaries of gravitational interaction. Poul Anderson set a novel, *World Without Stars*, on such an isolated star, but it seems to be another underutilized setting.

We *know* that spiral galaxies can spawn Earthlike planets, because here we are! In fact, it's possible only spirals can spawn life-bearing planets: They still have raw material for stars left, but are not so chaotic as the irregulars.

Even so, spirals don't seem to be particularly safe. A huge black hole seems to lie at the core of our Galaxy, and enormous gas clouds around the galactic center have been interpreted to be the debris from vast explosions in the galactic core, perhaps caused when a large clot of matter fell into the black hole. This is another scenario Niven has used in his "Known Space" series. Also, some other spiral galaxies seem to have extraordinary violent events occurring in their nuclei. Seyfert galaxies, for example, have extremely bright nuclei but otherwise look like ordinary spiral galaxies. So maybe a "Seyfert phase" is something every spiral galaxy goes through, once in a while, when for some reason all hell breaks loose in its core.

One estimate suggests the total energy released by a core explosion as one hundred million supernovas. If it all went off at once, that would be one hundred times as bright as a supernova only ten parsecs away, and presumably cause one hundred times the problems (page 145).

The core can't all go off at once, though. It's too big. The simplest argument is from light speed; one side of the core can't "know" the other part is exploding until the signal (shock wave?) gets there, and that signal can't travel faster than light. So even if the zone that explodes is a tiny (on galactic scales!) area a few hundred light years across, the light pulse from it will be spread over a few centuries. Which should make it manageable.

However: An explosion is not the only catastrophic event that could emerge from the galactic core. We think of an explosion as blowing off matter more or less uniformly in all directions—that is, it's roughly "isotropic." But certain "peculiar" (the astronomers' word for galaxies with unusual features) galaxies have some extremely violent events going on in them that are *not* isotropic. Huge jets of hot, ionized material, in some cases thousands of light years long, emerge from the cores of some such galaxies. A planet that blundered into such a jet, as its sun followed its orbit in its galaxy, might be in a bad way indeed.

How can such directed jets of hot material occur? One way is for matter to fall into a spinning black hole. The in-falling stuff forms a disk around the hole; because of conservation of angular momentum (page 43), it can't drop directly in. Similarly, high-energy radiation radiated by the hole, derived from the gravitational energy of the matter dribbling in from the inner part of disk, shoots out along the rotation axes in highly directed beams, like a gigantic firehose.

# CHAPTER 8

# Not as We Know It

## VOLATILE MIXTURES

As I've emphasized, differences in volatile content give major scope for variation in a world, both because they're a tiny percentage of planet's mass, and because their composition is much easier to finagle than the overall planet composition (page 97). So, I'll review some possibilities below.

## WETWORLDS

Our Earth is a wetworld. Such planets have lots of water; which means that their hydrogen ratio is high, and that they're reasonably oxidized, so that the hydrogen is combined with oxygen into water. Any carbon will be mostly in carbon dioxide or (equivalently) locked up in limestone. Of course, as we've seen even a generally "Earthlike" world can be very different from Earth, as with the "oceanworld."

So let's look at some even farther out variations.

### The Neon World

One would be a planet with an atmosphere rich in noble gases. Or to be realistic, an atmosphere rich in neon, since it's far and away the most abundant noble gas. As Poul Anderson years ago pointed out in his novel *The Man Who Counts*, such an atmosphere makes it easy to arrange *large* flying creatures, because you can make the atmosphere as thick as you want without having awkward geochemical (and biochemical) side effects. So, somehow we have to grow a protoplanet big enough that it starts to glom onto volatile matter out of the parent nebula (as did the gas giants in our own

System), but shut off its growth before it can catch much $H_2$ or He, so it doesn't just become a gas giant.

One way to halt the growth prematurely might be for the central star to enter its T-Tauri stage. This is a brief but very luminous phase that a forming star goes through, which blows away the remains of the nebula from which it and its planets condensed. Alternatively, maybe a major collision between protoplanets threw one into an orbit much closer to its sun, so its further growth was stunted. Of course, as with Titan, we could simply end up with a very water-rich world instead.

There's no evidence any of this came even close to happening in our System. We have a big (4.5 AU wide!) gap between a small rocky planet (Mars) and the biggest gas giant (Jupiter), with nothing in between but leftover debris. But of course, this doesn't prove it can't—or didn't—happen elsewhere.

## Clorox, the Chloroxygen World

Now let's look at an even farther-out variation, by way of considering the *halogens*, the group of elements including the toxic and reactive gases fluorine and chlorine. Just from their chemical properties, you could imagine that free fluorine and hydrogen fluoride (HF) might make up an analog to oxygen and water. That is, HF would form oceans and lakes, and would be the solvent in which biochemical reactions occurred. Presumably plant life would release free fluorine gas during photosynthesis, while animals would breathe in fluorine instead of oxygen. The planet Niflheim in H. Beam Piper's *Uller Uprising* used just this setup.

Chemically it's just fine. However: Fluorine is a very rare element. Although nucleosynthesis makes $^{16}O$ abundantly, fluorine-19, the only stable isotope of fluorine, is an out-of-the-way nucleus that's made only incidentally. For every fluorine atom, there are something over fifteen thousand oxygen atoms. And sure, geologic processes can be very effective at separating out elements, but there *are* limits!

On top of everything else, fluorine gas is so chemically active that it's going to be very hard to accumulate it in an atmosphere. It's a better oxidizer than oxygen (that seems oxymoronic, but it's true), so free fluorine gas replaces oxygen out of its compounds—including silicates. In other words, if you start with fluorine gas and an oxide, you soon have oxygen gas and a fluoride instead.

Chlorine breathers aren't likely either. To be sure, chlorine is less oxidizing than oxygen, so it doesn't replace oxygen right out of its compounds the way fluorine does. And chlorine is about five times as abundant as fluorine. However, its chemistry is quite a bit different.

For one thing, it doesn't react with organic matter very enthusiastically—much less so than does oxygen. On an atom basis, you get about six times as much energy by reacting carbon with oxygen instead of chlorine, and three times as much energy by reacting hydrogen with oxygen. (The energy of food comes largely from the carbon and hydrogen it contains.) So you can't really imagine critters "burning" food with chlorine to get energy, the way Earth critters "burn" food with oxygen.

You also *can't* imagine a chlorine atmosphere over seas of liquid hydrogen chloride. The chemistry is just not analogous, even if you could somehow gather enough chlorine together to try it. For one thing, liquid hydrogen chloride is *cold*. It freezes at $-114.8°C$, and boils at $-84.9°C$. The boiling point of chlorine itself is only $-101°C$—so the very breathing stuff in the atmosphere would condense out onto HCl ice! Obviously, this doesn't happen in the water-oxygen system; droplets of $O_2$ don't condense onto water ice. The small liquid range of HCl would also be a problem.

However, all is not lost. There may indeed be a way to set up a chlorine-bearing atmosphere, but as a variation on a generally Earthlike world. And such a hybrid has received no attention in SF, so far as I know.

So let's return to Earth. Over geologic time, geologic processes have gathered most of Earth's chlorine together in the ocean, in which it's present as the very stable chloride ion, $Cl^-$ (page 78). In fact, it takes quite a bit of energy to strip that electron away.

But suppose some plant in the oceans evolved the capability to make chlorine gas from chloride by stripping that electron away again, using the energy derived from food. (And, of course, a special enzyme system.)

Why would it bother? Well, say, as a defense mechanism. It could then incorporate the chlorine into its biomolecules to make itself a poor meal for predators—making its own natural chlorinated pesticides, if you will. But predators will eventually evolve a defense to that, too. Then, the continued escalation of the biological "arms race" may eventually result in plants releasing free chlorine—still as a defense mechanism, a natural gas attack.

You'd end up with what is still basically a water-oxygen world, like Earth, but with a smidgen of free chlorine in the atmosphere—a "chloroxygen" world. For starting out Earthlike, the planet hardly ended up that way! James Lovelock once noted that a major biocatastrophe, comparable to that caused by the first release of oxygen itself, would have occurred if some alga had "learned" to do this in the Precambrian.

Let's look at some of the effects. First, it will be smoggy. Chlorine is colored; as all the chemistry texts say, it's a "greenish yellow" gas. It absorbs blue light (and shorter wavelengths) strongly. But from space it probably won't look *too* un-Earthly, at least at first glance. It may just look kind of misty. Look through the atmosphere along the edge of the planet, where there should be a distinct green-yellow cast to the air.

In fact, light with wavelengths shorter than ~490 nanometers, which lies in the deep blue, actually photodissociates the atoms in a $Cl_2$ molecule. (Chlorine, like most elements that are gases, comes as molecules containing two atoms: $Cl_2$.) This photodissociation makes free chlorine atoms, which in turn will be highly reactive. Among other things, they'll probably make an ozone layer impossible, since chlorine atoms are very good at breaking ozone back down into ordinary oxygen. However, the chlorine itself may absorb enough UV to make up for no ozone.

Besides $N_2$, $O_2$, $CO_2$—and the dab of $Cl_2$—the atmosphere will contain traces of many other things, such as water vapor, HCl, and chlorinated organic compounds. (Including, no doubt, detectable amounts of phosgene, $COCl_2$. Phosgene is a useful starting compound for many industrial syntheses, but it's extremely toxic; like chlorine itself, it was used as a poison gas during World War I.)

Another quirk is that chlorine is heavier than oxygen and nitrogen. It's even heavier than $CO_2$. Thus it will tend to accumulate in low places and be an asphyxiation hazard. Caving will be a high-risk activity on Clorox. If there's a local civilization that buries its rulers in tombs *a la* Ancient Egypt, this phenomenon will help keep the tombs safe. For even the locals will get asphyxiated sometimes. Remember, they don't breathe chlorine! They're oxygen-breathers that can tolerate a lot of chlorine.

Chlorine also reacts with water, in what we might call the "Swimming Pool Reaction":

$$Cl_2 + H_2O = HCl + HClO$$
chlorine   water   hydrogen chloride   hypochlorous acid.

You've already guessed that this chloroxygen world has a dreadfully corrosive environment, and this is one reason why. Hydrogen chloride in water solution is hydrochloric acid. I call this the swimming pool reaction because it's used in large commercial swimming pools (and in municipal water supply systems) to disinfect them. Hypochlorous acid is a disinfectant—"Clorox" is a dilute solution of its salt sodium hypochlorite—and if you're dealing with a lot of water, it's much cheaper to add chlorine gas rather than hypochlorite itself. (In a swimming pool, though, you have to keep adding bases—sodium carbonate or "soda ash" is cheapest—to keep the acidity under control. Otherwise the hydrochloric acid keeps increasing and increasing, and the swimmers complain.)

So we'll have rivers, lakes, even oceans of a dilute acid and bleach solution. If the air contains, say, one percent chlorine, the acidity of surface water will be about like that of undiluted vinegar. Chemical weathering will be ferocious! Minerals will consist of lots of clays and quartz, and not much else. Limestone won't exist at all, because over geologic time all the carbonate will be fizzed back into carbon dioxide by the acidic surface water. (In fact, the standard field test for limestone is to drip acid on a rock and see if it fizzes.) This could be a problem; if it happens too fast, the world could end up baked in a heavy blanket of $CO_2$ like Venus. Either there must be few carbonate rocks to start with, or else their dissolution must happen slowly enough that the carbon can be cycled into organic matter.

What about biochemistry? Again we start with basically an Earthlike system, and add lots of chlorine tolerance. But that's a tall order: Earthlike living cells can't tolerate $Cl_2$ at all. Those reactive Cl atoms, made by photodissociation, are very good at glomming onto Earth-type biomolecules. So either the biochemistry will have to be very different, or else the shielding at the cellular level will have to be very good indeed. The latter possibility is not so unlikely as it may seem: Oxygen itself is highly toxic to the cell nuclei of terrestrial organisms, so that oxygen-breathing creatures like ourselves need elaborate mechanisms to protect the cell nuclei from the air.

Chlorine also reacts with lots of terrestrial-type organic compounds. It combines with hydrocarbons to make HCl, leaving a carbon residue, for example. So the organic molecules that do exist will be heavily chlorinated. Things like wood, for example, instead of being simply cellulose, will be like natural plastics. Tree trunks might be made of something like PVC (polyvinyl chloride, the white plastic used to make irrigation pipe). Shells, bones and teeth would be made out of something similar; they couldn't be made out of minerals like calcium carbonate or calcium phosphate, as they'd dissolve!

Plant photosynthesis would overall be about the same, in that its primary function would be to make oxygen (not chlorine!). But again the details will be very different. For one thing, the leaves won't be green, since green light is about the only thing that will come through the atmosphere—and again, something that *absorbs* green light will be any color but green (page 87). They'll probably look black to Earthly eyes, because they'll absorb most visible wavelengths. The leaves probably would have a "plasticky" look to terrestrial eyes, too; maybe they'd look like sun-rotted Hefty bags.

And the equivalents of flower perfumes, decay odors, the whole panoply of organic compounds put off by a living ecosystem: They would fit right into a toxic waste dump on Earth. PCBs, perfumes made of things like chlordane and DDT: all perfectly natural, and all, of course, perfectly nontoxic to the native life forms, which after all evolved with them and are tolerant to them.

As I've implied, too, there's no reason intelligence couldn't arise on a chloroxygen world. Oxygen metabolism, with or without chlorine, is high-energy and can support the overhead of a large multicelled organism—and of intelligence. But the sheer corrosiveness of the environment would also forestall technological development. Metals just wouldn't last long enough, even if you could smelt them in the first place. Even though a few noble metals—gold, platinum, a handful of others—don't react, they're rare and not very strong anyway. Try making a plow or a spear out of gold! The noble metals *are* good electrical conductors. Maybe the intelligent beings could develop an electrochemical technology, using ceramics for vessels. Without iron and copper, though, building massive generators will be difficult, so generating the electricity is likely to be a problem.

In addition, fires would just smolder, because chlorine atoms inhibit flame. So even fired ceramics wouldn't exist. Technology would thus be stalled out at the wood-and-stone level, even though by Earthly standards, the local "wood" would be a high-grade plastic.

Trapped in the Stone Age by the vagaries of the local chemistry. . . .

It'd be an interesting, but dangerous, place to visit, too. Although humans could probably walk around with a rubber suit and a special gas mask to strain out the chlorine, they'd die very slowly without such protection, for there'd be enough oxygen in the air to drag the process out.

And we'd have to be very careful of biocontamination. Suppose a simple, chloride-fixing microbe from a chloroxygen world accidentally got introduced to a planet like the Earth. If it were simple enough, this microbe would find Earth's environment bland but not hostile. After all, the bug is used to an oxygen-bearing atmosphere; indeed it probably needs free oxygen. Worse yet, it may find an Earthlike environment a paradise! There's water, oxygen, organic matter—and an awful lot of chloride that nobody wants just lying around.

The rabbits in Australia were subject to more natural population checks. And as the microbes multiply exponentially, they dump tons of homegrown chlorinated compounds into the terrestrial-type biosphere. . . .

A worse scenario than Crichton's *The Andromeda Strain*, for it leads to infection of the entire biosphere!

## NITROWORLDS

These are worlds where the dominant volatile element is nitrogen.

### The Ammonia World

Life-bearing planets probably require a liquid, because life needs a solvent in which all its multitude of chemical reactions can take place (page 104). Water fills the bill very well, not least because it's abundant. But is there anything else that might work?

One favorite alternative "thalassogen" ("sea former," a mellifluous coinage of Isaac Asimov's) is liquid ammonia ($NH_3$). Poul Anderson's world t'Kela in *Trader to the Stars* is one example, and Robert L. Forward's *Flight of the Dragonfly* (republished as *Rocheworld*) contains another.

Ammonia is also made from common elements, nitrogen and hydrogen, and so it's also common in the universe. Its properties are somewhat similar to water. It's a good solvent, for one thing. In fact, there's a whole technical literature on chemical reactions that take place in ammonia solution rather than water solution. This isn't just academic, either—quite a number of ammonia-solvent reactions are important in industry.

Ammonia is also liquid through a fairly long temperature range, over 40°C, and has a relatively high boiling point. At one atmosphere pressure, $NH_3$ freezes at $-77.7$°C and boils at $-33.4$°C. This means that an ammonia-ocean planet will be *cold*! (The boiling point's only *relatively* high.) Of course, since the liquid range is smaller than water's, ammonia won't be as flexible a thalassogen as is water. But, as we'll see, a real ammonia ocean will have a longer liquid range than does pure $NH_3$, because other things will be dissolved in it.

On the other hand, ammonia has problems as a thalassogen. One standard showstopper, for example, is that ammonia ice sinks in liquid ammonia. The fact that water ice floats on liquid water helps stabilize Earth's climate (page 105). However, if water ice sank, a layer of ice at the bottom of bodies of water might stabilize climate, too. It makes it hard to boil the ocean, for one thing, since you have to melt all that ice first. This is especially handy if you're orbiting a flare star! So maybe ammonia ice's sinking is not a showstopper after all. It makes the climate regulation different, but not impossible.

But there's at least one other severe problem: photodissociation by solar UV (page 71). Earth loses a bit of water this way, but the rate is low because of the "cold trap" in the upper atmosphere—most water freezes out before it gets high enough to be destroyed (page 71). Ammonia is even more easily broken up by UV than is water, and of course it freezes at a much lower temperature. Thus an ammonia planet's going to need a very effective cold trap indeed. A cool, type M "red" dwarf would help preserve the ammonia in the atmosphere, since such stars put out a lot less ultraviolet light than do G stars like the Sun. So now we can say that an ammonia-ocean world is not only cold, but has a "red" sun. Since such stars are cooler, too, this also makes it easier to arrange a cold world.

Another problem with ammonia oceans might be the greenhouse effect, because ammonia is a good greenhouse gas. You need *some* greenhouse effect, of course, to keep the oceans from freezing completely, but it might be easy to get too much of a good thing.

Ammonia might cause a runaway greenhouse, just as happened with water on Venus early in Solar System history (page 71).

So now we have a *thin* cold atmosphere on a small planet circling a dim red star. Maybe if the atmosphere's thin enough, the greenhouse can't run away.

The oceans won't even be all ammonia, either. Since water is so common, a world cold enough to trap ammonia will also traps *lots* of ordinary water ice. So our cold ammonia-world will also contain of lots of water ice.

Now, ammonia and water mix together easily. For this reason, ammonia gas is highly soluble in water at room temperature: "Household ammonia" solution is a dilute example. And conversely, at low temperatures quite a bit of water ice will dissolve in liquid ammonia. In fact, a little dissolved ice depresses ammonia's freezing point quite a bit—liquid ammonia and water have a "eutectic mixture," consisting of about 80 percent $NH_3$, that freezes around $-105°C$. Ammonia and water also make "mixed" ices, which are definite chemical compounds in which water and ammonia occur in a specific ratio.

So, our ammonia ocean is actually an ammonia-water ocean. It contains dissolved ice that acts a lot like antifreeze. Hal Clement touched on ammonia-water mixtures in his novel *Star Light*, as did Forward in *Rocheworld*. And, for a real live example in our own system: Saturn's huge satellite Titan may have a layer of liquid ammonia-water eutectic mixture, hundreds of miles thick, far below its solid surface.

And at this point we can see that even if you could arrange an ammonia (or ammonia-water) ocean, technology is going to be a problem.

Consider that with all that ice around, it will be hard to find *other* rocks—rocks for metal ores, or even just for building stone. Look again at those distant satellites in our own system, for example! Virtually all the "real" rock is buried under hundreds of miles of ice.

And even if you find some rock, getting metals out of ores will be extremely difficult. For one thing, there will be no fire! To see why, let's compare this with oxygen and water on our own world. On Earth, oxygen is split out of water by photosynthesis and accumulates in the atmosphere. So, presumably photosynthesis by ammonia-solvent life will split out nitrogen instead. But nitrogen, unlike oxygen, is almost inert chemically. Hydrogen and nitrogen *don't* burn to form ammonia the way hydrogen and oxygen burn to form water. They take a lot more coaxing than that to combine— and even then the atoms tend to come apart ("dissociate") again.

In fact, during World War I the Germans devised an expensive industrial process to make ammonia directly from hydrogen and nitrogen. The gases are forced together at high pressure and temperature, under which conditions some atoms reluctantly combine. That's in stark contrast to the way hydrogen and oxygen react to form water! [Then why did the Germans bother, especially in wartime? Because nitrogen compounds are extensively used in explosives, and Germany was cut off from nitrate imports, the previous source of nitrogen compounds, by the British blockade. Later (and still) this same process was used to synthesize fertilizers, which also contain lots of nitrogen compounds.]

And last, even if you can get metals out of rock, an ammonia-ice solution is highly corrosive toward many metals. When ice dissolves in ammonia, you get some ammonium ion ($NH_4^+$). Ammonium in ammonia is an acid; it dissolves many metals to give hydrogen. When liquid ammonia is used industrially for reactions, it's carefully freed of all dissolved water, because usually the water leads to unwanted side reactions.

Iron, for example, reacts with many ammonium salts! Hydrogen bubbles away while the iron dissolves. Now, sure, most metals don't bubble up into hydrogen right away. Although the ammonia solution will be corrosive, it generally won't react all that quickly. After all, water—especially with oxygen around—is pretty corrosive too! But even though iron rusts, it doesn't react so quickly that it's not useful on Earth. And similarly, iron (or copper, or brass) tools should last long enough to be useful in an ammonia environment.

But still, the corrosiveness of natural ammonia solutions isn't always taken into account by SF writers. And with the scarcity of any metal-bearing ores to begin with, it's unlikely an intelligent species on an ammonia world could develop any significant metalworking.

A cold world circling a red sun, trapped in a permanent Stone Age by the vagaries of the local chemistry . . . who says scientific world-building is dull?

## Nitroxy Worlds

Now let's look briefly at a completely different variation. Let's start by photodissociating all the water and assume we have a high nitrogen-to-oxygen ratio. This might eventually lead to lots of nitrogen oxides in the atmosphere—nitric oxide (NO) and nitrogen dioxide ($NO_2$). Both of these compounds are highly reactive (and highly toxic; they're major components of smog). In particular, they react easily with water to form nitric acid ($HNO_3$) and eventually nitrates. So if nitrogen oxides are abundant in the atmosphere, there won't be any free $H_2O$ around. Maybe, though, seas of nitric acid could exist—just as with seas of sulfuric acid on an oxidized, high-sulfur world.

Indeed, such a world would look a lot like the sulfuric acid world (page 168). Chemical weathering would be fierce; not many common minerals would be stable under those conditions. And this again would make it difficult for any intelligent species to develop past a Stone Age.

We know of no such world, but Mars once was speculated to have lots of nitrogen oxides in its atmosphere. A few of Niven's older stories treat such a Mars.

Of course, Earth also has lots of nitrogen in its atmosphere; almost four times the amount of oxygen (page 70). The reason the Earth didn't fall into the "nitroworld" scenario is only partly because we still have lots of surface water. Given time, the nitrogen and oxygen in our atmosphere *would* react to form nitrogen oxides and then nitrates. However, denitrifying bacteria are continually making nitrogen again from nitrogen-bearing compounds. In Hal Clement's *The Nitrogen Fix* this cycle had been destroyed. As with the "chloroxygen" world, this suggests that the dominant gases in the atmosphere of a life-bearing planet may have a lot to do with what biochemical cycles got established first.

## BRIMSTONE WORLDS

When Isaac Asimov coined the term "thalassogen" for those chemical compounds that could conceivably make oceans, he narrowed the candidates considerably by looking not just at their chemical properties but also at the abundance of their constituent elements. After all, oceans have to be made out of something reasonably common. But he overlooked some candidates, because he dismissed sulfur compounds. Although sulfur is a much rarer element than carbon, oxygen or nitrogen, under the right conditions even a fairly rare element can be concentrated by the fractionation processes in a planet, as is shown by Io (page 117). Even though the sulfur is just a thin surface veneer, a *surface* concentration is all we need to set up unusual conditions.

## The Sulfur Dioxide Sea

One sulfur-bearing candidate is sulfur dioxide, $SO_2$. Now, although some of Io's sulfur is combined into sulfur dioxide, under Io's temperatures the $SO_2$ is frozen at the surface. It's liquid only in the subsurface, where it helps drive volcanic "hot spring" type eruptions in much the same manner as water does on Earth. But maybe somewhere "out there" a somewhat bigger, warmer sulfur-world has liquid $SO_2$ right at the surface, forming lakes or even oceans. Such a world might be an even larger satellite of a giant planet. Or it might be a planet in its own right, a planet that started out rich in volatiles but that later lost most of them over geologic time.

So let's look at sulfur dioxide in more detail as a thalassogen. In many ways, it's like water (and ammonia). It also has a long liquid range (over 65°C) and a high boiling point: $-10°C$ under atmospheric pressure, and 15°C under a pressure of 2.5 atmospheres.

Sulfur dioxide is also a good solvent. In fact, just as with water or liquid ammonia, many chemical reactions can take place in liquid sulfur dioxide. Because of this, liquid sulfur dioxide is used in industry for various chemical syntheses, and for purifying hydrocarbons in oil refining.

Now for a key (and favorable) difference: As we saw for Io (page 117), sulfur dioxide, unlike water and ammonia, *isn't* vulnerable to photodissociation loss. This is how sulfur compounds can be concentrated onto a planetary surface in the first place: They're lost much less easily.

Sulfur dioxide is unlike water (but like ammonia) in another way, too: $SO_2$ ice sinks in liquid $SO_2$. But just as the fact that ammonia ice doesn't float on liquid ammonia may not be the problem that's sometimes thought, $SO_2$ ice sinking in $SO_2$ oceans may not lead to climatic disaster, either.

Sulfur dioxide has some other chemical quirks. For example, sulfur dioxide dissolves different substances than do water or ammonia, because its interactions with its solutes are quite different. So, the organic chemistry needed to build life forms in a sulfur dioxide sea will be very, very different from those in a water sea, or even from those in an ammonia sea. But that, of course, doesn't mean that life's impossible.

For another quirk, there won't be an oxygen atmosphere. $SO_2$ reacts with oxygen to give sulfur *tri*oxide, $SO_3$, which is a solid at room temperature. This reaction doesn't happen easily, but it still happens. It's done industrially here on Earth to make sulfuric acid. It also happens very slowly in our atmosphere: $SO_2$ released by volcanoes, or by coal-burning power plants from combustion of sulfur-bearing impurities in the coal, slowly turns into $SO_3$. *That* then makes acid rain when the $SO_3$ reacts with water.

So, to keep $SO_3$ from forming, however slowly, the sulfur-dioxide world will need extra sulfur around as an oxygen sink. The $SO_2$ sea will lap against shores of pure sulfur—if not everywhere, at least here and there. Io's $SO_2$ is protected in this way. Any sulfur trioxide that happens to form reacts with sulfur to make $SO_2$ again.

What *will* the atmosphere be made of, then? As I said above, hydrogen compounds will all be virtually gone, and the little bit remaining—the water, the organic compounds—will be dissolved in the $SO_2$ sea. Nitrogen gas is chemically unreactive and also fairly heavy, so it will no doubt make up some of the atmosphere. And there will also be a smidgen of the noble gases argon and (probably) neon, although helium, like hydrogen, will long since have been lost because it's so light.

But much, and probably most, of the atmosphere will also be sulfur dioxide, evaporated from the sea. This is a big difference from a water world: The compound that makes up the oceans also makes up a large part of the atmosphere! To be sure, water vapor is important in our atmosphere—it makes for most weather, of course—but it's only a minor constituent. By contrast, on the $SO_2$ world the very pressure of the air will be set by the average temperature of the oceans, because that will determine how much $SO_2$ can evaporate. At any particular temperature, vapor will evaporate from a liquid until the vapor pressure in the air reaches a certain point (page 67). On the $SO_2$ planet, the total air pressure will be pretty close to this equilibrium pressure. Thus, sulfur dioxide will behave rather like carbon dioxide on Mars (page 116).

Not having oxygen in the atmosphere also makes higher life forms improbable (page 107). Microbes and simple plants should be possible, though. Possibly a "sulfur trioxide-sulfur dioxide" cycle could power microbes. "Plants" could store energy by making sulfur trioxide, say, by some form of photosynthesis, and "animals" could react the sulfur trioxide with sulfur to give sulfur dioxide again.

In case you were going to ask, this cycle is utterly unknown for any actual living things on Earth! I've just proposed it on the basis of the chemical energy it could store. Although some Earth bacteria metabolize sulfur compounds, they do so in a very different way. Some use the oxygen from the sulfate ion ($SO_4^=$) to oxidize food while excreting hydrogen sulfide ($H_2S$) as a waste product. Others actually use the oxygen of the air to oxidize elemental sulfur or *sulfides*, direct compounds of sulfur and a metal, to generate energy. In all cases, though, such bacteria use basically the same biochemistry as ordinary Earth life; the sulfur metabolism is ancillary. Such organisms do suggest, however, the diversity that life processes can achieve.

Even if higher life forms could exist on the $SO_2$ world, developing a sophisticated technology will be a problem, because without free oxygen there will be no fire. Although $SO_2$ is a fairly reactive compound, it's not nearly so reactive as oxygen. In fact, it's just about as inconvenient as possible: $SO_2$ is just reactive enough to be pretty corrosive if you *do* manage to separate metal, yet it's not reactive enough to support a fire in the first place. For most things, anyway: certain metals, if finely enough divided, will burn in $SO_2$. They include potassium, magnesium and iron. Of course, all these will also burn in oxygen, at least under the right conditions: Try sticking a piece of steel wool in a flame sometime!

For an illustration of the problem, let's look at copper. Copper, like many familiar metals, has a high affinity for sulfur (that is, it's chalcophile; see page 48), so even on Earth most copper ores are just copper sulfides (mixed with a lot of other rock). And we'd certainly expect that copper sulfides could be present in the sulfur-world's crust. In fact, they might be a lot more common than on Earth, because there's so much sulfur around.

Now, how do we get metal out of such sulfide ores? On Earth, we start by heating the sulfides in air ("roasting," metallurgists call it). The sulfur reacts with oxygen to make sulfur dioxide, while the metal is left behind as an oxide. To free the metal, the oxide is later "cooked" with carbon; the oxygen and carbon combine to make carbon monoxide and leave the metal behind.

Obviously none of this will work if the air contains no free oxygen!

So, as with ammonia, we have the worst of both worlds: no fire, and no metal. Another world trapped in a Stone Age by the vagaries of the local chemistry.

## The Sulfuric Acid Sea

Seas of sulfuric acid ($H_2SO_4$)? That sounds completely preposterous. Sulfuric acid not only dissolves most everything in sight, it *reacts* with most everything in sight.

But on second glance the idea isn't quite so silly. Sulfuric acid is a lot like water: it's an excellent solvent, it has a high boiling point (~337°C), and it's liquid over a huge temperature range—over three times that of water.

How might such a world form? Well, just as with the $SO_2$ planet, we start with a world whose surface is sulfur-rich. This world, though, started out with a lot more oxygen than the $SO_2$ world. Consider a planet that started out relatively Earthlike, with a lot of water, but intense photodissociation by UV split up all the water vapor, so that the hydrogen escaped to space but the oxygen was left behind. Perhaps this planet orbits a hot, type F star, which puts out much more UV than the Sun. So the planet lost just its hydrogen while its oxygen was left behind, as happened in part on Mars.

Then the oxygen would sooner or later oxidize all the sulfur, not just to sulfur dioxide, but all the way to $SO_3$. *That* would then react with any remaining water to form $H_2SO_4$, sulfuric acid.

We have a partial Solar System analog of this scenario: the clouds of Venus. They're made of droplets of sulfuric acid. As Venus lost its water through photodissociation, lots of oxygen was left behind, and it oxidized sulfur to the point that sulfuric acid finally formed. Being bound up into $H_2SO_4$ droplets also preserves Venus's last smidgen of water from photodissociation. As this would also be true on a planet with $H_2SO_4$ oceans, we wouldn't lose quite *all* the hydrogen.

Of course, $H_2SO_4$ droplets in Venus's clouds are a far cry from having an $H_2SO_4$ ocean! But perhaps if Venus had started out cooler, had been less rich in $CO_2$, and had been *much* richer in sulfur, it might have sulfuric seas today too.

Obviously, the surface minerals on a planet where liquid sulfuric acid runs like water will be *very* different from Earth. Chemical weathering will be intense! Sulfuric acid reacts with most common minerals, breaking down their structures and extracting metal ions from them.

Surprisingly, we actually have an Earthly analog for such weathering, from hot spring deposits. Most terrestrial hot springs contain dissolved sulfur compounds, which oxidize into $H_2SO_4$ as they encounter oxygen near the surface. And the acidic waters then attack the rocks around them.

So we can get an idea of what the surface of an $H_2SO_4$ planet might be like by looking at hot spring minerals. As you might guess, only a few of the common minerals can resist such an acidic environment. Quartz (the common, stable form of crystalline silica, $SiO_2$) is one. Other common minerals, though, such as feldspars, crumble away. In fact they get changed into clay minerals—certain of which *are* stable, and which make up the cruddy, clayey or muddy material that's so ubiquitous in hot springs alteration. The individual crystals are so small that the material has a clay texture. Many Earthly ore deposits, by the way, are found in and around such altered rocks.

Other oxides besides quartz, which are rare minerals on Earth, might also be stable, including corundum (aluminum oxide, $Al_2O_3$). (The gem forms of corundum are more famous: they're sapphire and ruby.) Certain sulfates—salts of sulfuric acid—will also be stable, and maybe a few other salts. Not sodium chloride itself, though: the chloride in it reacts with $H_2SO_4$ to give HCl! So overall, the very rocks themselves will hardly be Earthlike.

As on the chloroxygen and nitroxy worlds, too, there will be no limestones. Again, then, carbon would have to be cycled into other compounds fast enough that a runaway greenhouse didn't develop.

This vitriolic sea will also be highly "salty": It will have dissolved lots of metal ions, to the point that nothing else can dissolve. In fact, sulfates will probably precipitate out, the way salts precipitate from extremely concentrated $H_2O$ brines on Earth such as the Great Salt Lake or the Dead Sea.

But even if some minerals could survive, could anything organic survive? Sulfuric acid reacts as enthusiastically with many organic compounds as it does with most minerals. For one thing, it dehydrates sugars to carbon and water: A standard lab demonstration is dripping $H_2SO_4$ onto a sugar cube. The cube crumbles into black carbon while steam wafts off from the heat of the reaction. It also breaks down many organic acids: Another Organic 101 demo is breaking down formic acid (HCOOH) into water and carbon monoxide by dripping sulfuric acid into a formic acid solution.

Still, $H_2SO_4$ doesn't react with *all* organic compounds. For example, alkanes (straight-chain hydrocarbons), like those in gasoline and natural gas, just bubble right through. The oil business uses this to purify them, by the way. It ionizes other organic compounds by adding a proton (hydrogen nucleus), but doesn't break them up. So this just says an alien biochemistry will need different building-block compounds. It doesn't say it's impossible.

And even if some system of organic compounds won't work, there is another interesting possibility: silicones. Of course, this class of compounds is much more famous for high-performance lubricants—not to mention starlet bosoms. But in fact they may be just the thing for a sulfuric acid environment: They're fairly stable chemically, and yet have the variety and complexity needed to be the basis of a biochemistry.

Silicones have a backbone made of alternating silicon and oxygen atoms:

$$\text{---- Si ---- O ---- Si ---- O ---- Si ----}$$

which looks just like the backbone in many silicate minerals. Unlike silicates, though, silicones are not known to occur naturally (so far, anyway).

Now, instead of the metal atoms stuck between the silicon-oxygen chains that silicates have, silicones have organic (carbon-hydrogen-oxygen) groups chains stuck onto the silicons, like this for example:

$$
\begin{array}{ccccc}
R & & R' & & R'' \\
| & & | & & | \\
\text{---- Si} & \text{---- O ----} & \text{Si} & \text{---- O ----} & \text{Si ----} \\
| & & | & & | \\
R^* & & R^{**} & & R^{***}
\end{array}
$$

where the R's and R*'s are various organic side chains. These groups need not be all the same; and for biochemicals, they certainly won't be, either! That's what gives them the variety and complexity—the information-storage capability—that may make silicones capable as serving as the basis of life.

H. Beam Piper's *Uller Uprising* proposed a silicone-based bio-chemistry, but the chemistry was wrong. The story suggested that silicones were favored evolutionarily because the planet was unusually silica-rich, but it would be hard to find a planet richer in silicon than the Earth itself (page 55).

In fact, silicates are very stable under the usual Earth-type conditions. To break them up—and keep them broken up—requires pretty rigorous chemical conditions. But "rigorous chemical conditions" is a good description of a sulfuric-acid environment! $H_2SO_4$ is capable of breaking up silicate minerals, and under such conditions silicones may have a chance of forming out of the debris.

As we saw, too, the sulfuric-acid planet will also be a highly oxidized planet. So, if some organism evolved oxygen-releasing photosynthesis, the atmosphere could accumulate free oxygen. Sulfuric acid is hardly going to burn! This is completely different from the $SO_2$ case, in which free oxygen can't accumulate. Maybe, therefore, something like the highly oxygen-rich atmosphere of Earth could evolve, to support complex, multicellular organisms like Earthly metazoans.

But even if intelligent life arises, it'll have *big* problems with technology. As on the chloroxygen and nitroxy worlds, what is it going to do for metal? Most metals react spectacularly with sulfuric acid. So any intelligent beings on the sulfuric acid planet are likely to be stuck there forever. Just as with the Clorox world, it's a way to get stuck in the Stone Age by the vagaries of the local chemistry. . . .

### Other Sulfur Worlds?

Hydrogen sulfide—the toxic, rotten-egg gas—is not likely, because it has a very low boiling point, and it's also easily broken up by UV light. But a more exotic idea yet would be molten sulfur itself as a thalassogen! Obviously such a world would be very hot, and thus a biochemistry may be difficult to arrange. But Io, with its sulfur lavas, may be an example, at least in places.

### CARBON (AND IRON?) WORLDS

Such worlds have more carbon than oxygen, so organic matter is left over once you make all the carbon dioxide or carbonate you can. Most nitrogen is present as gas, and there may be lots of water, too.

Saturn's giant moon Titan is a deep-freeze version. It's full of organic matter underneath that smoggy, nitrogen-rich air. So warm up a Titan, and what would you get? A mess! Titan is mostly ice underneath its surface. When it melted, we'd get a vastly deep, scummy sea. A very wet world indeed, but one with no free oxygen.

More interesting would be a carbon world without such an over-whelming amount of water. With a carbon-rich surface, obviously there's no oxygen atmosphere! But there should be water, hydro-carbons, nitrogen, even a little carbon dioxide in the air. All in all, we end up with something that looks like an anaerobic environment on Earth. And obviously a biochemistry could work just with fer-mentation reactions, the rearrangement of organic molecules to extract energy, as is done by many Earthly microbes.

As I said, a water ocean would be OK on a carbon world, but for something a bit more exotic, what about hydrocarbons instead? Seas of gasoline or kerosene! Liquid ethane ($C_2H_6$) may exist on Titan, and Isaac Asimov once proposed methane ($CH_4$—the sim-plest hydrocarbon) as a possible thalassogen. And Venus once was proposed to have massive amounts of hydrocarbons, too, some of which made up its clouds. So the idea's been kicking around for a while.

The problem with hydrocarbons, though, at least on a body rela-tively close to its sun, is that they're photodissociated easily. So they'll tend to be destroyed over geologic time (in retrospect, of course, this was a naive aspect of the Venus proposal).

Now, considering photodissociation also shows a big problem in forming a carbon world in the first place. If all the volatiles get "rendered down" by photodissociation to carbon-rich compounds, how do you get rid of the water while keeping other hydrogen compounds? As with hydrocarbons, other hydrogen compounds are photodissociated much more easily than water! And as we've seen, when you photodissociate water you leave behind the oxy-gen—and that makes the environment oxidizing.

### The Ironworld: "Cannonball"

So here's an even more exotic possibility: the ironworld. Suppose a *very* large impact blows off nearly all the rock from a fully formed planet, leaving just the iron core. (What happened to Mercury, only more so.) Metallic iron leads to a highly "reducing" (i.e., not oxidiz-ing) environment, so that carbon, hydrocarbons and such are stable. Even if there's not much left in the way of volatiles after the impact, surely smaller impacts by things like comets will plaster on more volatiles later. As far as that goes, some carbon will come dissolved in the iron.

So, now we have a solid body that will maintain a chemically reducing environment over geologic time. All that extra iron will soak up any excess oxygen, such as any made by water photodissociation.

We have another problem, though: Iron and water aren't stable together, at least over geologic time. Sure, we know iron rusts, especially if water's around, but that's basically a reaction with the oxygen in the air. But given time, iron will actually rip the oxygen out of water, leaving hydrogen behind.

Therefore, we need to find the ironworld (obviously its name is Cannonball!) a new thalassogen. Here's a suggestion that's untried in SF, so far as I know: oceans (well, lakes, anyway) of iron carbonyl (pronounced carbon-EEL), maybe containing some nickel carbonyl as well. (A "carbonyl" is a chemical compound of carbon monoxide.) At temperatures a bit above the boiling point of water (and under pressure) five molecules of carbon monoxide will react with one atom of iron to form iron pentacarbonyl, $Fe(CO)_5$. Similarly, four molecules of CO react with one atom of nickel to make nickel tetracarbonyl, $Ni(CO)_4$.

These bizarre compounds, members of a whole class of compounds formed by many metals, are highly volatile. Iron pentacarbonyl is a yellow liquid at room temperature that melts at $-10°C$ and boils about 103°C. Nickel carbonyl is even more volatile, boiling at 43°C. (Both compounds are also dreadfully toxic to terrestrial animals.)

Carbonyls decompose easily with heat. This is useful in some industrial processes: carbonyl decomposition can be used to purify iron or nickel, or to vapor-deposit very thin coats of the metals. It's a lot easier to move carbonyl vapor around, at only 100°C or so, than it is to move vaporized Fe or Ni metal at 3000°C or so!

And even though their thermal instability means carbonyls are easily photodissociated, that's not a big problem: Unlike hydrogen, carbon and oxygen are heavy atoms, so they won't be lost from the upper atmosphere.

Carbonyls aren't really stable, since carbon monoxide isn't really stable at low temperatures (as noted below). But volcanism on Cannonball will continually make CO, as long as the world is big enough to have ongoing volcanism; then, as the CO cools it will form carbonyls by reacting with all that iron and nickel. There's evidence of iron carbonyl formation in lunar lavas, so it can happen naturally. The lunar lavas actually have little crystals of iron metal in them, some of which looks to have been vapor-deposited from iron carbonyl.

So a steady-state system with a carbonyl ocean might work. And if living things *also* are making CO, that could stabilize the carbonyl oceans even more.

Here's a suggestion for a biochemical energy-storage mechanism based on carbon monoxide, CO. It's a little-realized fact, at least to non-chemists, that at room temperature and pressure carbon monoxide is unstable. It "wants" to react with itself like this:

$$2\ CO = C + CO_2$$

Under ordinary conditions, this reaction releases some sixty kilojoules of energy for every twenty-eight grams of carbon monoxide. The only reason it doesn't happen quickly—boom!—is that at ordinary temperatures the reaction rates are extremely slow.

(This reaction, which metallurgists call the "Boudouard reaction," can be a big problem in metallurgy, by the way. At modestly elevated temperatures the reaction *does* proceed: In fact, it goes like gangbusters and drops out a mess of solid carbon all over the place. This is called "sooting out" and is considered a no-no in such things as iron smelting.)

As you might guess, carbon monoxide *is* stable at high temperatures. That's why it's formed in combustion. It's made in the flame, and the flame gases cool so quickly (are "quenched") that the CO doesn't have time to react further. [And that's why CO is abundant in comets, too, at least to judge by the Halley data. The CO probably originally formed in a hot, thin gas cloud, such as one left by a supernova explosion, and has been preserved in "deep freeze" ever since. Comets are most likely leftover debris from our Solar System's formation that have been little altered since (page 109).]

Anyway, for comparison, fermenting glucose to lactic acid—a standard anaerobic respiration on Earth—releases only about nine kilojoules for every twenty-eight grams of glucose. So a photosynthesis that stores energy by making CO—and a metabolism that gets the energy back by making C and $CO_2$ from the CO—is not immediately ridiculous.

## EXOTICA

I'll conclude with some brief examples of outré worlds indeed. They're ruled by the same physical laws, but in much more unusual manifestations. With the background given in this book, you can appreciate what goes into such settings, and although designing such worlds lies outside the scope of this book, it will give you a start—or at least something to approach a grad student with!

Many years ago Hal Clement set a classic story *on* a brown dwarf (though that term wasn't then used) in his *Mission of Gravity*. To make the setting even more unusual, the brown dwarf, Mesklin, was rotating so rapidly as to cause extreme differences in surface gravity from the equator to the poles. For this reason the world was also highly distorted from a spherical shape. Even though Mesklin subsequently proved to have many details wrong (at the time Clement designed it, computers were hardly household appliances!) it remains a tour de force, and his essay "Whirligig World" on designing Mesklin is still well worth reading. It's been reprinted as an appendix in many editions of *Mission of Gravity*. The Mesklinites subsequently appeared in another novel, *Star Light*, on another intricate and highly un-Earthly planet.

Another unusual large world might be a "shriveled" gas giant. When the planet's parent star swells into a red giant, the extreme increase in luminosity might drive off most of the hydrogen and helium to leave a very different sort of world. For one thing, this might be an alternative way to get an atmosphere rich in neon. John Barnes, in *A Million Open Doors*, suggested such a scenario in passing, but so far as I know no one has used it in detail.

"Rogue planets," not associated with a star, have figured in stories such as Poul Anderson's *Satan's World* and "A Sun Invisible." Whether planets could accrete independently of a star is currently unknown. However, gravitational interactions in planetary systems will occasionally expel planets, especially during the chaotic time of late accretion, simply by happenstance—and such worlds might well be rocky instead of icy. They are another underutilized setting.

And last, Robert L. Foward's novels *Dragon's Egg* and *Starquake*, which postulate life on a neutron star, remain classics, although perhaps a bit far afield from classical world-building!

| | Mercury | Venus | Earth | Mars | (Ceres) | Jupiter | Saturn | Uranus | Neptune | Pluto |
|---|---|---|---|---|---|---|---|---|---|---|
| Mean distance from Sun (AU) | 0.387 | 0.723 | 1.0000 | 1.524 | 2.767 | 5.203 | 9.539 | 19.182 | 30.058 | 39.44 |
| (million km) | 57.9 | 108.2 | 149.6 | 227.9 | 413.9 | 778.3 | 1427 | 2869.6 | 4496.6 | 5900.1 |
| Year length (revolution period) (Earth days) | 89.97 | 224.7 | 365.26 | 686.98 | | | | | | |
| (Earth years) | 0.24 | 0.62 | 1.0000 | 1.88 | 4.6 | 11.86 | 29.46 | 84.02 | 164.78 | 248.4 |
| Tilt of orbit (°) | 7 | 3.39 | 0 | 1.85 | 9.7 | 1.3 | 2.49 | 0.77 | 1.77 | 17.2 |
| Eccentricity of orbit | 0.21 | 0.01 | 0.02 | 0.09 | 0.097 | 0.0485 | 0.0556 | 0.0472 | 0.0086 | 0.25 |
| Tilt of axis to orbit (°) | 0 | -2.6 | 23.5 | 24 | | 3 | 27 | 98.4 | 29 | 94 |
| Diameter (km) | 4878 | 12102 | 12756 | 6796 | | 139800 | 116900 | 50700 | 49100 | 3000 |
| (Earth = 1) | 0.38 | 0.95 | 1.0000 | 0.53 | | 10.96 | 9.16 | 3.98 | 3.85 | 0.24 |
| Mass ($10^{23}$ kg) | 3.3 | 48.7 | 59.8 | 6.42 | | 19000 | 5690 | 869 | 1030 | 0.135 |
| (Earth = 1) | 0.06 | 0.82 | 1.0000 | 0.11 | | 318.05 | 95.15 | 14.54 | 17.16 | 0.0021 |
| Density (Earth = 1) | 0.98 | 0.95 | 1 | 0.71 | | 0.24 | 0.13 | 0.23 | 0.30 | 0.16 |
| (g/cm³) | 5.42 | 5.24 | 5.52 | 3.94 | | 1.33 | 0.68 | 1.27 | 1.65 | 0.89 |
| Surface gravity (Earth = 1) | 0.38 | 0.91 | 1.00 | 0.38 | | 2.65 | 1.13 | 0.92 | 1.16 | 0.04 |
| (m/sec²) | 3.70 | 8.87 | 9.80 | 3.71 | | 25.93 | 11.10 | 9.02 | 11.39 | 0.40 |
| Escape velocity (km/sec) | 4.25 | 10.36 | 11.18 | 5.02 | | 60.20 | 36.03 | 21.38 | 23.65 | 1.10 |
| (Earth = 1) | 0.38 | 0.93 | 1.00 | 0.45 | | 5.38 | 3.22 | 1.91 | 2.12 | 0.10 |
| Rotation rate (sidereal day) (Earth days) | 58.65 | 243.01 | 0.99727 | 1.025954 | | | | | | 6.38755 |
| (hours) | | | 23.9345 | 24.6229 | | 9.92 | 10.66 | 17.24 | 16.11 | |
| Solar day (Earth days) | 175.974 | 116.7486 | 1.0000 | 1.0275 | | | | | | |
| (hours) | | | 24.0000 | 24.6597 | | 9.92 | 10.66 | 17.24 | 16.11 | 6.38 |
| Number of known natural satellites: | 0 | 0 | 1 | 2 | 0 | 16 | 17 | 15 | 8 | 1 |

| Satellite<br>Planet | Moon<br>Earth | Io<br>Jupiter | Europa<br>Jupiter | Ganymede<br>Jupiter | Callisto<br>Jupiter | Titan<br>Saturn | Triton<br>Neptune |
|---|---|---|---|---|---|---|---|
| Mean distance from planet<br>($10^3$ km) | 384.4 | 421.6 | 670.9 | 1070 | 1883 | 1221.85 | 354.8 |
| Month (revolution period)<br>(Earth days) | 27.3217 | 1.769 | 3.551 | 7.155 | 16.689 | 15.945 | 5.877 |
| Tilt of orbit to planet (°) | 5.15 | 0.04 | 0.47 | 0.195 | 0.281 | 0.33 | 23 |
| Eccentricity of orbit | 0.0549 | 0.0041 | 0.0101 | 0.0006 | 0.007 | 0.0292 | 0 |
| Diameter | | | | | | | |
| (Earth = 1) | 0.27 | 0.28 | 0.25 | 0.41 | 0.38 | 0.4 | 0.42 |
| (km) | 3476 | 3630 | 3138 | 5262 | 4800 | 5150 | 2705 |
| Mass | | | | | | | |
| (Earth = 1) | 0.012 | 0.015 | 0.008 | 0.025 | 0.018 | 0.023 | 0.004 |
| ($10^{22}$ kg) | 7.35 | 8.94 | 4.8 | 14.8 | 10.8 | 13.5 | 2.14 |
| Density | | | | | | | |
| (Earth = 1) | 0.61 | 0.65 | 0.54 | 0.35 | 0.34 | 0.34 | 0.38 |
| ($g/cm^3$) | 3.34 | 3.57 | 2.97 | 1.94 | 1.86 | 1.88 | 2.07 |
| Surface gravity | | | | | | | |
| (Earth = 1) | 0.17 | 0.18 | 0.13 | 0.15 | 0.13 | 0.14 | 0.08 |
| ($m/sec^2$) | 1.62 | 1.81 | 1.30 | 1.43 | 1.25 | 1.36 | 0.78 |
| Equatorial escape velocity | | | | | | | |
| (Earth = 1) | 0.21 | 0.23 | 0.18 | 0.24 | 0.22 | 0.24 | 0.13 |
| (km/sec) | 2.37 | 2.56 | 2.02 | 2.74 | 2.45 | 2.64 | 1.45 |
| Rotation rate (sidereal period) | 27.322 | 1.769 | 3.551 | 7.155 | 16.689 | 15.945 | 5.877 |

**TABLE 1a, b** Data on the Planets of the Solar System, and the Seven Large Satellites. Data adapted and recalculated from various sources, including Danby, Beatty et al., the two *Planetary Satellites* volumes in the University of Arizona Space Science series, and (for Neptune and Triton) E.C. Stone and E.D Miner in *Science*, 15 Dec. 1989.

| Spec Type | B-V | $T_{eff}$ (K) | Absolute Magnitude Vis. | Absolute Magnitude Bol. | Bolo. Corr. (BC) | Lum. | R | M | ρ (g/cm³) | Lifetime (years) |
|---|---|---|---|---|---|---|---|---|---|---|
| O5 | −0.35 | 40000 | −5.8 | −10.0 | −4.2 | 810000 | 18.7 | 35.9 | 0.008 | $4.4 \times 10^5$ |
| B0 | −0.30 | 30000 | −4.3 | −7.2 | −2.9 | 61000 | 9.2 | 18.2 | 0.033 | $3.0 \times 10^6$ |
| B5 | −0.16 | 16000 | −1.1 | −2.5 | −1.5 | 810 | 3.7 | 5.8 | 0.16 | $7.2 \times 10^7$ |
| A0 | 0.00 | 10000 | 0.8 | 0.3 | −0.5 | 64 | 2.7 | 3.0 | 0.22 | $4.7 \times 10^8$ |
| A2 | 0.06 | 9700 | 1.2 | 0.9 | −0.3 | 35 | 2.10 | 2.6 | 0.39 | $7.2 \times 10^8$ |
| A5 | 0.14 | 8600 | 1.9 | 1.6 | −0.3 | 19 | 1.94 | 2.16 | 0.42 | $1.2 \times 10^9$ |
| A7 | 0.20 | 8100 | 2.1 | 1.9 | −0.2 | 14 | 1.90 | 2.01 | 0.41 | $1.4 \times 10^9$ |
| F0 | 0.31 | 7300 | 2.6 | 2.5 | −0.1 | 8.5 | 1.82 | 1.75 | 0.41 | $2.1 \times 10^9$ |
| F2 | 0.38 | 6900 | 2.9 | 2.9 | 0.0 | 5.6 | 1.65 | 1.57 | 0.49 | $2.8 \times 10^9$ |
| F5 | 0.44 | 6600 | 3.3 | 3.3 | 0.0 | 3.9 | 1.50 | 1.43 | 0.59 | $3.7 \times 10^9$ |
| F7 | 0.50 | 6300 | 3.8 | 3.8 | 0.0 | 2.4 | 1.31 | 1.27 | 0.79 | $5.2 \times 10^9$ |
| G0 | 0.59 | 6000 | 4.4 | 4.4 | 0.0 | 1.4 | 1.10 | 1.09 | 1.17 | $7.8 \times 10^9$ |
| G2 | 0.64 | 5770 | 4.7 | 4.7 | 0.0 | 1.07 | 1.03 | 1.02 | 1.30 | $9.5 \times 10^9$ |
| G5 | 0.69 | 5600 | 5.1 | 5.0 | −0.1 | 0.81 | 0.95 | 0.95 | 1.53 | $1.2 \times 10^{10}$ |
| G8 | 0.72 | 5400 | 5.5 | 5.3 | −0.2 | 0.61 | 0.89 | 0.88 | 1.73 | $1.4 \times 10^{10}$ |
| K0 | 0.84 | 5200 | 5.9 | 5.8 | −0.2 | 0.41 | 0.78 | 0.79 | 2.31 | $1.9 \times 10^{10}$ |
| K2 | 0.92 | 4800 | 6.3 | 6.1 | −0.2 | 0.29 | 0.78 | 0.72 | 2.13 | $2.5 \times 10^{10}$ |
| K5 | 1.17 | 4400 | 7.4 | 6.6 | −0.8 | 0.19 | 0.74 | 0.64 | 2.23 | $3.5 \times 10^{10}$ |
| K7 | 1.34 | 4200 | 8.1 | 7.2 | −0.9 | 0.11 | 0.62 | 0.55 | 3.34 | $5.2 \times 10^{10}$ |
| M0 | 1.43 | 3900 | 8.8 | 7.8 | −1.0 | 0.061 | 0.54 | 0.48 | 4.24 | $7.8 \times 10^{10}$ |
| M2 | 1.52 | 3500 | 10.1 | 8.3 | −1.8 | 0.039 | 0.53 | 0.42 | 3.92 | $1.1 \times 10^{11}$ |
| M4 | 1.56 | 3200 | 11.1 | 8.8 | −2.3 | 0.024 | 0.51 | 0.38 | 4.04 | $1.5 \times 10^{11}$ |
| M6 | 1.62 | 2900 | 12.1 | 9.5 | −2.6 | 0.013 | 0.45 | 0.32 | 4.97 | $2.5 \times 10^{11}$ |
| M8 | 1.90 | 2500 | 16.0 | 11.8 | −4.2 | 0.0015 | 0.21 | 0.18 | 28.03 | $1.2 \times 10^{12}$ |

**TABLE 2** Some Properties of Main Sequence Stars. Headings are: *Spec. Type*, spectral type; *B-V*, color index, a value closely related to the spectral type and effective temperature; $T_{eff}$, effective temperature in kelvins; *Absolute Magnitude*, magnitude from a standard distance of ten parsecs; *Vis.*, visual magnitude; *Bol.*, bolometric magnitude; *Bolo. Corr. (BC)*, bolometric correction, added to the visual magnitude to get the bolometric magnitude; *Lum.*, luminosity (Sun = 1); *R*, radius (Sun = 1); *M*, mass (Sun = 1); ρ, density in grams per cubic centimeter; *Lifetime*, approximate lifetime on the Main Sequence, assuming the Sun's total life is $10^{10}$ years. Data adapted and recalculated from Allen, Lang and Swihart (see References).

# GLOSSARY

*absolute magnitude:* The brightness of a star from a standard distance of ten parsecs; *see* magnitude, absolute.

*accretion:* The processes by which planets form from a nebula around a star.

*albedo:* The reflectivity of a surface, from 0 for perfect absorber to 1 for perfect reflector.

*amino acids:* Compounds that are the "building blocks" of proteins.

*angular momentum:* A measure of the amount of "spin" in a physical system.

*apparent magnitude:* The brightness of a star as actually observed.

*atomic number:* The number of protons in an atomic nucleus.

*atomic weight:* Approximately the mass number (q.v.) of an atomic nucleus.

*basalt:* A dark volcanic rock relatively rich in iron, calcium and magnesium.

*binary stars:* Physical systems of two stars orbiting each other.

*black hole:* A mass whose gravity is so intense that not even light can escape.

*blackbody radiation:* Electromagnetic radiation emitted by an object merely because it's hot.

*bolometric magnitude:* Magnitude over all wavelengths, not just visible ones.

*brown dwarfs:* Bodies much larger than planets, but still too small to carry out continuous nuclear fusion in their cores.

*Cambrian:* Geologic period between about 540 to 510 million years ago, the beginning of the classic fossil record.

*carbonates:* Compounds containing the carbonate group, $CO_3^=$, which can be thought of as containing $CO_2$ in chemical combination with an oxide.

*carbonyls:* Compounds of CO and (usually) a metal atom.

*centrifugal "force":* The radially outward acceleration in a spinning reference frame.

*chalcophile elements:* Elements with an affinity for sulfur.

*chlorophyll:* The green pigment in plants that absorbs sunlight to carry out photosynthesis.

*chloroplasts:* The organelles (q.v.) in the cells of higher plants that carry out photosynthesis.

*convection:* The movement of heat by overturning that is induced by density differences between the hot and cool material.

*Coriolis effect:* A "sideways" push felt by a moving object in a spinning reference frame.

*Cretaceous:* Geologic period extending from about 145 to 65 million years ago that ended with the extinction of the dinosaurs.

*density:* Mass per unit volume.

*eclipses:* The obscuring of one celestial body by another.

*Eddington limit:* Maximum mass of a star (about one hundred Suns).

*effective temperature:* Temperature of a blackbody that radiates the same amount.

*elongation:* Angle between a planet and the Sun.

*epeiric seas:* Shallow seas covering a continent.

*eukaryotes:* Organisms having efficient oxygen-using cells with a discrete nucleus and specialized organelles.

*euxinic:* A sea whose deep water is anoxic.

*giant molecular cloud (GMC):* A vast diffuse "cloud" in interstellar space in which the gas is more concentrated than usual and so combined into molecules; star and planet formation result from the collapse and coalescence of a GMC.

*halogens:* "Salt-formers," group of chemical elements including fluorine and chlorine.

*hot spots:* Volcanoes on a terrestrial planet resulting from a long thin plume convecting from deep in the planet's underlying mantle.

*Ice Line:* Point in solar nebula where water ice became stable.

*ignimbrite (welded tuff):* Igneous rock deposited as extremely hot particles from erupted cloud (a nuee ardente, q.v.).

*inferior planet:* Planet with an orbit inside the Earth's.

*infrared light (IR):* Invisible light with wavelengths longer than red.

*insolation:* Amount of sunlight arriving on a surface.

*ions:* Atoms electrically charged due to gaining or losing electrons.

*isostasy:* Principle that high points on a planet are buoyed up by lighter rock beneath.

*isotopes:* Nuclei with the same number of protons but different numbers of neutrons, so that their chemical properties are nearly identical.

*Jovian planets:* Large gaseous planets far from the central star with many satellites and, commonly, rings.

*late heavy bombardment:* Intense bombardment by leftover planetesimals late in planetary accretion (but very early in Solar System history).

*light year:* Distance light travels in a year, approximately ten trillion kilometers or six trillion miles.

*lithophile elements:* "Rock-loving" elements, which have a strong affinity for oxygen and are found in the silicates and oxides making up common rocks.

*lithosphere:* Outer solid part of Earth consisting of crust and uppermost mantle that moves as discrete plates.

*Local Group:* The small group of loosely associated galaxies to which the Milky Way belongs.

*luminosity:* The amount of electromagnetic radiation a luminous object is out-putting.

*magma:* Molten rock within the Earth or other planet, called lava if it breaches the surface.

*magnitude:* Brightness of an astronomical object.

*main sequence:* Zone of stars "burning" hydrogen as their nuclear fuel.

*mass number:* Number of protons and neutrons in an atomic nucleus.

*mass-luminosity law:* Relation between mass and luminosity for main se-quence stars.

*Milankovich variations:* Cyclic changes in Earth's orbit resulting from pertur-bations.

*minerals:* The natural chemical compounds that make up rocks.

*mitochondria:* Organelles in eukaryotic cells that carry out respiration.

*neutron star:* Dead core left by a supernova explosion consisting of nuclear matter held together by gravity, more massive than the Sun but only a few kilometers across.

*neutrons:* The massive but electrically neutral particles in an atomic nucleus.

*nitrates:* Compounds containing the nitrate group $NO_3{}^-$

*novas:* Periodic exploding stars that are part of a red giant/white dwarf pair.

*nuee ardente:* "Glowing cloud," an erupted cloud of very hot gas with en-grained volcanic particles that may be molten; the source of ignimbrites.

*obliquity:* The tilt of a planet's axis with respect to its orbit.

*organelles:* Small separate structures incorporated in eukaryotic cells that carry out specialized functions.

*outer satellites:* Small, distant satellites that are probably captured asteroids.

*outgassing:* The release of volatiles from a planet in volcanic gases.

*parallax:* The shift in apparent position of an object as viewed from different places against a much more distant background.

*parsec:* A distance of 326 light years (*par*allax of one *se*cond).

*partial pressure:* The proportion of pressure due to a single gaseous contin-uent in a mixture, equal to the gas's proportion in the mixture.

*perturbations:* Changes in orbits due to the gravitational effects of other bodies.

*photodissociation:* The breaking up of a molecule by light, typically ultraviolet light.

*planetary nebulas:* The envelopes of gas blown off the cores of dying red giants.

*planetesimals:* Small "protoplanets" that grew as intermediates in planetary accretion.

*plasma:* A hot, electrically conducting gas consisting of a mixture of ions and free electrons (as star stuff).

*plate tectonics:* The dominant tectonics of Earth, in which the jostling of the edges of huge rigid plates of lithosphere (q.v.) causes most mountain-building and earthquakes.

*precession:* The "wobbling" of an axis of rotation.

*pressure:* Force per unit area.

*prograde:* Said of rotation or satellite revolution in the same direction as the planet revolves around the Sun.

*prokaryotes:* Single-celled organisms with more primitive cells containing dispersed genetic material and no specialized organelles; bacteria and cyanobacteria.

*proton:* The massive positively charged atomic particle that is a main constituent of atomic nuclei.

*r-process:* A nucleosynthetic process in which neutrons are added rapidly to preexisting "seed" nuclei.

*radioactivity:* The phenomenon by which unstable nuclei change into more stable forms with the release of energy.

*radius vector:* The line connecting primary and secondary masses in an orbit.

*red dwarfs:* Small, type M main sequence stars, redder than the Sun but not truly "red" to the eye.

*red giants:* Large aged stars, not truly "red," that have swelled greatly due to the accumulation of helium "ash" in their cores.

*refractory:* Said of materials with high melting and boiling points; opposite of "volatile."

*regressions, marine:* Low-stands of sea level.

*regular satellites:* Satellites that lie in the orbital plane of their parent planet and seem to form as a by-product of accretion.

*resonance:* The amplification or stabilization of motion when a driving force occurs nearly at the frequency at which the system would naturally oscillate (as with pushing a child on a swing).

*retrograde:* Said of rotating or satellite revolution in the opposite sense to that of the planet's orbit around the Sun.

*Roche's limit:* Limit within which a satellite is unstable to disruption by tidal forces.

*rogue planets:* Planets unassociated with a star.

*runaway glaciation:* A glaciation that amplifies itself uncontrollably due to the increasing albedo and consequent loess effective heating as the icecap grows.

*runaway greenhouse:* A greenhouse effect that amplifies out of control because of the increasing efficiency of the greenhouse as temperatures rise, as more and more greenhouse gases enter the atmosphere from the increased evaporation.

*"scumworld":* Planet on which only microbial life exists.

*sidereal day:* True rotation period of a planet.

*siderophile elements:* "Iron-loving" elements that tend to dissolve in the iron fraction because they're not easily oxidized.

*silicates:* Compounds of metals with a silicon-oxygen "backbone" that include nearly all important rock-forming minerals.

*solar day:* The time between successive appearances of the Sun at the same place in the sky.

*solar flare:* A gigantic eruption of high-energy subatomic particles from the Sun.

*solar wind:* A tenuous stream of subatomic particles continually emanating from the Sun.

*Stefan-Boltzmann law:* The physical law describing the total amount of radiation output by a blackbody.

*stellar winds:* A "solar wind" from another star.

*superior planet:* A planet with an orbit outside the Earth's.

*supernovas:* Gigantic explosions of super-massive stars at the end of their lives.

*superplumes:* Huge plumes of magma rising from deep in Earth's mantle.

*T-Tauri stage (of a forming star):* An intense stellar wind from a forming star.

*terrestrial (rocky) planets:* Small planets of rock and metal with thin atmospheres and few satellites that are near the central star.

*thalassogen:* A compound that can form oceans (from Greek "sea-former," coined by Isaac Asimov).

*tidal braking:* The slowing of rotation by tidal effects.

*tidal bulge:* The symmetric distortion raised by a tide on a body.

*tidal locking:* The stable locking of rotation by tidal action; the end result of tidal braking.

*transgressions, marine:* A rise in sea level.

*Trojan point:* The L-4 or L-5 "Lagrange" point, two stable positions for a third body that form equilateral triangles with a primary and secondary mass.

*two-body problem:* The basic orbit of one body around another under the influence of gravity.

*ultraviolet light (UV):* Invisible light with wavelengths shorter than violet.

*visible magnitude:* The magnitude (brightness) in visible wavelengths only.

*volatiles:* Compounds with low melting and boiling points that make up atmospheres and oceans.

*white dwarfs:* Tiny "dead" stars, the relict cores of red giants in which nuclear fusion has ceased.

*X-ray stars:* "Stars" outputting a great deal of energy as X rays.

# REFERENCES AND RESOURCES

As you no doubt have guessed, a book like this can aspire to no more than just "hitting the high spots" in a subject as broad as planetary science. The published literature on planetary science subjects has exploded in the last twenty-five years, too, from the results from space probes, improved ground-based studies and the revolution in the Earth sciences. So it can be a bit intimidating to approach, especially since so much information is squirreled away in specialist journals. Here, therefore, is a thumbnail sketch of *some* (by no means all!) references to start with if you need further information.

## GENERAL PLANETARY PHYSICS

Anderson, Don, *Theory of the Earth*, Blackwell Scientific Publications, 1989.

Bott, M.H.P., *The Interior of the Earth: Its Structure, Constitution and Evolution*, Elsevier, 1982.

Stacey, F.D., *Physics of the Earth*, 3rd ed., Brookfield Press, Kenmore, Queensland, Australia, 1992.

## GEOLOGY AND METEOROLOGY

Stanley, Steven M., *Exploring Earth and Life Through Time*, W.H. Freeman & Co., 1993. (*This is a textbook I've used in teaching historical geology that gives a current overview of the history of the Earth.*)

Wells, Neil, *The Atmosphere and Ocean: A Physical Introduction*, Taylor & Francis, 1986.

Lewis, John S., & Ronald G. Prinn, *Planets and Their Atmospheres: Origin and Evolution*, Academic Press, 1984.

Walker, J.C.G., *Evolution of the Atmosphere*, Macmillan, New York, 1977, 318 pp.

## PLANETARY GEOLOGY

Beatty, J. Kelly, and Andrew Chaikin, eds., *The New Solar System*, 3rd. ed., Sky Publishing Corp., Cambridge, MA, 1990, 224 pp. (*Consists of good overviews, each by a scientist expert on the subject.*)

Broecker, Wallace S., *How to Build a Habitable Planet*, 2nd. ed., Lamont-Doherty Geophysical Observatory, Palisades, New York, 1990. (*A guide to building an Earthlike planet by a noted geochemist.*)

Carr, M.H., R.S. Saunders, R.G. Strom, and D.E. Wilhelms, *The Geology of the*

*Terrestrial Planets*, NASA SP-469, 1984.

Chapman, Clark R., *Planets of Rock and Ice*, Scribner's, 1982.

Dole, Stephen H., *Planets for Man* (*Probably the first serious attempt at determining what makes up an Earthlike planet, but parts are now very dated, as it came out both before the plate tectonics revolution and the avalanche of planetary data from space probes.*)

Gillett, S.L., "Carbonosis: Organic Desiccation and the Fermi Paradox," *Analog*, pp. 74-84, Mar. 1993. (*This outlines the "carbonosis" scenario in detail.*)

Greeley, R., *Planetary Landscapes*, Allen & Unwin, 1987.

Hughes, David W., "Evolution of the Universe, Stars and Planets," in *Evolution and the Fossil Record*, K. Allen & D. Briggs, eds., Belhaven Press, London, 1989.

Melosh, H.J., *Impact Cratering: A Geologic Process*, Oxford U. Press, 1988. (*Now the definitive treatise on meteorite impact and its effects.*)

Murray, B.C., M.C. Malin, and R. Greeley, *Earthlike Planets: Surfaces of Mercury, Venus, Earth, Moon, Mars*, W.H. Freeman & Co., 1981, 387 pp.

Newsom, Horton E., and John H. Jones, eds., *Origin of the Earth*, Oxford University Press & Lunar and Planetary Institute, 1990.

Weaver, H.A., and L.A. Danly, eds., *The Formation and Evolution of Planetary Systems*, Cambridge Univ. Press, 1989. See George Wetherill's paper especially.

And last but hardly least, the twenty-odd volumes in the University of Arizona's marvelous Space Science series. These are collections of technical papers by experts in the field, and although they might be a bit intimidating, at least a few papers in each volume are "review papers," which give an overview of a subject. Titles include specific volumes devoted to particular Solar System bodies [e.g., *Mercury, Venus, Mars, Asteroids* (*I* and *II*), *Jupiter, Uranus* and *Comets*]. They also include more general topics of great potential SF interest, such as *The Galaxy and the Solar System, Saturn Satellites, Origin and Evolution of Planetary and Satellite Atmospheres, Near-Earth Resources*, etc., and on planetary system formation [*Protostars and Planets* (*I, II* and *III*); *Meteorites and the Early Solar System*].

## THE MOON

Cadogan, Peter, *The Moon—Our Sister Planet*, Cambridge Univ. Press, 1981.

Hartman, Phillips, & Taylor, eds., *Origin of the Moon*, Lunar and Planetary Institute, 1986.

Heiken, G., D. Vaniman, & B.M. French, eds., *Lunar Sourcebook: A User's Guide to the Moon*, Cambridge Univ. Press, 1991.

Taylor, S.R., *Lunar Science: A Post-Apollo View*, Pergamon, 1975.

————, *Planetary Science: A Lunar Perspective*, Lunar and Planetary Institute, Houston, 1982.

Wilhelms, D.E., *The Geologic History of the Moon*, U.S. Geological Survey, Professional Paper 1348, 1987.

**Hidden resources.** Useful results can be buried in unlikely places, too. One thing to remember when looking for planetary references is that, as an astronomy graduate student put it to me when I was a geology grad student, the planets have changed hands in the last thirty years. Most of the new studies on planetary science are showing up in the *geological* technical literature, rather than the astronomy literature. (In other words, *real* astronomers don't do planets!)

So, journals to watch (besides *Science* and *Nature*, the two general "overview" technical publications) include:

*The Journal of Geophysical Research*, especially the new "Planets" section.

*Reviews of Geophysics*

*Earth and Planetary Science Letters*

*Earth, Moon and Planets*

*Icarus, the Journal of Solar System Studies*

*Annual Reviews of Earth and Planetary Sciences*

*Annual Reviews of Astronomy and Astrophysics*

*Proceedings of the Lunar and Planetary Science Conference*. The Lunar and Planetary Science Conference is held every March in Houston, and these volumes summarize some of the information presented there. This conference started as "The Lunar Science Conference" in 1970 to present findings from the Apollo 11 samples, and has continued annually ever since.

## GENERAL ASTRONOMY

Berman, L., & J.C. Evans, *Exploring the Cosmos*, 5th ed., Little, Brown, & Co., 1986. (*This is a basic textbook with nice quotes, although it has occasional glitches in the tabulated data. I used it when I taught astronomy at a community college.*)

Swihart, Thomas L., *Astrophysics and Stellar Astronomy*, John Wiley & Sons, 1968. (*A good, albeit somewhat dated, treatise at the slightly more advanced level for those aggravating questions that the undergraduate texts don't quite answer.*)

Danby, J.M.A., *Fundamentals of Celestial Mechanics*, Macmillan, New York, 1964, 348 pp. (*A useful and relatively elementary treatment of celestial mechanics.*)

Allen, C.W., *Astrophysical Quantities*, Athlone Press, University of London, 1973. (*Standard reference on astronomical and astrophysical data.*)

Lang, Kenneth R., *Astrophysical Formulae*, Springer-Verlag, 1974. (*Standard reference on astronomical and astrophysical data.*)

To find data on specific stars and other astronomical objects, you can check any of a number of standard catalogs; e.g., *The Yale Bright Star Catalog, The Catalog of Nearby Stars, The Catalog of Visual Binary Stars*, and so on, which should be available at a large university library. They contain such data as positions, magnitudes, spectral types, distances and so on. Recently (and more usefully, perhaps), many of these catalogs have been put on CD-ROM. In particular, a single CD-ROM, *Selected Astronomical Catalogs, Vol. I*, which contains most of the basic catalogs, is available from the National Space Sciences Data Center, NASA Goddard Space Flight Center, Greenbelt, Maryland 20771. The catalogs are in ASCII text format readable by any standard personal computer.

Although I've advocated using spreadsheets for calculation, a number of specific programs for planet-designing also have been written. Most recently, Daniel Hatch has written a long BASIC program to automate planet design. It's available from him through the Science Fiction Writers of America (SFWA).

For the elements and their formation, a good general introduction is Cox, P.A., *The Elements*, Oxford University Press, 1989, 207 pp. It also has guides to some of the technical literature. *Annual Reviews of Astronomy and Astrophysics* also often has review papers on nucleosynthesis.

**Other resources.** Finally, of course, not only does your local university have a library where you might be able to find many of these references (and if they don't, they can get them via interlibrary loan), the staff is often a source of expertise. In particular, don't forget graduate students: They're often more approachable than the professors—and they're always looking for excuses not to work on their theses!

## STORIES AND NOVELS CITED

Novels are fairly easy to find. Even if they're out of print, they can be tracked down with a little effort in a large public library or used bookstore, since books are indexed by title and author. All the novels cited in this book also have one or more paperback editions, so that makes them even easier to locate.

Short stories, on the other hand, can be very difficult to locate because they're not indexed as such in (e.g.) a card catalog. In many cases, too, they've never been reprinted in anthology form, so their only published appearance has been an ephemeral one in the pages of a science-fiction magazine.

To make finding the stories easier, then, here is a list of places they've appeared. I've not tried to make an exhaustive list of anthology republications, but have simply listed a selection of relatively recent publications.

Anderson, Poul, "The Longest Voyage," in *The Hugo Winners, Vol. 1*; *The Best of Poul Anderson*; *The Many Worlds of Poul Anderson*; *The Analog Anthology #1*; *Winners* (Tor Books, 1981). (*It originally appeared in* Analog, *December, 1960, and won the 1961 Hugo award for best short fiction.*)

———, "The Queen of Air and Darkness," in *The Many Worlds of Poul Anderson*; *Nebula Award Stories #7*, *The Queen of Air and Darkness and Other Stories* (Signet, 1973); *Winners* (Tor Books, 1981). (*This story originally appeared in* The Magazine of Fantasy and Science Fiction, *April, 1971, and won the Nebula award.*)

———, "A Sun Invisible," in *The Trouble Twisters* (Berkeley Medallion, 1977). (*It originally appeared in* Analog, *April, 1966.*)

———, "Supernova" (a.k.a. "Day of Burning"), in *Beyond the Beyond* (Signet Books, 1969); *The Earth Book of Stormgate*; *The Many Worlds of Poul Anderson*. (*It originally appeared in* Analog, *January, 1967.*)

Asimov, Isaac, "Nightfall." According to one vote, this is the best SF story of all time and it has been reprinted many times. Some examples are *A Science Fiction Reader*; *The Road to Science Fiction #2*; *Classic Science Fiction*; *The Golden Years of Science Fiction (Second Series)*; and recently *Science Fiction: The Science Fiction Research Association Anthology* (HarperCollins, 1988). (*The story first appeared in the August, 1941, Astounding.*)

Clarke, Arthur C., "Exile of the Eons," in *Expedition to Earth*, 1953, which has been reprinted many times (e.g., by Ballantine, 1966). (*The story originally appeared in* Super Science Stories, *March, 1950.*)

Clement, Hal, "Whirligig World." This essay on the designing of the giant planet Mesklin for *Mission of Gravity* remains a classic. (*Originally appearing in* Astounding Science Fiction, *June, 1953, it has been reprinted as an appendix to many editions of the novel—e.g., Ballantine, 1978.*)

Goodloe, Lee, and Jerry Oltion, "Waterworld," *Analog*, pp. 12-56, March, 1994 (cover story).

Niven, Larry, "Inconstant Moon," in *All the Myriad Ways*; *The Hugo Winners, Vol. 3*; *Best Science Fiction for 1972*. (*This story won the Hugo award for best short story in 1972.*)

Oltion, Jerry, and Lee Goodloe, "Contact," *Analog*, pp. 12-71, November, 1991 (cover story). (*It was a nominee for the 1992 Nebula award for best novella and was reprinted, in digital format, on the compact disc Hugo and Nebula Anthology 1993, ClariNet Corp., San Jose, CA.*)

Shelley, Rick, and Lee Goodloe, "Because It's There," *Analog*, pp. 12-61, July, 1992 (cover story).

Utley, Steven, "The Glowing Cloud," *Isaac Asimov's Science Fiction Magazine*, pp. 108-160, January, 1992 (cover story).

# INDEX

Absolute magnitude, *see* Magnitude, absolute

Accretion, 45, 135; around binary stars, 148, 149; disk, 43, 44, 150; late, 46, 96, 97, 113, 115, 122, 175; of Earth, 55; of jovian planets, 44, 45, 109; of Jupiter, 44; of Mars, 46, 115; of Moon, 113; of planetesimals, 46; of rogue planets, 175; of satellites, 44, 48; of terrestrial (rocky) planets, 44, 48, 109

Adiabatic, 83

Albedo: and clouds, 83; and glaciation, 91, 101; and temperature, 66; defined, 66

Aldiss, Brian W.; *Helliconia* trilogy, 147

Amino acids, 105

Ammonia ($NH_3$), 165; and cold trap, 161; and photosynthesis, 162; and water, 162, 163; as common substance, 160; as greenhouse gas, 67, 161, 162; as volatile, 48; frozen, 161; in "early reducing atmosphere," 71, 95; ocean of, 160, 161, 162, 165, 166; photodissociation of, 71, 95, 118, 161, 165; properties of, 161, 163, 165; world, 160, 162, 163, 168

Ammonium ion ($NH_4+$), 163

Anderson, Poul, 53, 66, 74, 82, 119, 143, 146; *Ensign Flandry*, 70; *Fire Time*, 147; "The Longest Voyage," 118, 188; *The Man Who Counts*, 17, 19, 96, 154; *Murasaki* (planet design), 113; *Orbit Unlimited*, 66; *Planet of No Return (Question and Answer)*, 31; "The Queen of Air and Darkness," 19, 85, 188; *The Rebel Worlds*, 73; *Satan's World*, 51, 73, 86, 175; "A Sun Invisible," 135, 175, 188; "Supernova," 141, 146, 188; *Tau Zero*, 2; *Trader to the Stars*, 129, 160; *The Trouble Twisters*, 89; *A World Called Cleopatra*, 32, 51; *World Without Stars*, 152

Andes Mountains, 60

*Andromeda Strain, The* (Crichton), 160

Angular diameter, 136, 139, 143

Angular momentum, 27, 43, 45 conservation of, 13, 43, 153; in galaxies, 151; of Moon, 113

Anomalous satellites, *see* Satellites, anomalous

Antarctica; ice age, 101

Antipodal chaotic terranes, 47

Apparent magnitude, *see* Magnitude, apparent

Archean, 98, 107; and oceans, 91

Argon (Ar), 75; as volatile, 48; atmospheric, 64, 97; on sulfur dioxide world, 166

Asimov, Isaac, 160, 164, 172; "Nightfall," 146, 188

Asteroids, 43; and outer satellites, 110; as boiled out comets, 125; as leftover planetesimals, 46, 109; Trojan, 29, 31

Asthenosphere, 60; and oceans, 81

Atmosphere, 37, 54, 61, 63, 64, 68, 70, 71, *see also* Greenhouse effect; specific gases (e.g., oxygen, nitrogen); specific bodies; "early reducing," 71, 95; adiabatic profile, 83; ancient, 95, 98; and condensable phase, 83; and flight, 73, 74; and late heavy bombardment, 47, 48, 96; and life, 63, 64, 70, 98, 106, 107, 164; and magnetic field, 85; and ocean, 79; and Roche limit, 36; and Ross 128, 140; and solar flare, 85, 86; as secondary, 96; atomic weight of, 75; breathable, 64, 66; catastrophes, 83; circulation and continents, 84; climate and weather, 22, 81, 82; cold trap, 71, 72, 73, 95, 161; color of, 157; convection, *see* Convection, in atmosphere; dust in, 83; escape of, 12, 64, 69, 86, 173; evolution of, 64; exosphere, 64, 71; inversions, 83; maintenance, 52, 69, 77; of carbon world, 172; of Earth, 96; origin, 96; spacecraft, 63; structure, 73, 76; temperature, 75; thickness, 74, 76, 77

Atmosphere (unit of pressure), 63

Atomic number, 39; defined, 39

Atomic weight, 75; defined, 39; of atmosphere, 75

Auroras, 19, 85; and radio communication, 85

Axial tilt, *see* Obliquity

Axis (of rotation), 6, 17, 19, 20, 85, 102, *see also* Obliquity; precession of, 102

Bacteria, 63, 70, 104, 106, 164, 167

Barnes, John; *A Million Open Doors*, 175; *Mother of Storms*, 84

Basalt, 56; and hot spots, 56; flood, 47, 56, 57, 58, 59

"Because It's There" (Shelley & Goodloe), 60, 76, 188

*Big Planet* (Vance), 17

Binary stars, 12, 16, 136, 146, 147; accretion around, 148, 149; Alpha Centauri, 148; and asteroids, 148; and brown dwarf, 143; and Main Sequence, 150; and planets, 46, 146, 147, 148, 149; and Trojan planet, 31, 148;

cataclysmic binaries, 151;
contact binary, 150, 151;
formation of, 43, 44;
orbits, 44, 148; separation
147-150; Sunlike, 150
Biomolecules, 105, 156, 158,
159, 170, 171, 172; and
UV, 77; color of, 87
Black hole, 145; in galactic
core, 152, 153; in X-ray
star, 151
Black Sea, 103
Blackbody radiation, 66, 127,
129
Blish, James; *Earthman Come
Home*, 9
Blue-green algae, *see*
Cyanobacteria
Bode's Law, *see* Titius-Bode
Law
Bolometric correction, 132; of
Ross 128, 137
Bolometric magnitude, *see*
Magnitude, bolometric
Boron (B), 38
Boudouard reaction, 174
Bova, Ben, 86; *Test of Fire*, 86
Brimstone worlds, *see* Sulfur
worlds
Brown dwarfs, 31, 110, 129, 142,
143, 144, 175; and
Earthlike planet, 118,
138, 143, 144;
atmospheres of, 143;
defined, 141, 142;
hydrogen fusion, 142;
luminosity of, 144;
satellite of, 138; tidal
braking, 143
Burroughs, Edgar Rice, 73

Callisto (moon of Jupiter), 44,
118, 145
Cambrian, 95, 102, 107
"Cannonball" (hypothetical
planet), 172, 173, 174
Carbon (C), 39, 175;
abundance, 38, 52, 53,
165, 171; as volatile, 48;
cycle, 68; dioxide, *see*
Carbon dioxide;
formation of, 41, 144; in
biochemistry, 104, 156; in
limestone, 68; monoxide,
*see* Carbon monoxide; on
Cannonball, 172, 173; on
chloroxygen world, 158;

world, 171, 172
Carbon dioxide ($CO_2$), 39, 174,
175; and life, 63, 68; and
runaway glaciation, 91; as
greenhouse gas, 67, 68,
69, 72, 93; as volatile, 48;
atmospheric, 66, 68, 69,
70, 72, 93, 107; breathers,
105; clouds, 91, 93;
dissolved, 68, 69; in
ancient atmosphere, 95;
in carbonates, 68, 72; on
carbon world, 171, 172;
on chloroxygen world,
157, 158; on Mars, 116,
166; on sulfuric acid
world, 169; on Venus, 63,
72, 115, 168; on wetworld,
154; toxicity, 66, 95
Carbon monoxide (CO), 42,
167, 170, 173, 174, 175
Carbonate-silicate cycle, 52, 64,
68, 69, 72, 73, 79, 91; on
Mars, 116
Carbonates, 68, 69; limestone,
68, 69, 72, 113, 115, 154;
on carbon world, 171; on
chloroxygen world, 158,
159; on sulfuric acid
world, 169
"Carbonosis," 52, 185
Carbonyls, 173, 174
Cenozoic Earth, 94
Center of mass, 12, 13, 16, 23
Central America, land bridge,
100
Centrifugal "force," 81; and
equatorial bulge, 89; and
planet rotation, 11, 88;
and tides, 23
Chalcophile elements, *see*
Elements, chemical;
Chalcophile
Charon (moon of Pluto), 27,
125; as anomalous
satellite, 110
Chloride ($Cl^-$), 78, 106, 156,
160; on chloroxygen
world, 160
Chlorine (Cl), 78, 155, 158;
abundance, 78, 156; and
ozone ($O_3$), 86;
compounds, as fire
retardants, 70; gaseous
($Cl_2$), 156, 158; and Earth
life, 88, 106, 156-159; on
Earth, 78, 156

Chlorophyll, 87
Chloroplasts, 107
Chloroxygen world, 88, 106,
155, 157, 158, 160, 164,
169, 171; and
intelligence, 159; and
technology, 159
CHON, *see* Elements, chemical;
CHON
*City and the Stars, The* (Clarke),
73
*City of Illusions* (LeGuin), 20
$Cl_2$, *see* Chlorine (Cl), gaseous
($Cl_2$)
Clarke, Arthur C., 124; *The City
and the Stars*, 73; "Exile
of the Eons," 73, 188;
*Imperial Earth*, 5; *Prelude
to Space*, 89; *The Songs of
Distant Earth*, 79, 98
Clement, Hal, 175; *Mission of
Gravity*, 11, 175; *The
Nitrogen Fix*, 70, 106, 164;
*Star Light*, 162;
"Whirligig World," 188
Climate, *see* Atmosphere,
climate and weather
Climatic zones, 17, 19
Clorox, 158
Clouds, 68, 83, 84, 88, 143, 144;
carbon dioxide, 91;
cometary, *see* Comets;
giant molecular, *see* Giant
molecular cloud; on
Venus, 63, 168, 172;
water, 68, 83
CO, *see* Carbon monoxide
$CO_2$, *see* Carbon dioxide
Cobalt (Co), 49, 53, 55
Color; and temperature, 127,
129; metal compounds,
87; of biomolecules, 87,
140; of planet, 87; of sky,
87, 88, 157; of stars, 88,
129, 137
Comets, 7, 125, 126, 174; and
atmosphere, 47, 96, 173;
as leftover planetesimals,
109, 125, 174; Kuiper
Cloud, 125; Oort Cloud,
125
Common proper motion
(CPM), 147
"Contact" (Oltion & Goodloe),
1, 129, 150, 188
Continental distribution, 83, 85,
94, 98, 99, 100; and ice

ages, 101, 102; and supercontinents, 98
Continental drift, *see* Plate tectonics, continental drift
Convection: and plate tectonics, 59; in atmosphere, 81-83; in ocean, 81, 84 103; superadiabatic, 83
Core: of planet, 9, 10, 11, 50, 53, 55, 85, 109, 114, 123, 172; of spiral galaxy, 151, 152, 153
Coriolis effect, 81, 82, 84, 88
Cretaceous, 99, 102
Crichton, Michael; *The Andromeda Strain*, 160
Crust (of planet), 50, 53, 114, 167; and lithosphere, 55; continental, 54, 55, 58, 79, 98, 116; oceanic, 54, 79; of Earth, 51, 52, 53, 54, 55, 56, 59, 64, 68, 69, 79, 98
"Cueball" world, 51, 52
Cyanobacteria, 98, 106

Deep time (antiquity of earth), 95
"Deepocean," 118; on Europa, 118
Degrees Kelvin, *see* Kelvins
Density, 10, 11, 12, 29, 54, 114, 117, 125; and surface gravity, 4, 10, 11, 55; of core, 10; of stars, 136
Desertification, 73
Deuterium ($^2$H), 142
DNA, 104, 105, 107
*Door Into Ocean, A* (Slonczewski), 79
Double planets, 36, 113, 118, 122; Pluto-Charon, 125; stability, 36, 138
Double stars, *see* Binary stars
*Dragon's Egg* (Forward), 145, 175
Dryworld, 79; aged, 73; and inversions, 83; and plate tectonics, 73, 81; hot, 72
*Dune* (Herbert), 73

Earth, *see also* more specific reference; atmosphere of, 63, 64, 70, 71, 97; rotation of, 27, 89, 90
*Earth Book of Stormgate* (Anderson), 74

Earthlike satellite, 118
*Earthman Come Home* (Blish), 9
Earthquakes, 60, 61; and Moon, 112
*Earthsea* trilogy (LeGuin), 80
Eccentricity (of orbits), 48; and Milankovich variations, 102; and tides, 25, 28, 117, 138; binary stars, 44, 147, 148; defined, 13; effects of, 20, 21, 102, 140; Mercury, 114
Eclipses, 124
Eddington limit, 141
Effective temperature, 135, 139; defined, 129; of Sun, 135
Electromagnetic radiation, 61, 127
Electromagnetic spectrum, 61
Electrons, 38; and chemical properties, 38; and color, 87
Elements, chemical, 37, 38, 39, 40, 129; abundance, 37, 38, 49, 53, 96, 104, 117, 160, 164; atmophile, *see* Elements, chemical, volatile; Volatiles; chalcogenides, 49; chalcophile, 48, 49, 53; CHON (carbon-hydrogen-oxygen-nitrogen), 38, 104, 118; definition, 38; formation of, 40, 41, 42, 51, 144, 151; fractionation, 48-50, 155; geochemical classes, 48, 50; heavy elements, 38, 41, 53, 135; in crust, 52, 55, 68, 79; lithophile, 48, 49, 50; nomenclature, 39; nutrient, 51, 73, 104; "oxyphile," 49; radioactive, 52, 55, 97; siderophile, 48, 49, 50, 53; volatile, 48, 49
Ellipse, 13
Elliptical galaxies, *see* Galaxies, elliptical
Elongation, 110; and morning/evening stars, 110; of Trojan, 31
*Ensign Flandry* (Anderson), 70
Enzymes, 156; defined, 105
Epeiric seas, 99
Epithemis (co-orbiting satellite

of Saturn), 34
Equatorial bulge, 9, 11; and perturbations, 22, 23, 89, 124
Escape velocity, 12, 64
Ethane ($C_2H_6$), on Titan, 118, 172
Eukaryotes, 107
Europa (moon of Jupiter), 91, 117, 118, 123, 143; resonance, 36
Euxinic, 104
Evening star, 110; Trojan body as, 31
"Exile of the Eons" (Clarke), 73, 188

Fire Time (Anderson), 147
Flight, *see* Atmosphere and flight; Surface gravity and flight
Flight of the Dragonfly (Forward), 160
Flood basalt, *see* Basalt
Fluorine (F), 155, 156; gaseous ($F_2$), 155-156
Forward, Robert L.; *Dragon's Egg*, 145, 175; *Flight of the Dragonfly*, 160; *Rocheworld*, 36, 129, 162; *Starquake*, 145, 175; *Timemaster*, 138

Galaxies, 8, 12, 42, 43, 141, 142, 151; elliptical, 152; expelling stars, 152; irregular, 152; Magellanic Clouds, 152; peculiar, 153; Seyfert, 152; spiral, 41, 42, 151, 152; types, 151
Ganymede (moon of Jupiter), 118, 145; resonance, 36
Gas giants, *see* Jovian planets
Giant molecular cloud, 41, 42; and brown dwarf, 142
Glacial age, *see* Ice ages
Glaciers, 19, 20, *see also* Ice ages; equatorial, 19
"Glowing Cloud, The" (Utley), 58, 188
GMC, *see* Giant molecular cloud
Gondwanaland (ancient continent), 100
Goodloe, Lee; "Because It's There," 60, 76, 188;

"Contact," 1, 129, 150, 188; "Waterworld," 1, 118, 145, 188
Gravitational constant (G), 9, 10, 12, 13
Gravity, 6, 8, 16, 21, 23, 29; and GMCs, 42; and Ice Line, 44; and tides, 23, 25; escape velocity, *see* Escape velocity; forcing bodies into spheres, 9; of planetestimal, 46; orbits, *see* Orbits; resonance, 32; surface, *see* Surface gravity
Greenhouse effect, 67, 72, 77, 78, 91, 161, *see also* Atmosphere; specific bodies; specific gases

H-R diagram, *see* Hertzsprung-Russell diagram
Half-life, 40, 41; potassium-40 ($^{40}$K), 97
Halogen breathers, *see* Chlorine (Cl$_2$) breathers, fluorine (F$_2$) breathers
Halogens, *see* Fluorine (F), Chlorine (Cl)
Hawaii, 56
Heinlein, Robert A., 73
Helium (He), 97; abundance, 37, 38, 53; as nuclear "ash," 38, 40, 133, 135, 143; as volatile, 48, 49; condensation of, 45; escape of, 64, 97, 166, 175; formation of, 40; from radioactive decay, 41, 97; fusion of, 40, 144; helium-3 ($^3$He) (in small star), 143; in jovian planets, 109, 116, 122; in stars, 37; on Earth, 97
*Helliconia* trilogy (Aldiss), 147
Hemoglobin, 87
Herbert, Frank; *Dune*, 73
Hertzsprung-Russell (H-R) diagram, 133
Himalayas, 60
Horizon distance, 16, 17
"hot poles" (on Mercury), 114
Hot spots, 47, 56; and superplumes, 99
Humid landscape; ancient, 108
Hurricanes, 84
Hydrochloric acid, 158

Hydrogen (H), 39; abundance, 37, 38, 42, 53, 104, 160; as volatile, 48, 49; chloride, *see* Hydrogen chloride (HCl); condensation of, 45; fluoride, *see* Hydrogen fluoride (HF); formation of, 40; fusion, 7, 38, 40, 133, 142-144; gaseous (H$_2$), 42, 64, 71, 97, 116, 163, 166, 173, 175; heavy, *see* Deuterium ($^2$H); in biochemistry, 104, 156; in jovian planets, 109, 116, 122; in stars, 37; molecular, *see* Hydrogen, gaseous (H$_2$); on wetworld, 154; sulfide, *see* Hydrogen sulfide (H$_2$S)
Hydrogen chloride (HCl), 158, 159, 169; ocean of, 156; on chloroxygen world, 157; properties of, 156
hydrogen fluoride (HF); ocean of, 155
Hydrogen sulfide (H$_2$S), 49, 106, 171
Hypochlorous acid (HClO), 158

Ice, *see* Water, properties of
Ice ages, 21, 22, 91, 101, 102, 103, 107; Milankovich variations, *see* Milankovich variations; runaway glaciation, 91, 93
Ice Line, 44, 45
Ice world (terrestrial), 91
Iceworld (distant satellite), 118, 123, 145
Ignimbrite, 58
*Imperial Earth* (Clarke), 5
"Inconstant Moon" (Niven), 86, 188
Inferior planet, *see* Planets, inferior
Infrared light (IR), 61, 66, 67, 132, 139
and Ross 128, 140
Inorganic carbon cycle, *see* Carbonate-silicate cycle
Insolation, 102
Io (moon of Jupiter), 44, 117, 122, 165, 171; as sulfur world, 117, 165, 166; internal heating of, 117;

orbit of, 117; resonance, 36; sulfur dioxide on, 117, 165
Ions, 78, 86, 149, 156, 169; defined, 38; in stars, 129
Iron (Fe), 39, 51; abundance, 38, 49, 50, 53; and ammonia, 163; and carbonyl, 173, 174; and color, 87, 116; and technology, 52; as chalcophile element, 50; as lithophile element, 50; as siderophile element, 49; in brown dwarf clouds, 143; in core, 9, 10, 50, 53, 55, 85, 109, 172; in crust, 51, 52, 53, 55; in lunar lavas, 174; in mantle, 55, 79; in technology, 52, 53, 159; isotopes, 39; on Mars, 116; on sulfur dioxide world, 167; rusting of, 163; stability of nucleus, 38, 49, 144, 145; world (Cannonball), 171, 172, 173
Irregular galaxies, *see* Galaxies, irregular
Isostasy, 60
Isotopes, defined, 39

Janus (co-orbiting satellite of Saturn), 34
Japan, 60
*Jem* (Pohl), 50
Jovian planets, 46, 116; *see also* specific bodies; specific topics; atmospheres of, 116; defined, 109
Jupiter, 7, 109, 116, 122, 155; and brown dwarfs, 141; and late heavy bombardment, 45, 46, 148; and Mars, 46; formation of, 44, 45, 46; satellites of, 44, 117, *see also* Europa; Ganymede; Io; Callisto; Trojan asteroids, 29, 31

Kelvins (K) (temperature scale), 5
Kepler's Laws, 13, 20, 21, 45, 115, 137; law of areas, 13
*Key Out of Time* (Norton), 80

L-4, L-5 points, *see* Trojan points
Lagrange points, 29, *see also* Trojan points
Late heavy bombardment, 20; and atmosphere, 47, 96; and Jupiter, 45, 46; and plate tectonics, 47; and volatiles, 48; defined, 47; on Moon, 47, 112
Lava, *see also* Basalt; Magma; Melting; Volcanism; defined, 56
LeGuin, Ursula; *City of Illusions*, 20; *Earthsea* trilogy, 80
Life, 70, 104, 105; and atmosphere, 63, 64, 70, 95, 98, 106, 107, 164; and boron, 38; and liquid ammonia, 162; and liquid sulfur dioxide, 165; and liquid water, 80, 104; and magnetic field, 85; and Mars, 115; and plate tectonics, 80; and potassium, 116; and technology, 108; and UV light, 77; Archean, 98; as source of conflicts, 3; at Ross 128, 140; biochemistry, 38, 104; crises, 100, 106; detection, 70; history of, 106; in Archean, 98; in spiral galaxies, 152; multicellular, 98, 106, 107, 135; needs liquid, 160; nutrient elements, 51, 52; on chloroxygen world, 159; on Earth, 66, 80, 94, 95, 104, 106, 107, 116; on Europa, 118; on fluorine (F₂) world, 155; on iceworld, 123; on jovian planets, 116; on land, 77, 80, 107; on neutron star, 145, 175; on oceanworld, 79; on sulfur dioxide world, 166, 167; on sulfuric acid world, 171; on Titan, 118; tenacity of, 57
Light year, 4, 8
Limestone, *see* Carbonates, limestone
Lithophile elements, *see* Elements, chemical;

Lithophile
Lithosphere, 55, 56, 59; defined, 55; of Mars, 115
Local Group, 151
"Longest Voyage, The" (Anderson), 118, 188
Lowell, Percival, 73
Luminosity, 131, 132, 133, 135, 140; defined, 131; increase of Sun's, 72, 135; inverse-square law, 131; Main Sequence, 133; of brown dwarf, 144; of contact binaries, 150; of red giant, 144, 175; of Ross 128, 137; of Sun, 131; of Tau Ceti, 131, 133

Magma, *see also* Basalt; Lava; Melting; Volcanism; defined, 56
Magnetic field; and auroras, 85; of Earth, 55, 85-87; of stars, 149, 150
Magnitude, 130; absolute, 128, 130, 131, 137; 128, 130-132, 135, 137; defined, 130; of Sun, 130, 131; visual, 128, 131, 132, 137
Main Sequence, 37, 40, 133, 135, 141; and binary stars, 150, 151; and star mass, 133; star lifetimes on, 135
*Man Who Counts, The* (Anderson), 17, 19, 74, 96, 154
Mantle, 50, 54, 55, 99; and hot spots, 56; and lithosphere, 55; of Earth, 55, 59, 60, 79, 80
Mars, 77, 115, 155, 164; and late heavy bombardment, 47; as "accretion-starved" world, 46, 115; as run down, 64, 69, 73, 77, 117; atmosphere of, 48, 115, 116; climate of, 116; CO₂ on, 166; color of sky, 88; core of, 85; crust of, 116; "dying," 73; hot spots, 56, 115; obliquity variations, 22, 116; orbit perturbations, 22; oxidation of, 116, 168; perturbations of, 116; photodissociation on,

116; satellites of, 124; tectonics, 115
Mass number, defined, 39
Mass-luminosity law, 133, 136, 137
Mediterranean Sea, 100, 103; and salinity, 103; dry, 76
Melting: at depth, 55, 56, 57, 60; from meteorite impact, 58; of iceworld, 123; of Miranda, 122, 123; of Triton, 27, 123
Mercury, 47, 114; "hot poles," 114; as inferior planet, 110; as morning/evening star, 31, 110; atmosphere of, 114; elongation of, 110; mega-impact on, 46, 114, 172; motion of Sun, 21, 115, 140; orbit of, 114, 115; orbital eccentricity, 28, 114, 117, 140; rotation of, 114, 115; satellites of, 28, 36, 138, 143; solar day, 114, 139; tidal braking, *see* Tidal braking, of Mercury; tidal locking, *see* Tidal locking, of Mercury
Messinian crisis, 100
Metazoans, 107
Methane (CH₄), 88, 106; as greenhouse gas, 67; as thalassogen, 172; as volatile, 48; atmospheric, 70; in "early reducing atmosphere," 71, 95; photodissociation of, 71, 95
Milankovich variations, 22, 23, 102, 119
*Million Open Doors, A* (Barnes), 175
Minerals, 49
Miranda (moon of Uranus), 122, 123; orbit of, 122
*Mission of Gravity* (Clement), 11, 175
Mitochondria, 107
Molecules, defined, 39
Month, 125
Moon, 23, 112, 115, 117, 122; and late heavy bombardment, 47, 112; angular diameter, 110, 136; as angular momentum bank, 113; as

anomalous satellite, 110; as another world, 114; as rocky world, 112; colonies on, 74; eclipses, 124; effects of, 22, 23, 102, 112, 113; flood basalts on, 47, 56; horizon on, 17; in habitable zone, 79; month, 125; orbit of, 27, 124; origin, 46, 48, 97, 113; phases of, 110, 112; revolution period, 124; rotation of, 27; satellite of, 23; size, 112, 113, 117; successive moonrises, 124; telescopes on, 70; tidal braking, *see* Tidal braking, and Moon; tidal locking, *see* Tidal locking, and Moon; tides, *see* Tides, lunar; Trojan point, 29

Moonrises; time between, 123

Moons, *see* Satellites

Morning star, 110; Trojan body as, 31

*Mote in God's Eye, The* (Niven & Pournelle), 97

*Mother of Storms* (Barnes), 84

Mt. St. Helens, 56, 58

*Murasaki* (Anderson et al.), 113, 138

N₂, *see* Nitrogen (N), gaseous (N₂); atmospheric

N₂O, *see* Nitrogen (N); oxides of; nitrous oxide (N₂O)

Neon (Ne), 96; abundance, 38, 96; and atmosphere origin, 96; as volatile, 48, 49; atmospheric, 96, 154, 175; formation of, 41; on sulfur dioxide world, 166; world, 154

Neptune, 88, 122; and Titius-Bode Law, 43; formation of, 45; orbit of, 123; satellites of, 27, 122, *see also* Triton

Neutron star, 16, 145, 175

Neutrons, 38, 40, 41

Nickel (Ni), 38, 49, 50, 53, 55; and carbonyl, 173

"Nightfall" (Asimov), 146, 188

Nitrates, 70, 106, 163, 164; on nitroxy world, 164

Nitric acid (HNO₃), on nitroxy

world, 164

Nitrogen (N); abundance, 38, 52, 96, 160, 165; and explosives, 163; as volatile, 48; cycle, 70; formation of, 41; gaseous (N₂), 63, 64, 66, 70, 75, 86, 95, 106, 118, 123, 157,162, 164, 171, 172; in biochemistry, 104; isotopes, 39; on nitroworlds, 160; oxides of, 86, 106, 164

Nitrogen dioxide (NO₂), *see* Nitrogen (N); oxides of

*Nitrogen Fix, The* (Clement), 70, 106, 164

Nitrous oxide, *see* Nitrogen (N); oxides of

Nitroworlds, 160

Nitroxy world, 88, 164, 169, 171; and technology, 164

Niven, Larry, 9, 11, 96, 152, 164; "Inconstant Moon," 86, 188; *The Mote in God's Eye*, 97; *World Out of Time*, 95

NO₂, *see* Nitrogen (N); oxides of

Norton, Andre, 94; *Key Out of Time*, 80

Novas, 151; as sites of element formation, 40, 51; defined, 151; early Solar System, 42

Nuclear winter, 83

Nucleosynthesis, *see* Elements, chemical; formation of

Nucleotides, 105

Nucleus, atomic, 38, 39

*Nuee ardente*, 58, 59

O₂, *see* Oxygen (O)

Obliquity, 17, 19, 20, 91; and equatorial glaciers, 19; and ice ages, 22; and snowpack, 19; initial, 20, 47, 48; of Earth, 19; of Earthlike satellite, 119; of Uranus, 19, 122; stabilization, 23, 113; variations, 20-23, 47, 102, 116

Ocean basins, 54, 79

Ocean, convection, *see* Convection, in ocean

Oceans, 61, 72, 73, 78, 79, 91,

95, 97; ammonia, *see* Ammonia (NH₃), ocean of; and carbonate-silicate cycle, 72; and chlorine (Cl), 78, 156; and common elements, 164; and ice cover, 105; and life, 80; and plate tectonics, 73, 80; and Ross 128, 140; and supercontinents, 99; as heat bank, 84; boiling of, 71, 72, 84; carbonyls, *see* Carbonyls, ocean of; circulation and continents, 84; color of, 88; distribution, 83, 98; from iceworld melting, 123; hydrogen fluoride, *see* Hydrogen fluoride (HF), ocean of; on chloroxygen world, 158; on Earth, 78, 156; on Triton, 123; on Venus, 72; oxygenated, 84; salinity, 78, 100; sulfur dioxide, *see* Sulfur dioxide (SO₂), ocean of; sulfuric acid, *see* Sulfuric acid (H₂SO₄), ocean of; tides, *see* Tides, ocean; warm and saline, 89

Oceanworld, 79, 80, 98, 154; and technology, 80; Earth as, 80

Oltion, Jerry; "Contact," 1, 129, 150, 188; "Waterworld," 1, 118, 145, 188

Olympus Mons, 56, 115

*Orbit Unlimited* (Anderson), 66

Orbital eccentricity, *see* Eccentricity (of orbits)

Orbits, 11, 12, 16, 23, 27, 29, *see also* specific bodies; and gravity, 8; close binary stars, 149; co-orbiting satellites, 34; during accretion, 46; ellipse, 13; geosynchronous, 124; law of areas, 13; Milankovich variations, *see* Milankovich variations; of Earthlike satellite, 122; of inferior planets, 110; of planetesimals, 46, 96; of superior planets, 112;

parallax from, 8; perturbations of, *see* Perturbations; planets and binary stars, 148; resonance, 34, 36; rings, 32; satellite, 23; stability, 21, 46; tidal decay of, 138, 143, 149, 150; Trojan, 29, 31, 110, 143; two-body problem, 12, 21

Organelles (in eukaryotic cells), 107

Organic compounds: and color, 87

Outer satellites, *see* Satellites, outer

Outgassing, 96, 97

Oxygen (O), 39, 49, 50; abundance, 38, 49, 52, 104, 155, 165, 171; and ozone ($O_3$), 78, 107; as lithophile, 49; as volatile, 48, 49; formation of, 41, 144; gaseous ($O_2$), 63, 64, 66, 68, 70, 75, 84, 86, 95, 96, 98, 101, 103, 105-108, 155-160, 163, 166-168, 171-173; *see also* Photosynthesis; in biochemistry, 104; in crust, 55; isotopes, 39; on Io, 117; on Mars, 116; on Titan, 118

Ozone ($O_3$), 77, 78, 86, 95, 107, 146; in atmosphere, 86; on chloroxygen world, 157

Pangea (supercontinent), 98, 100

Parallax, 8

Parsec, 8

Partial pressure, 63; and liquid, 67; of constituents in breathable atmosphere, 64, 66

*People of the Wind* (Anderson), 74

Permo-Triassic extinction, 100

Perturbations, 22, 25, 31, 102, 119, *see also* specific bodies; Milankovich variations; Orbits; Tides; Tidal braking; and obliquity variations, 20, 47; and rotational variations, 47; and tides,

25, 27, 28, 32; by binary stars, 149; by passing star, 123, 125, 147; cyclical, 22; equatorial bulge, 89; from irregularities, 23; of Earth, 102; of planetesimals, 46; of satellites, 124; of Solar System, 123; resonance, 36; secular, 22

Phases (of planet), 6, 110, 112, 125

Phosgene ($COCl_2$), 157

Photodissociation, 64, 71; and "early reducing atmosphere," 71; and hydrogen loss, 71; and Ross 128, 137; and spectral type F star, 73, 168; and sulfur dioxide ($SO_2$), 117; and water loss, 71, 72, 73, 164, 168, 173; as cause of oxidation, 116, 168; of ammonia ($NH_3$), 71, 95, 118, 161, 165; of carbonyls, 173; of chlorine ($Cl_2$), 157, 158; of hydrocarbons, 172; of methane ($CH_4$), 71, 95; of sulfur dioxide ($SO_2$), 165; on carbon world, 172; on Earth, 73; on Mars, 116; on nitroxy world, 164; on sulfuric acid world, 168; on Venus, 72, 115, 168

Photosynthesis, *see also* Oxygen (O), gaseous ($O_2$); and carbon dioxide, 70; and cold conditions, 93; and energy storage, 105; and oxygen ($O_2$) release, 63, 68, 98, 106, 162; non-oxygen-releasing, 106; on ammonia world, 162; on Cannonball, 174; on chloroxygen world, 159; on fluorine ($F_2$) world, 155; on sulfur dioxide world, 167; on sulfuric acid world, 171

Piper, H. Beam; *Uller Uprising*, 155, 171

*Planet of No Return (Question*

*and Answer)* (Anderson), 31

Planetary nebulas, 145; as sites of element formation, 40, 51, 53, 145; early Solar System, 42

Planetesimals, 46, 125; accretion of, 46; asteroids and comets as leftover, 46, 125; defined, 46; Mars-forming, 46; orbits, 46; Pluto and Charon as, 125; Triton as, 122

Planets, *see also* specific planets, accretion of, *see* Accretion; as "wandering" stars, 110; contrast with stars, 7; double, *see* Double planets; formation of, *see* Accretion; inferior, 110; of binary stars, *see* Binary stars, planets; powering tectonics on, 40, 52, 55, 117; superior, 112

Plasma (as star stuff), 149

Plate tectonics, 50, 51, 54, 55, 59, 79, 91; and continental distribution, 98; and late heavy bombardment, 47; and life, 80; and oceans, 73, 80, 81; and recycled seawater, 96; and superplumes, 99; convergent boundaries, 60; defined, 59; on Mars, 116; volcanism, 58

Pluto, 7, 8, 27, 125; and Titius-Bode Law, 43; orbit of, 114

Pohl, Frederik; *Jem*, 50

Potassium (K); as lithophile element, 49; deficiency, 51, 116; in crust, 51, 55; potassium-40 ($^{40}K$), 55, 97

Pournelle, Jerry; *The Mote in God's Eye*, 97; *Warworld* series, 144

Precession, 102, 119

*Prelude to Space* (Clarke), 89

Pressure: of atmosphere, 63 units of, 63

Prograde; orbit, 122; revolution, 25; rotation, 139

Prokaryotes, 106

Proper motion, 147

Proteins, 105
Protons, 38, 40, 85, 86; and
    atomic number, 39
Proxima Centauri, 135, 147, 148
Pulsar, as neutron star, 145

Quartz, *see* Silica (SiO₂), quartz
"Queen of Air and Darkness,
    The" (Anderson), 19, 85,
    188; *Question and Answer*
    (Anderson), see *Planet of
    No Return*

R-process, 41, 51
Radioactivity, 61, 97; alpha-
    radioactive, 41, 97; as
    planetary power source,
    40, 41, 48, 52, 55;
    radioactive nuclei, 40
Radius vector, 13
*Rebel Worlds, The* (Anderson),
    73
Red dwarfs, 129, 135, 143; and
    ammonia planet, 161,
    162; as flare stars, 140;
    brown dwarf in orbit, 138;
    color of, 129, 137;
    infrared output, 132;
    lifetimes of, 135, 141;
    luminosity of, 132, 138;
    planet around, 136; Ross
    128, 137; tidal locking by,
    138
Red giants, 20, 144, 145; and
    "shriveled" world, 175;
    and habitable planet, 145;
    as sites of element
    formation, 40; in nova
    pair, 151; in X-ray star,
    151; lifetimes of, 144;
    luminosity of, 144; mass
    of, 144
Refractory, 45, 109
Regressions, marine, 80
Regular satellites, *see* Satellites,
    regular
Resonance, 32; defined, 32;
    Jovian satellites, 36, 117;
    Miranda, 122; orbital, 34,
    36; tidal, 28
Retrograde; revolution, 27, 28,
    90, 124; rotation, 90, 115,
    139
Revolution period, 16, 17, 27,
    90, 137, 139, 140, *see also*
    Year; and rotation period,
    90; Mercury, 114;

retrograde, 124; Ross 128
    (star), 140; sidereal, 123,
    124, 125; Sun in Galaxy,
    152; synodic, 123
Rings, 31, 32, *see also* Shepherd
    moons; and Earthlike
    planet, 32, 33, 34
Roche's limit, 29, 33, 138, 150
*Rocheworld* (Forward), 36, 129,
    160, 162
Rodinia (supercontinent), 98
Rogue planets, 175
Ross 128 (star), 137, 138, 139
Rotation, 6, 21, 27, 37, 89, 123,
    *see also* Axis (of rotation);
    specific bodies; and
    Coriolis effect, 81, 82; and
    equatorial bulge, 9, 11,
    22, 89; and late heavy
    bombardment, 20, 47;
    and magnetic field, 85;
    and tidal braking, 27; and
    tidal lock, 21, 27, 28;
    centrifugal "force," 88;
    changes in, 47; day and
    night, 88; double planet,
    138; of Sun, 150;
    prograde, 139;
    retrograde, 90, 115, 139;
    sidereal, 89, 90, 123, 124,
    125; slow, 89; solar, *see*
    Solar day; tidal lock, 118
Runaway glaciation, *see* Ice
    ages
Runaway greenhouse, 68, 71,
    72, 78, 84, 115; ammonia,
    162; on sulfuric acid
    world, 169

*Satan's World* (Anderson), 51,
    73, 86, 175
Satellites, 110, *see also* specific
    bodies; Shepherd moons;
    accretion of, 44, 48; and
    Ross 128, 141; and tidal
    effects, 25, 27, 28;
    anomalous, 110; co-
    orbiting, 34; eclipses,
    124; motions of, 123;
    outer, 110; regular, 44,
    110, 122; resonance, 36;
    Trojan points, 29
Saturn, 116, 122; rings, 31, 32;
    satellites of, 29, 34, 118,
    162, 172, *see also* Titan
Scale height, 74, 75
Schmidt, Stanley, 94, 104

Scientific notation, 5
"Scumworld," 95, 98, 107, 108
Sea level; and ocean basins, 79;
    change, 99, 101, *see also*
    Eperic seas;
    Transgressions;
    Regressions; and ice age,
    102, 103
Seafloor spreading, 98, 99; and
    marine transgressions,
    99; spreading centers, 60
Seasons, 17, 19, 21, 81, 91; and
    binary stars, 147; and
    eccentric orbit, 20, 21;
    and rings, 33, 34; and
    Ross 128, 141; on
    Earthlike satellite, 118,
    119
Semimajor axis, 13, 16
Semiminor axis, 13
Sheffield, Charles; *Summertide*,
    36
Shelley, Rick; "Because It's
    There," 60, 76, 188
Shepherd moons, 32, 34
Sidereal day, *see* Rotation,
    sidereal
Sidereal rotation period, *see*
    Rotation, sidereal
Siderophile elements, *see*
    Elements, chemical;
    siderophile
Silica (SiO₂), 56, 158; and
    silicones, 171; on sulfuric
    acid world, 169; quartz,
    52, 169
Silicates, 58, 79, 117, 155, 171;
    and silicones, 170;
    defined, 49; in brown
    dwarf clouds, 143
Silicon (Si), 49; 38, 171; as
    lithophile, 49; in crust, 55
Silicon dioxide (SiO₂), *see* Silica
    (SiO₂)
Silicones, 170, 171; as
    biomolecules, 171
SiO₂, *see* Silica (SiO₂)
Sky; color of, 87
Slonczewski, Joan, 80; *A Door
    Into Ocean*, 79
SO₂, *see* Sulfur dioxide
SO₃, *see* Sulfur trioxide
Soda-water sea, 69
Solar day, 89, 90, 124, 125, 139,
    *see also* specific bodies
Solar eclipse, 124
Solar flare, 86; effects of large,

86, 87
Solar wind, 85
*Songs of Distant Earth, The*
    (Clarke), 79, 98
South America, 60; placental
    invasion, 100
Spectral type, 129, 132, 133;
    defined, 129; of Ross 128,
    137; of Sun, 129
Spectroscopy, 42, 70, 129
Spiral arms, *see* Galaxies, spiral
Spiral galaxies, *see* Galaxies,
    spiral
Spreading center, *see* Seafloor
    spreading
Stable nuclei, 40
*Star Light* (Clement), 162
*Starquake* (Forward), 145, 175
Stars, 6, 7, 9, 13, 45, 127, 152;
    and auroras, 85; and
    planet formation, 6, 43,
    45, 46, 142; and UV
    output, 73, 78; and year,
    17; angular diameter of,
    139; as blackbodies, 127;
    as suns, 6; binary, *see*
    Binary stars; color of, 88,
    129, 132, 136-138;
    composition, 37, 38;
    contrast with planets, 7;
    density of, 136; diameter
    of, 135; dim, 20, 28, 117,
    135, 136, 137, 141, 143,
    144, 150; element
    formation in, 40, 41, 43;
    flares on, 86, 140, 161;
    formation of, 37, 40, 41,
    42, 43, 152; fuel of, 7, 133,
    144; habitable zone, 72,
    79; hot, 45, 46, 73, 85, 86,
    136, 141, 168; in galaxies,
    151; isolated, 152;
    lifetimes of, 7, 20, 42, 135,
    141, 144; luminosity of,
    131, 132, 133, 135, 138;
    luminous, 7, 20, 135, 141;
    magnetic fields of, 149;
    magnitudes of, 130, 131;
    mass of, 16, 20, 31, 133,
    137; massive, 7, 40, 41,
    42, 141, 145; nearby, 6, 8,
    70, 137, 143; old, 7, *see
    also* Red giants; on H-R
    diagram, 133; on Main
    Sequence, 37, 40, 133,
    144; parallax of, 8; red
    dwarfs, *see* Red dwarfs;

red giants, *see* Red giants;
    Ross 128, *see* Ross 128;
    spectral type, *see* spectral
    type; Sunlike, 54, 78, 132,
    135; temperature of, 133,
    135; vs. brown dwarf, 142;
    warming by, 66, 132, 137,
    144; white dwarfs, *see*
    White dwarfs; X-ray, 151
Steam: atmosphere of, 72; in
    volcanism, 56, 58, 117
Stefan-Boltzmann law, 127
Stellar winds, *see also* Solar
    wind; close binary stars,
    149; from red giants, 40
Sulfur (S); abundance, 38, 164;
    as chalcogenide, 49; as
    chalcophile element, 49;
    as volatile, 49;
    compounds, as
    thalassogens, 164;
    dioxide, *see* Sulfur
    dioxide (SO₂); in Earth
    life, 167; ocean of, 171; on
    Io, 117; on Venus, 168;
    trioxide, *see* Sulfur
    trioxide (SO₃); world,
    117, 164, 165, 167, 171
Sulfur dioxide (SO₂), 165, 166,
    168, 171; atmospheric,
    166; cycle, 166, 167;
    escape of, 117, 165; ocean
    of, 165, 166; on Io, 117,
    165; properties of, 165;
    reactivity, 167; world,
    166-168
Sulfur trioxide (SO₃), 166, 168;
    cycle, 166, 167
Sulfuric acid (H₂SO₄);
    biomolecules, 170;
    formation of, 166, 168; in
    Venus clouds, 63, 168;
    ocean of, 164, 168, 169;
    properties of, 168;
    reactivity, 169, 170, 171;
    salts, 169; silicones, 170;
    terrestrial hot springs
    analog, 169; weathering,
    169; world, 168, 171
    and technology, 171
Sulphur, *see* Sulfur
*Summertide* (Sheffield), 36
Sun, 133, 135, *see also* Stars;
    Solar; aging of, 144, 145;
    ancient, 96, 135; angular
    diameter, 110, 136;
    distance of, 7; effective

temperature, 135; in
    Milky Way Galaxy, 152;
    magnitude of, 130, 131;
    mass of, 7; rotation of,
    149; spectral type, 129
"Sun Invisible, A" (Anderson),
    135, 175, 188
Sunspot cycle, 149
Supercontinents, 98, 99
Superior planet, *see* Planets,
    superior
"Supernova" (Anderson), 141,
    146, 188
Supernovas, 42, 53, 145, 174;
    and element formation,
    41, 42, 146; and galactic
    core explosion, 152; and
    star formation, 42; early
    Solar System, 42; effects
    of nearby, 145, 146, 147;
    luminosity of, 145, 146
Superplumes, 99
Surface gravity, 4, 5, 10, 11, 55,
    60, 63, 64, 76, 77, 78; and
    flight, 74; defined, 10; on
    brown dwarf, 175;
    variations, 11, 23
Swimming pool reaction, 157,
    158

T-Tauri stage (of forming star),
    155
Tau Ceti, 131, 132, 133
*Tau Zero* (Anderson), 2
Terrestrial (rocky) planets,
    112, *see also* specific
    bodies; specific topics;
    defined, 109
*Test of Fire* (Bova), 86
Tethys (moon of Saturn), 29
Tethys (seaway), 100
Thalassogen, 160, 164, *see also*
    specific compound
Thorium (Th), 41, 50, 51, 52, 55,
    97
Tidal braking, 20, 25, 27, 33, 36,
    47, 122; and "double
    planet," 28, 138; and
    Moon, 27, 28; and
    satellite orbits, 138; of
    Mercury, 114; of Venus,
    47, 115
Tidal bulge, 11, 24, 27, 36;
    binary stars, 136, 149
Tidal heating, 27, 117; of
    Europa, 117; of Io, 117; of
    Miranda, 122; of Triton,

27, 123

Tidal locking, 21, 27, 138; and brown dwarf, 143; and Moon, 27, 138; and red dwarfs, 138; and Ross 128, 138, 140; of Mercury, 28, 89, 114, 138; of Venus, 89; Pluto-Charon, 27

Tides, 23, 24, 25, 141; "storm tides," 113; and Roche limit, 29; and third body, 28; and Titius-Bode Law, 44; as evolutionary driver, 112; lunar, 23, 24, 25, 28, 112, 113, 138; ocean, 24, 25, 28, 84; Ross 128, 138; scaling of, 24, 25; solar, 24, 25, 28

*Time Machine, The* (Wells), 73

*Timemaster* (Forward), 138

Titan (moon of Saturn), 118, 155, 162, 172; atmosphere of, 118

Titius-Bode law, 43

*Trader to the Stars* (Anderson), 129, 160

Transgressions, marine, 80, 99

Triton (moon of Neptune), 122, 123, 124; as anomalous satellite, 110; capture of, 122; destruction by orbital decay, 28; orbit of, 122; tidal melting of, 27, 123

Trojan point, 29, 31; "daystar," 112; Earthlike planet, 31, 143; elongation, 110

*Trouble Twisters, The* (Anderson), 89

Turtledove, Harry, 77; *A World of Difference*, 66

Two-body problem, *see* Orbits, two-body problem

*Uller Uprising* (Piper), 155, 171

Ultraviolet light (UV), 61, 77, 78, 132, 157; and photodissociation, 71, 73, 137, 161, 168, 171; and Ross 128, 139

Units (of measurement), 4, 5, 7, 8, 12, 61, 63, 90

Uranium (U), 38, 41, 49, 50, 51,

52, 55, 97

Uranus, 88, 122; formation of, 45; obliquity, 19, 23, 122; satellites of, 122, see also Miranda

Urey, Harold, 95

Utley, Steven; "The Glowing Cloud," 58, 188

Vance, Jack; *Big Planet*, 16

Venus, 61, 72, 115; as daytime object, 112; as inferior planet, 110; as morning/evening star, 31, 110; atmosphere of, 47, 63, 68, 69, 72, 113, 115; clouds, 63, 168, 172; core of, 85; elongation, 110; greenhouse effect on, 63, 115, 158; rotation of, 47, 90, 115, 139; runaway greenhouse, 68, 71, 72, 162; satellites of, 28, 36, 138, 143; tidal braking, *see* Tidal braking, of Venus; tidal locking, *see* Tidal locking, of Venus; water on, 71, 72, 168; year, 90

Visual magnitude, *see* Magnitude, visual

Volatiles, 61, *see also* Atmosphere; specific compounds; and late heavy bombardment, 47, 48, 97; defined, 48; in atmosphere, 97; in jovian planets, 109; on terrestrial planets, 109; variation in, 78, 97, 154

Volcanic arcs, 58, 60

Volcanic gas; as steam, 58, 117

Volcanism, 52, 55, 56, 58, 60, 69, 96, 98, *see also* Basalt; Hot spots; Lava; Magma; Melting; Outgassing; and fractionation, 50, 56; on Cannonball, 173; on Io, 117; on Moon, 112

*Warworld* series (Pournelle), 144

Water, *see also* Oceans; Glaciers; Atmosphere; abundance, 44, 104; and

life, 63; and nitrogen oxides, 164; loss of, *see* Photodissociation; Atmosphere, escape of; on ammonia world, 162, 163; on Cannonball, 173; on Mars, 116; on sulfuric acid world, 168; properties of, 104, 105, 165; surface, 69, 81

Water vapor: as condensable phase, 83; as greenhouse gas, 67, 68, 71; as volatile, 48; atmospheric, 68, 166; equilibrium with liquid, 67; in ancient atmosphere, 95; in atmosphere, 95; on chloroxygen world, 157

Waterworld, 123

"Waterworld" (Goodloe & Oltion), 1, 118, 145, 188

Weather, *see* Atmosphere; Climate and weather

Welded tuff, *see* Ignimbrite

Wells, H.G.; *The Time Machine*, 73

Wetworld, 154

"Whirligig World" (Clement essay), 175, 188

White dwarfs, 145; in nova pair, 151

*World Called Cleopatra, A* (Anderson), 32, 51

*World of Difference, A* (Turtledove), 66

*World Out of Time* (Niven), 95

*World Without Stars* (Anderson), 152

X-ray stars, 151

Year, 17, 21, 90, *see also* Revolution period; and seasons, 17, 19, 20; insolation, 19, 102; length, 4, 16, 20, 21, 90; Ross 128 (star), 137, 139, 141

Zones, climatic, *see* Climatic zones

CPSIA information can be obtained at www.ICGtesting.com
Printed in the USA
BVOW08s0917121213

338943BV00001B/9/A